2:05

$ 49.95

CONTEMPORARY
PUBLIC FINANCE

CONTEMPORARY PUBLIC FINANCE

Nicholas V. Gianaris

PRAEGER

New York
Westport, Connecticut
London

336
GH3c

Library of Congress Cataloging-in-Publication Data

Gianaris, Nicholas V.
  Contemporary public finance / Nicholas V. Gianaris.
    p.   cm.
  Bibliography: p.
  Includes index.
  ISBN 0–275–93044–0 (alk. paper)
  1. Finance, Public.   I. Title.
HJ141.G53   1989
336—dc19   88–25186

Library of Congress Catalog Card Number: 88–25186
ISBN: 0–275–93044–0

First published in 1989

Praeger Publishers, One Madison Avenue, New York, NY   10010
A division of Greenwood Press, Inc.

Printed in the United States of America

The paper used in this book complies with the
Permanent Paper Standard issued by the National
Information Standards Organization (Z39.48–1984).

10   9   8   7   6   5   4   3   2   1

TP

To the memory of my parents
Vasilis and Dimitra

"The ideas of economists and political
philosophers, both when they are right
and when they are wrong, are more
powerful than is commonly understood."

John Maynard Keynes, 1936

Contents

Tables and Figures

Preface

With an ever-growing public sector in the United States and in almost all market economies, the subject of public finance acquires more and more importance not only in matters of financing government expenditures but also in matters of countercyclical policy. As governments are troubled by budget deficits, inflation, and unemployment, and as international transactions grow rapidly under flexible exchange rates, policymakers have difficulty implementing domestic economic policies to correct undesirable trends. Although solving these problems with fiscal measures alone is difficult, proper policies of public finance have a significant effect on economic stability and employment to improve public welfare.

Government expenditure and tax changes play a vital role in determining income and wealth distribution, investment allocation, and growth performance. Recent policies emphasizing reduction in inflation and increase in factor productivity have resulted in changes and reforms on spending and taxation in order to enhance production incentives and increase governmental revenue. Such policies aim at discouraging rapid growth of the bureaucratic public sector, encouraging competition, and stimulating saving for financing productive investment even at the sacrifice of vital social programs.

Moreover, the phenomenon of an increasing proportion of the aged in our population presents new problems of financing social security and transfer payments. In light of further increase in public demands and the need for effective fiscal management and welfare considerations on a local level, an up-to-date survey of state and local goverment financial problems is imperative.

Market economies with a large private sector, including the United States, move gradually toward larger public sectors mainly because of partial market failure. Planned economies with a large public sector move toward decentralization and large private sectors primarily because of bureaucratic inefficiencies.

This indicates a notable trend toward structural similarities in different fiscal systems. This is an important but largely neglected area of public finance.

The main questions to be considered in this book are these: What is the proper size, if any, of the public sector compared to the private sector to maximize economic efficiency and social welfare? What types of government expenditures and taxes will lead to stable prices and high employment? What is the economic impact of public sector activities in a democratic framework? And, what is the relationship of domestic fiscal policy to international finance?

This book combines normative rules to guide public sector decision making and positive economic analysis to study government activities on expenditures, taxation, and other fiscal measures relative to the allocation, distribution, and stabilization functions in the economy. It provides all the important material required for a textbook on public finance and incorporates tax reforms and deficit problems that challenge students and researchers alike. In addition to brief historical perspectives, the book encompasses recent theoretical considerations and real world practices.

I would like to express my indebtedness to Professors Ernest Block, Clive Daniel, George Gianaris, Laurence Krause, Sylvester Lewis, Victoria Litson, James Martin, Gus Papoulia, Adamandia Polis, John Roche, Dominick Salvatore, and Paul Voura, as well as the tax specialists and exchange rates experts George Alikakos, George Balodemos, Steven Rusko, and Christos Tzelios for their stimulating comments during the preparation of this book. Many thanks to my students of public finance and other related courses, who laid the foundation for my studies on public sector economics. Bill and Mike Gianaris, Nicholas Notias, Mario Karonis, Ted Kasapis, Loula Logus, Mike Stratis, and Maria Guerrier provided valuable services in reviewing, typing, copying, and other technical support.

CONTEMPORARY PUBLIC FINANCE

2:25

1

Introduction to Public Finance

OVERVIEW

Basic Concepts and Functions

Public finance deals with the activities of the public sector. The public sector includes all the governmental units (federal, state, and local)[1] as well as all public enterprises. The subject matter of public finance is the study of the expenditures, taxes, borrowing, and regulating activities of governments and public authorities. As such, public finance is part of the field of economics, which deals with the allocation of scarce resources to competing ends. It is related to both macroeconomics—with such common topics as stabilization and growth policies—and microeconomics, which encompasses welfare economics and income distribution as well as the distinction between social and private goods that touches both macro and microeconomics.

In more detail, public finance studies governmental spending and taxes and their effects on allocation of resources, distribution of income, and stabilization of the economy. Public finance is influenced by and influences activities in international trade and finance—functions that have largely been neglected in the past and are acquiring growing importance at present. Moreover, it has a whole network of indirect effects not only on economics but on political science and philosophy as well. However, this volume concentrates primarily on budgetary revenue and expenditures and their effects on the economy.

The U.S. economy is a mixed system that involves both sectors, private and public. The interaction of these two sectors necessitates an analysis of the characteristics and the basic operations of the private sector, in addition to a thorough study of the public sector. Such an analysis includes the market forces of supply and demand under competitive and monopolistic conditions and the effects of governmental activities upon them. It seems that the private sector, which Aristotle supported, and the "invisible hand" of the free market mechanism, which Adam Smith promulgated, present some disadvantages from a social point of view, and the public sector is needed to supplement them.

The public sector generally intervenes in the market to provide public goods, redistribute income, and in the private sector correct distortions such as monopoly and externalities. But the public sector may be less efficient than the private sector and do more harm than good. This may be so because bureaucrats may try to maximize selfish gains and not the welfare of society. Also, the government may not always be responsive to the wishes of the majority that elected it.

Many economic problems are better solved by free markets and the private sector. Free markets determine prices and quantities through the supply and demand mechanism, but they are not a panacea. A number of current social problems and economic inconsistencies simply cannot be solved effectively by a competitive market. They may be better organized and coordinated by non-market institutions or the public sector (including state and local units of government). From this perspective a clear understanding of the limitations of the free market is needed for a rational public policy.

In the process of analyzing the functions of public finance, a number of questions will be raised. These include the following:

- What are the historical and sociopolitical trends that determine the present status of the public sector?
- What are the interactions of the public and the private sectors and the intergovernmental fiscal operations?
- Who bears the main tax burden, and what types of taxes are levied?
- How do public sector spending and taxation influence the economy from the viewpoint of employment, price level, and growth?
- What is the importance of budget deficits and the national debt?
- What is the relationship between fiscal policy and international finance?

Scope of the Book

The previous section dealt primarily with some basic concepts and functions of public finance. The following sections of this chapter deal with theoretical aspects and practical applications of government expenditures and revenue as well as fiscal policy implications.

The remainder of the book is organized in three parts: Part I surveys historical trends and welfare considerations, the size of the public sector compared with the private sector, government expenditures, and intergovernmental activities. Part II discusses public sector revenue. Taxation, which is by far the main source of public sector revenue, is reviewed in terms of theoretical principles and the distinction among different kinds of taxes. Also reviewed are the role and magnitude of the underground economy, social security financing, and the effects of tax changes upon the economy as a whole. Finally, Part III examines countercyclical measures, budget deficits, and the national debt. Also considered in this part of the book is the relationship of fiscal policy to international finance, a largely neglected area. In this domain we are confronted with a terra nova in public finance.

The main characteristics and innovative features of the book include (1) a brief historical review to give students a basic foundation and a comprehensive knowledge of the long-run trends of public finance; and (2) with a "looking forward" approach, a consideration of recent crucial fiscal issues such as the growing public versus private sector, excessive goverment expenditures, tax structure and reforms, the federal and the state-local fiscal systems, social security problems, the countercyclical use of public finance, and the international aspects of fiscal policy.

Using a combination of theoretical and empirical information, the text brings clarity to some dull subjects in straightforward language. It makes analogies between the U.S. public finance system and other fiscal systems and considers their notable trend toward structural similarities.

The text covers the up-to-date material required for a junior-senior course in public finance and can also be used as a supplementary text in related courses, particularly microeconomic analysis, macroeconomic policy, and international finance.

NEED FOR PUBLIC SECTOR FUNCTIONS

Every person is born free but gradually comes under social restrictions. Initially, an individual's survival requires the protection and provisions for livelihood made through the family, which can be considered as the primary unit in society. The union or association of individuals and families creates the city and eventually the state.

Progressively, villages and city-states developed as independent economic and political units with their own governments or public authorities. With the growth of population, many villages and cities established separate states where the functions of the public sector increased and became more complicated.

In modern societies everyone places part of his or her freedom and power under a common will of the state and becomes part of society. The state, in turn, provides protection for each member of its society. This is what Jean Jacques Rousseau considered as the basic tenet of the "social contract."[2] As natural power has been transformed into political power, natural instincts have been replaced by social justice, which has made the human being more polite and cooperative.

Historically the size of the public sector has increased in comparison to the private sector, and discussions about the optimum size of the public sector developed and have continued. In the process of such discussions the goal has been to finance governmental services in such a way that additional expenditures, the marginal costs, for each public purpose equal additional or marginal benefits.

Although there is strong criticism against public sector spending, it has been proven that as income increases, demand for government services increases, and this despite the fact that private industry spends a great deal in advertising expenditures in order to create new and more intense wants for private goods. The demand for public services includes, among other social activities, defense, administration of justice, social security, and other services of health, education, and welfare which are vital for the functioning of modern societies. If such public services are insufficient and of poor quality, the private sector and the economy as a whole will not perform well.

However, one may ask, Is it proper for the public sector to undertake economic activities where the private sector fails? Or can better results be achieved by getting the goverment's dead hand out of some economic activities?

Private sector performance, through the market mechanism, seems to be more effective in certain areas of the economy where individual incentives play a vital role. It may be argued that civil servants in the public sector are equally subject to the same or even more serious shortcomings encountered by private entrepreneurs, particularly in sectors with a long history of bureaucracy. Probably, government subsidization of new private ventures through easy loans, matching grants, tax rebates, and the like, may have greater significance than direct public intervention.

Although the best government is that which governs least, as Thomas Jefferson suggested, it is difficult to assume that an economy with a nonexisting or limited public sector would be able to resolve the complex problems of present economies. Modern concern about individual behavior in a society of economic interdependencies, consumer protection in a monopolistic market structure, and improvement in the environment and the quality of life require collective or government action. As long as some individuals are not ethically reasonable in respecting equal freedoms and rights for others, some form of public policy is necessary.

There are economic functions that the market mechanism cannot perform alone and for which corrections and guidance by the public sector are needed. Government regulations or other measures are required to provide the legal framework in which private enterprises can operate efficiently and remove obstacles to free entry and competitive practices. At the same time, instances of possible inefficiencies in competition, especially in cases of economies of scale and decreasing cost, as well as expected advantages of "externalities," should be considered by public policy.

Government laws and regulations are needed to secure the conditions of factor and product market competition; to provide the legal framework for exchanges; to adjust the smooth transmission of property rights; and to help achieve price stability, high employment, and economic growth.

Allocation

The allocation function provides for the division of resource use between social and private goods. On many occasions the market is inefficient or fails to provide the goods needed through the market mechanism. For example, under conditions of monopoly, where there is one seller of a product, or of oligopoly, where a few sellers control the market, there are no voluntary exchanges. In such cases, where there are no competitive markets with many buyers and sellers, as in telecommunications and electric utilities and other natural monopolies, government intervention is justified in order to control monopolistic power and protect the public against unjust prices and other quantitative restrictions. Similar government controls are needed on firms that pollute the environment or engage in the production of unhealthy products.

Social goods may be provided by the public sector or produced by such public enterprises as transportation authorities and public power corporations as well as by other nationalized firms, which prevail primarily in socialistic economies and Western Europe. Moreover, social goods may be provided either by the national or central government or by local authorities through revenue and expenditure activities. For example, national defense and space exploration are functions of the federal or central government, while garbage collection and street lighting belong to the city or other local governments. The provision or production of social goods by the public sector requires expenditures that the users must pay. However, people try to pass the cost of social products to others and thus become "free riders." The government must then coerce payment through taxation. People can, though, influence production decisions according to their preferences through ballot voting in place of dollar voting.

To determine how much of a public good to make available, governmental units should compare benefits and costs associated with different quantities of the good. However, people do not have the same preference and find it difficult to agree on what is the optimal amount of the good. In democratic societies decisions are made through the majority vote, but in some nondemocratic or dictatorial societies decisions are made by an oligarchical team or a dictator. Local authorities normally decide on matters in their jurisdiction, but there are certain public goods and services, such as defense or space exploration, about which the central government decides. To improve efficiency and welfare, decentralization policies must strive for a balance between expected benefits and possible lower costs from larger numbers of participants; that is, such policies must consider the advantages of economies of scale in the allocation process.

Distribution

In a market system the well-being or welfare of individuals depends primarily on ownership of scarce resources that may be the result of wealth accumulation from work, profit making, or inheritance. Because of differences in resource ownership, some individuals possess more wealth and have better opportunities to satisfy their wants than others. This results in distributional inequalities. Such differences may also appear because of market failures. Even if distribution of income takes place according to factor productivity in a competitive economy, ethical and moral considerations may demand an income and wealth distribution different from that based on purely economic principles.

The aim of achieving a more equitable income and wealth distribution provides another reason for government intervention in the economy. Redistribution may be implemented through taxation and transfer payments. Specifically, progressive taxation and taxes on luxury goods may be levied against high-income people, while income transfers and subsidies for basic necessities may be provided for low-income people. By political voting, people can influence the patterns of income and wealth distribution toward certain standards of equity and a more egalitarian society.

Governmental income maintenance programs serve to transfer income and services to citizens who live in poverty and thereby reduce extreme inequalities. Such programs, which are financed by taxes, affect the aged, the disabled, the veterans, the unemployed, and other poor people with low or no income. Government benefits may take the form of subsidies to individuals producing certain goods and services, including price support for farmers, loan guarantees for businesses, and tax deductions and credits to encourage certain types of investment and other activities. The whole pattern of fiscal policy regarding government spending, taxation, and regulations, influences, directly or indirectly, the distribution of income among individuals or groups.

Government transfers can be made in money or in kind (food stamps, public housing, free school lunches, legal assistance). In competitive markets the distribution of money income depends on the ownership of productive resources and the prices of services from these resources. However, because of market imperfections, union influences, and other discriminatory practices, there are inequalities in work opportunities, education, and wages. To correct such imperfections and distortions in the economy, government interventions and regulations are used.

Close to half the aggregate money income is received by the highest fifth of U.S. households and only about 5 percent by the lowest fifth. Although a more "equitable" distribution of income is justifiable, care should be taken to avoid losses in work incentives and efficiency. Given such considerations, welfare policies should be replaced with workfare programs.

Stabilization and Growth Policies

On many occasions budgetary expenditures and taxation are used to stabilize the economy and increase the rate of real economic growth. Government spending can be a source of stimulus. However, increasing taxes can have a contractionary effect on the economy as money is siphoned off the public. Government borrowing for deficit financing can also have a contractionary effect, unless there are excess savings in the private sector. And budget outlays may result in higher imports instead of increasing domestic demand and stimulating the economy. The budget's interaction with the economy is thus complex, and so the consideration of other variables such as income elasticities of domestic demand and imports may be needed.

When government expenditure or revenue grows equiproportionately with the Gross National Product (GNP), neutral growth in government occurs. All else being equal, growth in government expenditures that is higher than in the GNP leads to expansionary movements in the economy. On the other hand, if tax revenue grows more rapidly than the GNP, the result is a contractionary effect (fiscal drag). Thus, the countercyclical effects of the budget are obvious. However, the timing of fiscal measures plays a pervasive role in economic stabilization and as such should be seriously considered in decision making. Otherwise, such fiscal measures may turn out to be procyclical and aggravate recession or inflation, instead of being countercyclical.

The goals of full employment and price stability are difficult to achieve through the market mechanism. Economic fluctuations or business cycles, with increasing economic activities, or booms, and economic declines, or recessions, are usual in the United States and in other market economies. To correct undesirable fluctuations public policy guidance is required.

To avoid deep recessions similar to that of the 1930s (the Great Depression), Congress passed the Employment Act of 1946, which states that "it is the continuing policy and responsibility of the Federal Government to use all practicable means . . . to promote maximum employment." This act was amended with the Full-Employment and Balanced Growth Act of 1978, known as the Humphrey-Hawkins Act, to make the responsibility of government on matters of employment and growth more specific.

From the 1940s to the present years, the U.S. government frequently borrowed funds to finance expenditures. It followed the prescription of John Maynard Keynes by using deficit spending to stimulate the economy. However, heavy deficit spending during the Vietnam War and later led the U.S. economy to double-digit inflation. This combined with a series of oil crises and other structural bottlenecks produced low rates of economic growth and high rates of unemployment (stagflation). To cope with the dilemma of the Scylla of recession and the Charybdis of inflation, the government has used various measures of fiscal policy, along with monetary policy. These have included wage-price guidelines, wage-price controls, investment credits, and other expenditures and tax-induced income policies.

The main task of policymakers is to coordinate fiscal policy in an optimal or normative way to achieve major economic objectives and avoid conflicts of group interests during policy implementations. Thus, if the objective is to stimulate demand and increase employment, low-income groups with a high propensity to consume should be given greater spending power, independently of the mix of social goods supplied and the benefits derived. In cases of anti-inflationary policies, the opposite prescription should be used. If, on the other hand, a high rate of economic growth is the objective, investment should be encouraged, since growth depends primarily on capital formation. If the private sector is unable to finance and implement related investment projects, then the public sector should introduce incentives for capital formation or invest in public projects.

In addition to using fiscal policy measures, policymakers must implement monetary policy measures to achieve successful short-run stability and long-run growth. Such monetary measures, which include discount rates, open market operations, reserve requirements, and credit and other controls, affect domestic as well as international transactions. Thus, for example, high interest rates together with reduction in government spending and/or tax increases can be used to reduce inflation and attract foreign capital. The opposite prescription can be used to increase employment and income. Therefore, a mix of fiscal and monetary policies should be used properly to complement each other in problems of stabilization and economic growth.

Previous government efforts to stimulate or reflate the economy only through demand management have at times resulted in high rates of inflation without achieving steady economic growth and high levels of employment. It would seem that for an economy to come out of the orbit of stagflation, emphasis on investment, together with demand management, is required. Such an investment policy would improve supply conditions to satisfy additional demand and avert chronic inflation and budget deficits, which undermine business confidence and real growth. Although existing built-in stabilizers limit economic fluctuations somewhat, a proper mix of government policies can be achieved through the use of such discretionary measures as investment grants, tax credits, and allowances or state guarantees. Depending on the particular circumstances that prevail at that time, a whole arsenal of fiscal and monetary measures can be used for a proper combination of demand and investment management so that extensive budgetary and balance-of-payment deficits will be reduced or eliminated. These policies should be coordinated with other trading-partner countries so that an orderly foreign exchange market and international economic cooperation are promoted. Economies are linked to one another by trade, and capital flows and domestic policies affect and are affected by policies in other countries. Thus, mutual trade cooperation and foreign exchange market coordination require similar institutional arrangements and commonly accepted business ethics to promote trade and investment.

Future tax and other fiscal policies should consider, for example, the problem U.S. manufacturers face as a result of foreign competition. A number of U.S. industries, particularly the steel, auto, shoe, and textile industries, which have lost much of their efficiency and productivity, demand that the government build tariff walls and make restrictions to keep out similar products made abroad. However, protectionist measures may cost the United States more jobs in the long run as other nations reciprocate with trade barriers.

COORDINATION OF GOVERNMENTAL ACTIVITIES

The expansion of the public sector as a result of the ever-increasing demand for governmental services (including those provided by regional and local units of government) requires increasing amounts of tax revenues. In spite of arguments against the public sector, which may be justified on the grounds of growing bureaucracy and inefficiency, public expenditures continue to increase proportionately more than the overall economy. The financing of such growing government services requires large amounts of revenue in the form of direct, or income taxes, and indirect, or consumption, taxes. From that point of view, structural changes and reforms in the public sector can raise needed revenue and improve public services, reduce bureaucracy, and simplify the complicated tax system.

Recent inflationary pressures have led to significant distortions in the tax system. In periods of inflation the public sector absorbs more and more taxes, especially those on income, to finance growing government expenditures, despite criticisms against low productivity in this sector. For that reason, arguments for tax reduction, tax indexing, and the introduction of tax incentives to stimulate the economy are widespread.

In recent years, there has been a growing interest in proposals for taxing consumption expenditures as an alternative to taxing income mainly because U.S. tax laws have overly subsidized consumption in the past. Indirect taxes, which include turnover taxes, value-added taxes, tariffs, and sales taxes, are primarily expenditure taxes and as such are affected by changes in consumption, imports, and inflation.

Consider the three main alternative means of financing public expenditures, that is, taxation, money creation, and bond issuance. It would seem that the first alternative is the most anti-inflationary. Money creation, in contrast, is clearly inflationary when it exceeds the real rate of economic growth, given that at present velocity also tends to be high; and government bond issuance increases the debt of the country.

To maintain high levels of employment and low rates of inflation, that is, to reduce or avoid stagflation or even slumflation (negative economic growth and inflation), large amounts of resource-related investments must be financed by the public and the private sectors. Moreover, new investment is needed to replace capital equipment worn out through depreciation, especially in such industries as transportation and communications, and to introduce new technology and innovations for high productivity. Given these considerations, it is argued that economic policy in general and public finance in particular should be directed toward the supply side, emphasizing productive investment more than demand. Along these lines it would seem, then, that the Keynesian emphasis on effective demand has run its course and is inappropriate in cases where the economy operates under inflationary pressures.

The prevalence of bureaucracy and political favoritism in public enterprises,

has brought rise to strong arguments in support of denationalization and dis-
mantling, instead of the erection of welfare-state structures, even though such
a policy of privatization may add to unemployment. At the same time, that
private enterprises are reluctant to engage in long-term productive investment
and prefer to invest in short-term ventures for quick profit may require increased
investment activities by the public sector.

Goverment regulation and/or subsidization play an important role in agricultural and industrial growth policies. In any case, economists and social scientists
can hardly avoid the conclusion that objective factors call for a mixed economic
regime involving both private and public components in the process of development. Some degree of subordination of extreme individualism to collective
or group decision making, a sort of self-discipline and togetherness, may be
needed for long-term growth. Also, some training toward consensus and cooperation in effective decision making on economic and social matters, in a
democratic framework, may be required for higher economic efficiency. Given
this point of view, public sector services may play a vital role in coordinating
economic and social objectives. Advocates of economic planning believe that
the dilemma of inflation and unemployment, as well as bottlenecks or shortages,
could be avoided or limited with a strong public sector. However, others think
that in such a system a self-appointed elite of bureaucrats will try to regulate
the private sector and thus lead to more inefficiencies and bottlenecks.

It would seem imperative that for better economic efficiency and consumer
protection, individual and collective activities should be combined to achieve
high levels of productivity and a workable balance between the private and the
public sectors. Given this point of view, one would expect that workers' and
managers' joint participation in decision making would increase incentives for
production and reduce government intervention for work protection and similar
measures. Such employee sharing of authority as well as responsibility, as another
alternative to public and private sectors, should not lead to another form of
bureaucracy and operational drawback. Probably, comanagement would be effective on matters of overall strategies such as macroplanning, human relations,
investment projections, and market orientation in each enterprise, but not on
tactical and day-to-day operational activities that require quick decisions. The
government can use fiscal policy measures to encourage such trends of employee
ownership and revenue and decision sharing and thus avoid some of the disadvantages of the private sector and the laissez-faire mechanism while at the
same time avoiding many bureaucratic traps of the public sector. Such an innovative system has been successfully introduced in other countries, notably
Japan.

THE ROLE OF GOVERNMENT IN THE CIRCULAR FLOW
OF INCOME

The public sector interacts with the private sector in our mixed economic
system. It not only diverts private income to public use but also contributes to

Figure 1.1
Circular Flow of Income and Expenditures

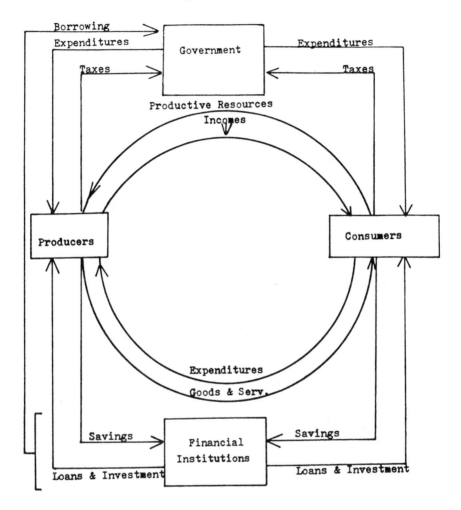

the flow of income through government expenditures. Figure 1.1 shows a circular flow of income between producers and consumers. Enterprises or producers pay income (wages, rent, interest, and profits) in return for the services of productive resources (labor, land, capital, and entrepreneurship), as shown in the upper part of the diagram. Whereas, the consumers or the public spend a large portion of the income they receive to pay the producers in return for goods and services they buy, as the lower part of the diagram shows.

However, a part of the income received by the public is saved and, primarily through financial institutions, is channeled back to the producers or consumers in the form of loans and investment. Another part of income is absorbed by government in the form of taxes and is channeled again into the economy through government expenditures. We assume that the foreign sector is incorporated into the circular flow.

If the summation of incomes received is equal to the total spending, equilibrium is maintained in the economy. From that point of view, banking policy and fiscal policy play an important role in facilitating the circular flow of income and expenditures and affecting equilibrium. If the sum of savings (S) plus taxation (T) is higher than the sum of investment (I) plus government expenditures (G), that is, if $S + T > I + G$, then the economy is expected to decline because of the lack of sufficient spending and effective demand. Vice versa, if investment and government spending are larger than savings and taxation, demand is stimulated and the economy moves toward full employment. If overspending takes place, that is, if spending levels are higher than required by full employment, then the result would be an increase in nominal or inflationary income, not real income. Inflationary pressures, though, may start even before the full employment level is reached, mainly because of structural rigidities and allocative bottlenecks in the economy. Therefore, one of the main goals of fiscal policy, along with monetary policy, is to pursue full employment with price stability. (Later chapters deal with this topic in more detail.)

In recent years, government expenditures in the United States and many other countries have exceeded government revenues or taxes. To finance the resulting budget deficits, the government borrows funds from the economy through selling bonds, notes, bills, and other securities to the public and to businesses. That is, the government absorbs savings from the circular flow of income through borrowing, instead of raising taxes, to finance such deficits, thereby postponing the payment burden for later years and accumulating more debt.

In addition to income and expenditure flows, the public sector interacts with the private sector in the factor and the products markets of the economy. The government uses factor inputs and produces goods and services that are provided to the public without a direct charge. However, the financing of the production and supply of such goods and services takes place primarily through taxes or borrowing, not through sales, as happens in the private sector market.

PRODUCTION POSSIBILITIES AND SOCIETY'S PREFERENCES

The allocation of resources between private and public sectors plays an important role in economic growth and social welfare. The interaction of supply and demand among the different sectors of the economy and the positive or negative externalities (indirect benefits or costs) generated by the public sector should be considered, together with government controls and regulations, to determine the most efficient intersector resource allocation and the optimum utility or satisfaction to be pursued in a democratic society.

The total production of goods and services depends on the amount of resources

Figure 1.2
Production Possibility and Preference Curves for a Society

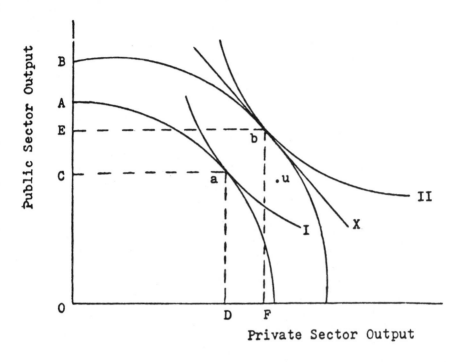

Private Sector Output

(land and natural resources, labor, capital, entrepreneurship), the productivity
or efficiency per unit of resources, and the gains from foreign trade. The limited
amounts of productive resources, along with unlimited human wants, leads to
the necessity of optimal resource allocation. Such allocation can be made by the
private sector, operating through the market mechanism of supply and demand,
or by the public sector, operating through the revenue and expenditure activities
of the government.

Assuming full employment of factors of production or resources, a country
can achieve a certain amount of output of private and public goods. The country's
production possibilities, however, can be raised by an increase in the quantity
and quality of natural, human, and capital resources and by improving its stock
of technological knowledge.

Figure 1.2 shows the production possibility frontiers and the consumer's indifference curves regarding public and private sector outputs. With the output
of the public sector measured vertically and that of the private sector horizontally,
curve A shows the best possible combinations of both kinds of outputs that can
be produced at full employment of factors of production. If all resources are put
into public sector output, the largest possible output would be equal to OA at
production possibility curve A and vice versa for the private sector. If OC of

public sector output is produced, the largest possible output of private sector output would be OD, and so on.

Economic growth, through increments of factor resources and technological improvements, brings about a shift of the production possibility curve from *A* to a new curve, *B*, which indicates the possibility of higher production of public and private sector outputs. The concave to the point of origin of the production possibility curves means that both public and private outputs are produced under conditions of increasing costs. In order for an economy to exploit its productive potential fully, not only sufficient demand must be generated, but proper changes in the allocation of resources should be made. Then the economy will be able to achieve the maximum combination of factors and products, that is, to reach the highest productive potential with the available factors of production. If there is unemployment or underemployment (disguised unemployment), then the country is not utilizing its maximum productive potential and the economy will be operating inside the curve, such as point *u*, for example.

Social indifference curves I and II represent the preferences of the members of a society as well as their effective demand for public and private goods. Such demand is affected, not only by income and wealth possessions, but also by political representation that is determined mainly by voting power, lobbies, and pressure groups. These indifference curves are convex to the point of origin, reflecting a diminishing marginal rate of substitution (MRS) between public and private goods; that is, smaller amounts of public goods are exchanged for the same amounts of private goods as one moves downward along the indifference curves.

At the higher production possibility curve *B*, members of society can move to a higher indifference curve. As long as their preference or demand for public goods is growing proportionately more than that for private goods (as it did in all the postwar decades, as will be shown later), their higher, new indifference curve II would not be parallel to the previous indifference curve I. The new output mix demanded would shift from point *a* to point *b*. Here the ratio of public to private goods demanded and produced in the economy, OE/OF, is higher than that of point *a*, OC/OD. Line X, which at point *b* is tangent to both the production possibility curve *B* and the indifference curve II, shows the marginal rate of substitution of consumers (members of society)—or the slope of the indifference curve II—and the marginal rate of transformation in production—or the slope of the production possibility curve *B*. Point *b* is the best point of production and consumption, that is, the point of optimal intersector allocation, where the production possibility curve *B* is tangent to social indifference curve II, providing OE in public sector output and OF in private sector output.

The market mechanism, as the best planner in resource allocation, would determine the products to be produced so that in selecting from among the products considered, consumers would achieve the most possible satisfaction out of their income allocation. Then, under competitive conditions, producers or sellers would try to equate marginal cost with marginal revenue, that is, the

extra cost with the extra revenue from an additional unit product; whereas consumers would try to equate the marginal rate of substitution with the price ratios
of the products in question. However, in our nonperfect markets, policymakers
may modify product mixes through controls or fiscal and monetary measures.

The benefits of private goods, such as bread or shoes, are totally internalized;
whereas the benefits of public goods, such as defense or the clean up of pollution,
are wholly external. In the first case benefits and costs are subject to the market
mechanism of supply and demand, but benefits of social or collective goods are
not subject to the price mechanism. In reality however, mixed situations of
private and social benefits exist.[3]

The main economic objective is to achieve efficient allocation of resources in
production and maximize the satisfaction of the consumers. In a Robinson Crusoe
economy, things are somewhat simple. A single individual will try to use available resources in such a way so as to produce the goods that maximize satisfaction. But in the real world are many consumers, and the question is how to
organize production and distribution so as to maximize the satisfaction of most
or all of them. In other words, the question is how to achieve Pareto's efficiency,
how to have an economic arrangement in which no one can improve his or her
welfare without worsening the welfare of others.[4] Then an increase in efficiency
can be achieved by changing the mix of output or the size of the public sector
so that the position of an individual or a group of individuals can be improved
without hurting others.

From the viewpoint of total consumer or social satisfaction, it is argued by
the supporters of income equality that a dollar taken away from a rich person
and given to a poor person would increase total social utility. Critics of income
equality, on the other hand, argue that inequality provides work and creative
incentives as well as greater amounts of saving and investment. According to
them, under a completely equalitarian system, society would be dull and stagnant.

PART I

THE PUBLIC VERSUS THE PRIVATE SECTOR

2

Development of the Public Sector and Welfare Economics

A BRIEF HISTORICAL SURVEY

For thousands of years people lived in nomadic tribes, traveling over relatively wide areas for hunting and food gathering, with no conception of property in land and no collective ruling or governmental authority. The family was the first social unit. Gradually, around 5000 B.C., nomadic tribes settled down and established villages. The village or collective life necessitated some form of public ruling or government. Tribal chiefs or kings and rulers used slaves for the construction of irrigation and other projects and imposed heavy taxes or contributions upon their subjects to build the Pyramids, the Great Wall, luxurious temples, and monuments and to support large armies and many servants. This type of public expenditure was mostly associated with bureaucracy, inefficiency, and waste of productive resources.

Greco-Roman Period

In ancient Greece, groups of villages grew into larger units or cities known as city-states (sixth century B.C. and later). Each city-state (polis) was an independent political and economic unit and had its own laws, its own army, and its own public finance. To fulfill their duty, citizens had to participate in government. This was the system of democracy, which prevailed in Athens and other Hellenic city-states, wherein decisions on public expenditures and revenues were made by the majority of citizens. However, at certain times there prevailed other forms of government, especially those of despots or tyrants and oligarchies, under which people were oppressed and freedom was lost. It was in these city-states that the concept of democracy, as an ideal political system, was developed.

The constitution of Solon (sixth century B.C.) abolished bondage and gave citizens a share in the government in a democratic fashion. The income class of the people determined their eligibility for public office.

As the number of public officials increased and more citizens participated in rotation in the city-state assembly (Ecclesia) for pay, government expenditures grew rapidly and reserves were reduced. Moreover, in order to support the people who fled from the countryside into Athens, the government used more public funds (Theoricon or Theoric Fund). Such a welfare system and other deficiencies in public finance demoralized the citizens, increased the proportion of idle persons, destroyed the treasury, and accelerated the decline of Athens. Similar trends can also be seen today in countries with growing welfare systems.

Plato in his *Republic* said that the true creator (of the state) is necessity, which is the mother of invention. The city arises because of the division of labor that is the result of natural inequalities in human skills and the multiplicity of wants. Happiness or the good life, according to Plato, must include all the people, while "poverty results from increase of man's desires, not from diminution of his property."[1]

Based on the writings of Xenophon, an Athenian politician named Euvoulos supported the idea of a fair distribution of the tax burden and suggested reduction in public controls and regulations for free movement of foreign capital, improvement in the balance of trade, and vitalization of the construction industry and the commercial activities of the city-state. The policy prescriptions of Euvoulos were for the reduction of the public sector in favor of the private sector.

Aristotle (384–322 B.C.), a student of Plato, argued that the state is the union of families and villages and aims to insure the good life; it is a creation of nature, and man is by nature a political animal. He was in favor of private ownership as a stimulus to productive incentives and criticized Plato's support of public ownership. He thought that "common ownership means common neglect."[2]

In terms of public finance, the Roman period (31 B.C. to A.D. 476) is characterized by efficient public administration, the construction of public works, especially highways, and high military expenditures to support large army units. The state's recognition of juristic persons or public entities was an important contribution to the creation and expansion of the corporate form of modern enterprises. In the long run, the possession of large estates (*latifundia*) by the wealthy class and the nobles, the inefficiency of slave labor, extensive state regulation such as controls on wages and just prices (*justum pretium*), and the introduction of heavy taxation to pay for large public expenditures contributed to the decline of the Roman Empire.

Feudalism, Mercantilism, and Physiocracy

During Europe's Medieval period (A.D. 476 to about 1500), great administrative powers were placed in the hands of the owners of large estates (including the Church), which became new political and economic units. This was the manorial or feudalistic system.

The landlords exercised extensive authority, acting as independent rulers and forming their own laws and courts, while the serfs worked for the lords. Further, secular authority and Canon Law of the Church preserved the concept of fixing a maximum or just price, as Thomas Aquinas advocated.[3] Also, regulations against forestalling, usury, and other trade practices were imposed by the authorities and the guilds, which later acquired monopolistic powers. With the support of the state, the captialist system was spread and colonialism emerged.

Commercial expansion by monopolies and colonialism nurtured the new doctrine of mercantilism (1550—1776) mainly in Britain and Germany, advocating, among other things, the supremacy of the state over the individual for the support of exports and the accumulation of precious metals to finance large armies for foreign wars.

However, the Physiocratic school (1756–78), which appeared primarily in France toward the end of the era of mercantilism, advocated economic freedom and competition with limited or no governmental regulations.[4] Only through economic liberalism or nonintervention (laissez-faire), which is in conformity with the natural order, can society best achieve progress. Any intervention would result in misallocation of resources and inefficiency.

In his *Wealth of Nations* (1776), Adam Smith pointed out that division of labor increases productivity but it also creates the need for greater mutual help and dependence of each member of society. Such mutual help and cooperation comes automatically under private property and the free market system, or laissez-faire, which is the best planner of resource allocation. As members of society try to achieve their own interests, they are led as if by an invisible hand to promote the interest of society as a whole.[5] Contrary to the mercantilistic support of strong states, Smith thought that government interference and monopoly are associated with bureaucracy, corruption, and inefficiency and as such they are harmful to the progress of nations. The economy should regulate itself through competition between buyers and sellers, instead of being regulated by the state.

Although Smith supported the laissez-faire or free enterprise system, as the Physiocrats did, he recognized that certain functions should be performed by the public sector, that is, by the state. Such functions are the following:[6]

1. Protection of society from violence and invasion by other societies, that is, national defense.

2. Protection of every member of society from injustice or oppression by other members, or administration of justice.

3. Erection and maintenance of those public institutions and those public works that cannot be established or maintained by any individual or small number of individuals.

4. Meeting the expenses needed for the support of the sovereign, which depend on the political structure of the nation.

In addition to defense and domestic security or law and order for the protection of individuals and property as important functions of government, Smith listed a number of public works such as roads, bridges, canals, harbors, coinage, and post office operations to be performed by the state. He observed that as societies advance in civilization, governments became increasingly involved in defense and other functions. Such functions, he maintained, need collective undertakings and cannot be provided by private companies on a profitable basis.

Other classical economists, primarily Thomas Malthus, David Ricardo, and John Stuart Mill, agreed with Adam Smith that the free market mechanism, and not public controls, is the best system of resource allocation. According to Mill, however, continuous progress requires security of persons against violence and arbitrary power of government as well as the association of producers and consumers in the form of cooperatives. Mill believed that the government would provide more public works than Smith suggested. Such public works would also include, according to Mill, irrigation projects, canals, and schools.

Contrary to the arguments of Adam Smith and the classical school that growth of the agricultural sector was to be stressed first to produce surplus food for the industrial workers, Freidrich List advocated (1841) a balanced growth among agriculture, manufacturing, and commerce and wanted the state to bring this balance into existence, since this could not be done under a laissez-faire policy, which he rejected. For a transitional period, List thought, state protection of some domestic industries (infant industries, for example) was necessary for the industrialization of the country. Tariffs and other protective measures would gradually be reduced, however, as the country reached higher stages of development.[7] Countries already in the highest stage (agricultural, manufacturing, and commercial development) would adopt free trade and abandon governmental protection in favor of competition. Protection would also be reduced through economic confederations and unions similar to the customs union between the German states (Zollverin) in 1834. List thought, moreover, that the subordination of individual interests to the state would bring about better economic and social results—ideas that were similar to those of Adam Müller and that provided the rationalization for the Nazi state.

Arguments in Favor of the Public Sector

Saint-Simon, Charles Fourier, Karl Marx, and other socialist writers took advantage of the negative features and failures of early laissez-faire and free market economies and proposed a thesis that private ownership and the free market system were the root evils of social life. For that reason they suggested and supported a system of state-directed economy. Wealth concentration by the private sector and automation in the production process would lead to high unemployment, underconsumption, and ever-increasing economic crises. Periodic crises would intensify until common or state ownership of the means of production finally replaced private ownership. Then what was left of capitalist institutions would gradually disappear and the state would wither away. In its place would evolve a classless society representing the acme of perfection that would last forever.[8]

This tenet of equality in welfare underlines the egalitarian thought of Rousseau and is similar to the Utopia of Plato's ideal state. In contrast, Thorstein Veblen, a U.S. economist, believed that the development of institutions would not stop and the friction of old and new habits and institutions would continue in an evolutionary process.

Later Marxist and conservative critics argued that the growth of the fiscal system carries the seeds of destruction of the capitalist system. To Marxists, the ratio of public expenditures (and therefore taxation) to total national production must rise to absorb overproduction by the private sector. According to Adolph Wagner, however, public expenditure must rise because interdependence of economic activity requires increasing public sector involvement. Also, progress requires expanding social services.

During the eighteenth century, when the naked laissez-faire system prevailed, unemployment, misery, and inequality were widespread. Gradually, though, many governments introduced welfare reforms and reduced extreme polarizations in income and wealth distribution. Today, countries that practice some form of the Marxian or complete state control system, such as in the Soviet Union and in the Eastern European countries, have suppressed consumption in favor of public sector investment and rapid growth. This same process was followed by the capitalist countries in their own early stages of development, though with higher inequality in income distribution. Extensive capital formation in these economies has taken place though forced saving or taxation by the state. However, economic progress and a better distribution of income and wealth in market economies tend to broaden ownership and modify the economy toward a mixed (private-public) system.

Reforms to Traditional Fiscal Systems

Contrary to the classical model, which calls for the private sector and the market mechanism to solve problems of underconsumption and unemployment, reformed fiscal systems call for the public sector to use fiscal and monetary measures to stimulate the economy toward full employment. Since one of the main reasons of recessions or depressions is lag in effective demand, the role of government in supplementing inadequate spending by the private sector is obvious. According to John Maynard Keynes, in the case of slackening economy and growing unemployment, the government or any other public institution should increase its spending, mostly in investment to increase demand and stimulate production and employment. Such government spending, which would be covered primarily by deficit financing, would have a multiplier effect, generating income several times the amount originally spent. Also, monetary authorities should influence production and employment through changes in interest rates or other policy tools. In the case of recession and unemployment, an interest rate lower than the return on investment would encourage new investment.

Keynes believed that fiscal policy, that is, government budget manipulation, would exert greater influence on income and employment than monetary policy. Government spending in public works and other projects would be necessary in case of severe unemployment, even if they are of doubtful utility (such as digging holes in the ground and filling them again). However, government is not to do things which individuals are doing.[9]

Many countries are developing increasingly into dual economies, that is, joint partnerships of private enterprises with goverments. The private sector concentrates on the production of material goods, while the public sector provides a wide range of services (welfare state services), such as social security, health, education, and community projects. It is argued that this private-public partnership will enable countries and populations to reach high levels of development.[10] However, the growing reliability on the public sector for investment and other spending may lead to gradual expansion of the public sector at the expense of the private sector and eventual government controls on many or all sectors of the economy.

Recently a new form of organization has appeared. This is the world of large corporations, which itself is served by the private and the public sectors instead of serving them. The consumer, the government, and the market accommodate themselves to the needs of the producer's organization. National or international corporations may dominate the state; the state, in turn, will secure the ends and goals of the corporations, providing training for research scientists, engineers, and skilled personnel, as well as protective legislation, to make the system continue to work.

Advanced industrial technology goes together with organization or bureaucracy. In many instances economic and even political power may be exercised by smaller inner or managerial groups and impersonal bureaucracy, regardless of the fiscal system considered. Wealth and political power and economic decisions may be concentrated in the hands of a small minority, bureaucrats or executives, excluding the masses from many incentives for improvement.[11] Owners of companies and corporations may, at the same time, be parliamentary representatives, ministers, or military leaders of the country, controlling or influencing governmental decisions on matters of public finance, social justice, and economic growth. In such cases where extensive economic or political power accrues to a few individuals, whether in the public or the private sector, national policies may be influenced toward one or another direction, regardless of the desires of the majority of the population.

Empirically, a growing public sector was the long run trend in the United States and in other market economies. On the average the proportions of GNP spent by government (including state and local government) increased year after year, as did public revenue to finance such expenditures. The old saying about the certainty of death and taxes is true, but recently the public sector seems to have reached a plateau in its growth and even to retreat in favor of the private sector.

THE WELFARE PRINCIPLE OF PARETO'S OPTIMALITY

Welfare Considerations

The main economic goal of each society is prosperity and happiness for its members. This can be achieved through higher levels of production, security, equal opportunities, dignity, and freedom. This is the subject matter of welfare economics.

The effective use of active fiscal and monetary policy and the successful management of demand contributed to the continuation of progress under the market system. Income policies in the form of price and wage determination or productivity guidelines, tax cuts, investment incentives, and a variety of subsidies introduced to attain maximal welfare for the society tend to make the economy more public or social and less private. In contrast, reforms, which are characterized by the introduction of new institutional arrangements, tend to increase social utility within a democratic framework where individualism and the private sector predominate in the economy. It has been thought that much economic centralism is responsible for bureaucracy, poor quality, and low labor productivity. As the economy moves to higher levels of development, enterprises require more autonomy on such vital matters as borrowing funds, employment, investment, production, and sales reforms, which means a movement toward the private, rather than the public sectors.

Although economic and political considerations on fiscal matters usually go together and it is difficult to separate one from the other, it becomes more and more obvious, particularly with the growth of social awareness, that economic considerations are gaining importance in matters of social welfare. The dilemma is to formulate a satisfactory welfare system and provide income support for the poor without creating work disincentives. Ethical or value judgments and concepts of aggregate individual utilities may be applied to attain the Pareto-optimum norm of social welfare.

Pareto optimality, the welfare principle of the Italian economist Vilfredo Pareto (1848–1923) states that optimum economic efficiency and social welfare would be attained when no one could be better off without making someone else worse off. In this case, each consumer's utility or satisfaction is maximized given the utility levels of all other consumers.[12]

Figure 2.1 shows the conditions of maximization of welfare of two consumers for two commodities, A and B (Edgeworth Box). The first consumer will try to improve his or her position by moving to higher indifference curves (a combi-

Figure 2.1
Optimization of Consumers' Welfare Box

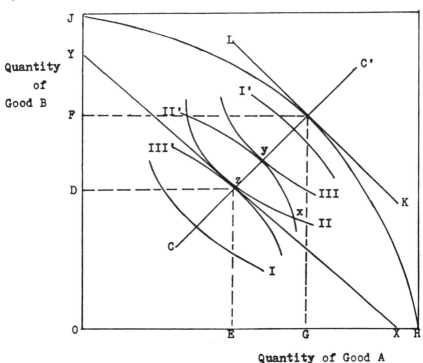

Quantity of Good A

nation of the two goods) I, II, and III successively; and the second consumer, by moving from I' to II' and to III'. Any point in the box (x, y, or z, for example) represents a possible combination of A and B between the two consumers. However, point y is better than point x because the first consumer moves to a higher indifference curve, III, while the second consumer remains in the same curve, II'. Any movement toward the contract line CC' will increase the welfare of the consumers. The choice then would be between y and z. Assuming a rate of exchange OX of A for OY of B, the price line XY shows the possible combinations or exchange ratios of the two goods. Point z, at which the price line is tangent simultaneously to the highest indifference curves each consumer can reach, represents the optimum possible combination in the sense that neither consumer can move to a higher curve without pushing the other to a lower one. This is the concept of Pareto's optimum, which was further developed primarily by A. P. Lerner, Oscar Lange, and John Hicks. At this optimum point, the marginal rate of substitution (MRS) between the two consumer goods is equal to the ratio of their marginal utilities (MU) or their prices (P). That is:

$$MRS_{AB} = \frac{MU_A}{MU_B} = \frac{P_A}{P_B}$$

Suppose, for example, the two consumer goods A and B are beef and pork, respectively, and the price of beef is two dollars per pound while that of pork one dollar. In order to gain one unit of beef, the consumer must give up two units of pork. The marginal rate of substitution of beef for pork is two to one, which is directly related to the prices and the marginal utility of these two commodities and inversely related to the quantities exchanged. In other words, two units of pork are exchanged per unit of beef because the utility or satisfaction from beef, and therefore its price, is double as compared to pork. The same is true for a bundle of private goods (A) in exchange for a bundle of public goods (B).

Moreover, the marginal rate of substitution between the two commodities at point z is equal to their marginal rate of transformation, as the tangent to both indifference curves of the two consumers (XY) is parallel to line KL, which is tangent to the production possibility curve (HJ). At point z, which is the best point of utility (welfare) maximization of the two consumers, the first consumer will receive OD of good B and OE of good A, while the second consumer will receive DF of B and EG of A.

With the same reasoning, the marginal rate of transformation (MRT) of factors producing goods A and B is equal to the ratio of the value of their marginal product (MP) or their prices (P), that is, wages for labor and interest for capital. Thus, for labor (L) and capital (K), we have

$$MRT_{LK} = \frac{MP_L}{MP_K} = \frac{P_L}{P_K} = \frac{w}{r}$$

where w stands for the factor price of labor (wages) and r for the factor price of capital (interest).

Utility Approach

As with private goods, the same thing occurs with public goods: The more we have a public good, the less we desire it. This means that the utility or satisfaction from each additional unit of a public good we use declines. Therefore, we are willing to pay lower prices or taxes for more units. Thus, the marginal disutility of tax payments increases as more and more units of a public good are allocated. Assuming full employment of factors of production, the more the allocation of public goods, the less the allocation of private goods.

To have optimal intersector allocation of public and private goods, or to attain maximal welfare for society, as Arthur Pigou envisioned, the marginal utility of a good should be equal to the marginal disutility of payment for that good, either in the form of price in the case of a private good or in the form of tax in the case of a public good.[13] Marginal disutility of tax payment may be considered equal to the opportunity cost of private goods foregone.

Figure 2.2 shows the growing total utility (TU) from the use or consumption

Figure 2.2
Public Goods Allocation: Utility Approach

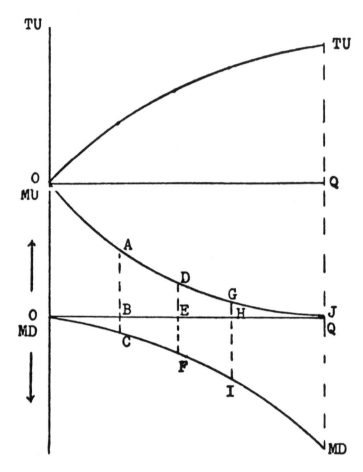

of public goods up to a saturation point, where the tangent at the TU curve is parallel to the horizontal quantity (Q) axis. As more and more units of public goods are used, total utility increases, but at lower rates, since the tangents at each point along the (TU) curve give smaller and smaller angles. This means that the marginal utility (MU) declines gradually until it reaches zero at point J. On the other hand, the marginal disutility (MD) of tax payments increases with the increase of quantity. At point A, marginal utility is higher than marginal disutility ($AB > BC$) and it pays to use more budget expenditures for the public good, until marginal utility is equal to marginal disutility ($DE = EF$). At point E the economy achieved optimal allocation of public goods. Beyond E, consumption of additional quantities of public goods is associated with declining marginal utilities and growing marginal disutilities to the extent that it does not

Figure 2.3
Price and Output under Perfect Competition

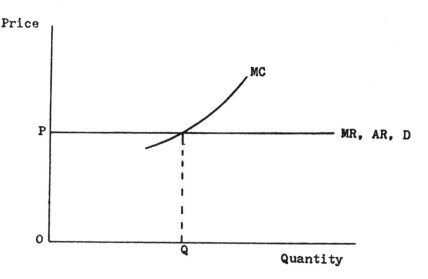

pay to use more. Thus, at point *H* there is overallocation of public goods and underallocation of private goods (MU < MD). At point *B* the opposite (MU > MD) occurs. At both last points *B* and *H* there is nonoptimal allocation of public goods and society does not attain maximal welfare.

COMPETITIVE AND MONOPOLISTIC PRICING

Beyond the distribution and stabilization functions of governments, their intervention in the economy may be justified also on resource allocation grounds. In such cases, the public sector would implement policies to supplement market failures and achieve social optimum outputs.

Under conditions of perfect competition, average revenue and marginal revenue are the same and are represented by a horizontal demand curve, as Figure 2.3 indicates. In such a pure competitive model, there are many sellers and buyers, a homogeneous product, free entry, free movement of factors and products, and perfect knowledge of the market so that the producer is a pricetaker not a pricemaker and the consumer's sovereignty prevails. In this model the market is the best planner of resource allocation and the principle of profit maximization, under which marginal cost (MC) of the firm equals marginal revenue (MR), coincides with the optimum resource allocation. In that case, marginal cost equals average revenue (AR), as well.

However, mixed economies, such as that of the United States, are more and more departing from the model of perfect competition and moving toward a monopolistic market structure, primarily under the model of monopolistic com-

Figure 2.4
Price and Output under Monopolistic Competition

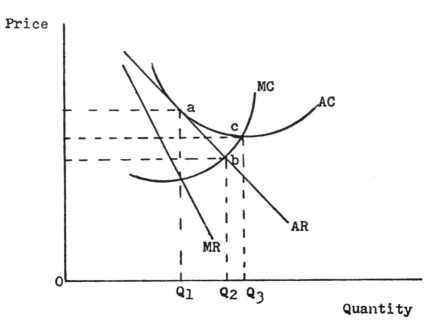

petition. In that model a relatively large number of firms are producing or selling differential products such as cloth, shoes, food products, and entertainment. Because of the differentiated products, imperfect competition prevails in the market, so that average cost equals average revenue at *a*, determined by the vertical (broken) line drawn upward from the point where marginal cost equals marginal revenue, as Figure 2.4 shows. Because of free entry in the market, the seller of differentiated products is forced to a nonprofit tangency of average cost curve to the demand curve at point *a*, with a price-quantity combination where profit maximization or loss minimization prevails. In this case, the firm operates at point *a*, with an average cost higher than the lowest possible cost per unit at point *c*, that is, with idle capacity. However, the government can subsidize the firm to expand production to the optimal social point *b* (MC = AR) with quantity Q_2, or even to Q_3, where marginal cost equals average cost (MC = AC). Also, it can implement demand stimulation policies and achieve a parallel shift of the demand or average revenue curve up to the lowest AC point (*c*).

On the other hand, under an oligopolistic market structure, which prevails largely in the United States, a few sellers control the largest part of trade. This does not lead to optimum production for the benefit of society. Oligopolists are afraid to cut prices because of the expected retaliatory action by others. Therefore, they face a kinked demand curve and a vertical marginal revenue curve. They maximize profits by producing at the MC = MR point, and they do not reduce prices even when their marginal and average costs are reduced as a result of technological improvement or other cost-saving innovations.

Under perfect competition the community enjoys a consumer's surplus. Because of low prices, consumers can buy more and pay less per unit than what they are willing to pay. However, when monopolies charge higher prices, determined by the profit maximization principle (MC = MR), the consumers lose more in surplus than the monopolies do in profits because of the inefficiency involved.

In private goods, an individual can consume a good if he or she pays for it. Marginal benefit to the consumer from such a good, which is wholly internalized, is equal to the marginal cost. However, in public goods this is not the case and their nature of joint consumption makes pricing very difficult or impossible. All individuals of a nation must consume the total amount of a public good or service, say defense, regardless of how much each one is willing to pay for it (nonexclusion).

In the private sector, total industry (market) demand of a private good, such as meat or gas, can be found through the horizontal summation of individual demands. In this case, individuals can be excluded from consuming a divisible private good if they do not like to pay for it. However, in a public indivisible good, such as administration of justice or police protection, total demand can be found by a vertical demand summation of the demands ($a + b = c$) for this public or social good, as Figure 2.5 indicates. Points a and b show the marginal benefits to individual consumers and the prices they would be willing to pay, respectively. Here all individuals consume equal amounts of a public good even if some of them are not paying for such a good (free riders). In these nonexclusion cases, since consumers try to avoid payment, the public sector will finance such jointly consumed goods through taxation or other compulsory means.

EXTERNALITIES

Market prices may give biased information to society about certain economic activities, either overstating benefits or understating costs and vice versa. There may be external benefits not reflected in the costs incurred in the production units, or there may be private economic activities that affect people other than those directly involved. For example, a firm's production of chemical goods may pollute the air of the surrounding area or the water running nearby and thus inflict costs on people who are not involved in the production or consumption of these products. The firm that pollutes the air or the water is imposing a negative externality on the individuals who breathe the air or use the water. Another example of a form of economic activity that has characteristics of both "privateness" and "publicness" is education. Economic benefits accrue to students who are expected to pay for their education; but also society at large benefits from an educated population. From that point of view, education should

Figure 2.5
Demand Summation for a Public or Social Good

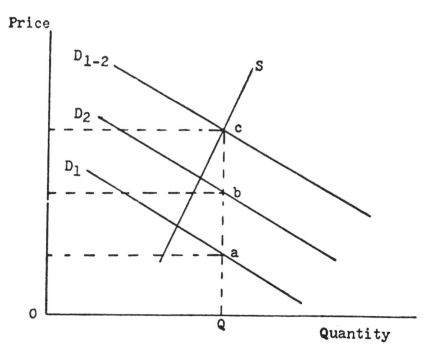

be supported or provided by the public sector beyond that paid by individuals (up to the point where marginal costs equal marginal private benefits). As Alfred Marshall pointed out, the economic value of even one industrial genius may be sufficient to cover the expenses of education of a whole town.

Even an ideal system of perfect competition may fail to achieve an efficient allocation of resources because of the existence of positive or negative externalities, since benefits or costs are not reflected in prices.[14] Therefore, corrective government measures are needed in the form of subsidies, fines, and regulations to adjust prices for the use of certain resources. Here, efforts are needed to bring local governmental boundaries and jurisdictions in line with the extension of externalities to avoid undesirable spillovers or neighborhood side effects. The private sector can deal with externalities without public sector intervention if it internalizes such externalities by forming sufficiently large units to abosrb the consequences.

As Arthur Pigou (1918) pointed out, social benefits and costs have both internal (private) as well as external (public) effects. When social beneficial effects exceed private benefits, there is positive externality. A government subsidy to compensate a private firm for higher production than a free market would support is demonstrated in Figure 2.6. Curve D_1 (pseudo-demand) shows external (non-

Figure 2.6
Internalization of Positive Externalities

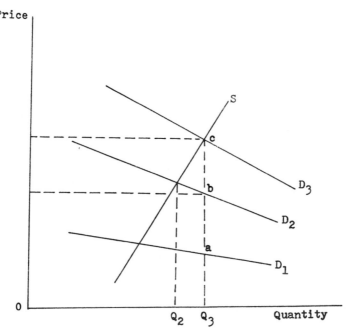

Figure 2.7
Internalization of Negative Externalities

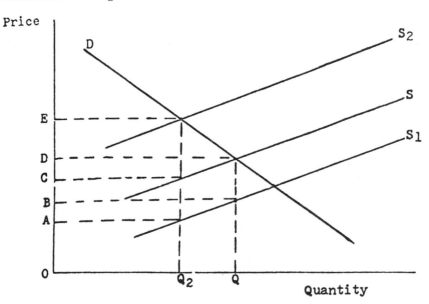

33

priced) benefits, while D_2 represents the market demand for the priced benefits. The vertical summation of the two curves in D_3 represents total social benefits generated from this good, and the government pays a subsidy bc equal to Q_3a. The firm now produces a higher quantity (OQ_3) than that supported by the free market (OQ_2).

Internalization of negative externalities or external costs is shown in Figure 2.7. The market equilibrium of supply and demand for a product, say steel, shows the price per unit (OD) in which nonmarket costs, such as pollution, are not considered. A corrective action through a government penalty tax to reduce pollution, for example, would result in a shift of the supply curve from S to S_2 which includes external costs indicated by the curve S_1. The new price OE includes or internalizes the anti-pollution tax or cost CE (equal to OA), which reduces output from OQ to OQ_2 and the associated negative externality (pollution) by AB.

Under the principle of profit maximization, private enterprises are not motivated to take corrective actions to protect the public from unhealthy by-products such as air, water, land, and noise pollution, or to avoid rapid depletion of vital resources. In such cases, the public sector must use the political process to improve resource allocation and social welfare.

A familiar example of externalities is that of an owner of beehives who receives external benefits in the form of free nectar from the neighbor's apple blossoms to produce honey, and the apple grower who receives free pollinating services to increase his apple crops.[15]

Negative externalities, or external costs, may occur when there is common property or when property rights are not adequately defined. Thus, when a firm pollutes the air, the people living next to it cannot sue the firm for pollution damages, and so external (uncompensated) costs are imposed on the neighboring individuals. Thus, for example, landlords in the polluted neighborhood might lower the rent they charge for their property. Such externalities prevent economic efficiency and Pareto's optimality of leaving someone better off without worsening the position of others.

In large-number externalities, which modern industrial nations face, government intervention is required in the form of taxes, regulations, or subsidies if efficiency is to be improved. In single or small-number cases, individuals may negotiate and establish property rights and bargain related remunerations for negative externalities if the cost of internalizing them exceeds the welfare gains (Coase Theorem).[16] For example, smokers may in some way compensate non-smokers in a nonsmoking compartment of a train or a plane for their permission to smoke. Or a cattle raiser may privately compensate a neighboring wheat farmer whose crop has been damaged by cattle straying into the wheat field.

CONGESTION AND ALLOCATION OF PUBLIC GOODS

Economic goods can be classified as pure private, quasi-private, club goods, and public (social) goods. In pure private goods benefits are divisible, consumption is determined according to the price mechanism, the exclusive principle applies, and the free-rider problem is largely avoided. In such goods, the consuming unit is one individual, a family, or a small group able to reach an agreement without governmental intervention. A toothpaste, a beefsteak, or a shirt are examples of such goods, where voluntary exchanges prevail.

A quasi-private or quasi-public good is a partially private and partially public good, with some benefits divisible and some indivisible, for which exclusion is partially possible. For example, university education may be a publicly provided private good, with partial or no payment, with which not only the individual students but society as a whole may benefit. Another example of quasi-private good is that of flowers in front of a house that are enjoyed privately by the owner as well as publicly by the neighbors and the people passing nearby. For some of such "impure" goods, exclusion may be possible but undesirable or costly. Such cases may involve levying tolls for new roads or installing meters for water supply and charging new service-users a fee, although the associated marginal costs may be small or zero.

Pure public goods provide indivisible benefits that are jointly and equally consumed by large groups, where the exclusion principle does not apply. Such goods, which include national defense and administration of justice, require government allocation intervention. In some cases, the government may interfere to allocate or distribute certain divisible goods through direct supplies or subsidization, although the market can do that. Postal services, low-cost housing, electricity, transportation, or food stamps and school lunches may be included in the categories of such (merit) goods.

The benefits obtained from the joint consumption of a public good fall as more persons use the good simultaneously. If many people migrate into an area, or use the services of a public good, crowding or congestion may occur. The optimal number of users (the members of a club, for instance) of a public good is achieved when marginal benefits from the last unit supplied equal marginal cost.[17] Members of groups or cooperative organizations of people with identical tastes compose such clubs, and the public goods they consume are "club goods." They may include tennis clubs, golf societies, members of swimming pools, and other collective forms of consumption-ownership groups which are subject to congestion and exclusion is possible. As the membership of such a club increases, the benefits per member can initially rise but eventually will decline. This is similar to the law of diminishing returns, where increases in the units of a varying factor, keeping another factor fixed, would eventually lead to a decline in the marginal product. It thus may be beneficial for a region or a country to encourage an immigration of new residents or inversely to restrict the number of residents, depending on whether the optimal size of sharing the output of certain common facilities has been achieved.

3

Size of the Public Sector

CHANGES IN THE PUBLIC SECTOR

The Increasing Public Sector in the United States and in Other Market Economies

By nature, men and women are normally neither giants nor dwarfs. Likewise, in order to be efficient a state should not be too big; neither should it be too small, for it must be able to sustain itself. There seems to be a maximum size that should not be exceeded by any state or other authority. However, in some cases that state becomes very large and tends to be similar to what Thomas Hobbes described in his *Leviathan*: a giant or monsterous technical person. In this case, the relationship of the state and its members becomes loose and cumbersome and frequently governments collapse under their own weight as people try to regain their freedom.

As Rousseau pointed out, when the government is far away from the local people, it becomes more inhuman, more demanding, and oppressive. More governing authorities are created between the people and the central government, more tax revenues are required to pay for growing public expenditures, and inefficiency and bureaucracy increase. In such cases, there is more confusion in applying state laws and regulations, more arbitrary and oppressive actions by in-between bureaucrats, and more corruption, which is difficult for the state to correct. On the other hand, people in great distance from the central authority feel isolated and abandoned; their virtues are disregarded and their talents ignored. As politicians and policymakers become overwhelmed by the plethora of cases they must deal with, they let the bureaucrat clerks implement policy measures, thus increasing confusion and corruption.[1] It is the task of political leaders to establish an equilibrium between the ideal and the real and to make the state mechanism less oppressive and more efficient.

For the last two centuries the United States and other Western nations have experienced public sector growth larger than that of the private sector. The gradual increase in public spending is due to the enlargement of government activities or functions in providing social services such as internal and external security, education and welfare, subsidies to agriculture, environmental protection, and other activities, producing goods and services with the characteristics of publicness and a growing social interest in their allocation.

About a century ago Adolph Wagner, a German political economist, promulgated the hypothesis that social progress in industrializing nations causes a proportionately higher growth of government, or the public sector, than growth of the overall economy.[2]

Although Wagner's law of the expanding state activity explains important long-term trends, it was criticized as a self-determining theory of the state that omits the influence of wars, inflations, and other disturbances that push government expenditures to successively higher plateaus.

In addition to Adolph Wagner's predictions of a growing public sector as a result of economic development and the continued pressure for social progress, Ernst Engel, another nineteenth-century German economist, seemed also to expect growing public expenditures and outlays for sundries, yet falling proportions of family consumption spending, with greater income. Moreover, Pigou thought that the public sector would grow with increasing national income and wealth,[3] while Alan Peacock and Jack Wiseman presented empirical evidence supporting a regular growth of governmental activity mainly because of shifts of expenditures and revenues to new, higher levels in cases of wars and social disturbances with no return to the previous lower levels (this is the displacement effect).[4]

On the other hand, Richard Musgrave argues that as the size of population that shares a public good rises, the relative tax price of the good is expected to fall, giving an elasticity higher than one, as the percentage change in demand for this good becomes larger.[5] Similarly, William Baumol, in his model of unbalanced economic growth, expects a faster growth of the public sector than the private sector primarily because of the strong political demand for the maintenance of public goods and the ever-increasing portion of labor force shifted to the public sector.[6]

Economic growth in modern industrial societies leads to more specialization, impersonalization, and interdependencies in economic and social life that require a larger and more efficient public sector. Furthermore, industrialization and modern technology require large amounts of capital and long-run fixed investment in public utility projects (natural monopolies), which the private sector, interested primarily in short-run profits, may hesitate or may be unable to undertake.

Rapid technological changes and new social problems may force governments to intervene and seek proper solutions (this is the inspection effect). Directly or indirectly, the displacement and/or the inspection effects frequently lead to the concentration of economic activities in the public sector at the expense of the private sector.

Market economies, like those of the United States and Western Europe, are characterized by the dominance of the private sector. They have, nonetheless, a sizable and growing public sector. In such mixed economies, the existence and growth of the public sector is justified primarily because of the growing monopolization of the market and the failure of the free market mechanism to perform well in the allocation and distribution of resources and products in certain sectors and industries of, primarily, the public domain.

Many central economic and social issues cannot be handled adequately by the market mechanism and call for public policy measures. It seems that public policy, like it or not, is necessary in our modern society to solve some of its complicated problems. There are public or semi-public institutions and enterprises that are directly or indirectly under government control and regulations. For example, of a semi-public character are the giant retirement plans for doctors, lawyers, engineers, and other groups from many walks of life—those who possess a prominent place in society. Management of these plans, which is appointed by member voting and largely regulated by the government, can influence investment and even social policies through the use of large portfolio holdings.

A new economic tendency or necessity, which appeared recently with great force in the United States and other market economies, is that of bailing out or rescuing troubled enterprises by providing and rescheduling state loans or though capitalizing and controlling problematic firms. Such firms include Lockheed, Chrysler, Continental Illinois, Amtrak, Eastern Railroads and Conrail, Home Savings Bank in Ohio, Old Court Savings and Loan Association in Maryland, savings banks in Texas and elsewhere, and probably other auto, steel, and airline companies, as well as banks with problem loans to Argentina, Mexico, Brazil, and other debtor nations. This bailing-out phenomenon took place in Italy during the Mussolini era and is presently taking place in Britain, France, Germany, Spain, Greece, Turkey, and even Japan, where the governments struggle to keep moribund enterprises alive to avoid extensive unemployment.

The Decreasing Public Sector in Planned Economies

Socialist or planned economies have a tendency toward the denationalization of small industries and retail stores and the redistribution of some state lands to the private sector in order to provide high incentives to increase productivity. This trend of reducing the public sector can be observed in almost all planned economies, but particularly in China and the Eastern European countries, including the Soviet Union through its recent openess (*glasnost*) and reconstruction (*perestroika*). In these command economies, privatization and self-management seem to be more attractive than nationalization. It is also suggested that even nationalized industries in the United States and other market economies be handed over to a mutual fund in which every citizen would have shares that could be introduced in a free market.[7]

One of the main problems policymakers have to face in these economies is how to achieve planned targets while at the same time allowing more autonomy to search for and apply new techniques and innovations. Like Adam Smith's invisible hand in capitalist markets, what is required is an invisible foot to jolt managers into the introduction of new technology. However, bureaucracy in the public sector still continues to thwart efforts to promote innovations and increase efficiency.

To stimulate efficiency and increase production, planned economies have started to reorganize their economic mechanisms. This includes giving more autonomy and promoting self-sufficiency for state enterprises by adjusting production to related market demand, reducing or eliminating subsidies, and increasing material reward to the workers with high productivity. This economic strategy, named the new mechanism, aims at the improvement of quality and an increase in productivity through more cooperative competition, or competitive cooperation, and less inflexible controls. Also, the institution of property is gradually enlarged to include retail trade and housing, in addition to small plots in agriculture. Indeed, the private agricultural plots and the growth of small numbers of livestock, as recently permitted, are more reliable sources of food than state stores. It can thus be said that one volunteer worker is worth two or more of those who are pressed into production service.

Planned economies are under pressure to liberalize their economies by removing subsidies from a number of consumer products and allowing prices to fluctuate, that is, to be adjusted to the market forces of supply and demand, as well as by giving more freedom to the private sector. The main goals of these new policies are to reduce bureaucracy; unload government budgets from their heavy burden of subsidies, which are responsible for a drain of about one-third of total revenue; and make production enterprises stand on their own feet.

A striking example of the reduction of the public sector in favor of the private sector is the new policy of China, which gradually abandons traditional blind and sterile ideology in favor of pragmatism and economic realism. In this way, Chinese policymakers try to reduce price subsidies on consumer goods that absorb about 40 percent of the state budget.

In the industrial sector, some enterprises in planned economies have begun to adjust wages to the productivity of workers. In many enterprises the job tenure system that compensates workers regardless of their performance is still stifling productivity. On the other hand, workers and employees who exceed their quota receive extra rewards and vice versa for those who do not meet their quota. To encourage investment in industry, the government provides tax holidays and other incentives to foreign investors and supports joint ventures to attract new technology and modernize production, as is practiced also in Western countries.

The government will concern itself primarily with macroeconomic goals, leaving microeconomic decision making to the enterprises, which will pay taxes instead of passing profits to the state. With this denationalization and gradual deregulation of many industries and rural and urban services, policymakers aim at the reallocation of labor and resources to the most efficient enterprises.

Recently, trends of self-management, decollectivization, and privatization of small-scale industries can be observed in planned economies, notably in China, Hungary, Romania, Yugoslavia, and to a lesser extent in the Soviet Union.[8] Increasing numbers of workers earn their living without going through the Party or government bureaucracy. In order to encourage workers to increase production, the central authorities are forced to reduce controls, especially in industries where individual incentives are needed.

Employee Ownership as an Alternative to Private and Public Sectors

The limitations of the private and public sectors and the avoidance of extremes—or the pursuit of the mean in freedom and welfare, as Aristotle and the Pythagorians advocated centuries ago—may be pursued through a new system of employee ownership and enterprise decision making. An economic system in which working people participate in enterprise decision making may be considered as a healthy basis for an effective democratic way of life with more political freedom, less inequality, and higher efficiency. What is presently said, that ''in capitalism man exploits man, in communism it is the other way around,'' may be avoided in such a system.

In recent decades a remarkable development in industrial organization has been introduced in a number of countries, including the United States, signifying a deviation from both the private and the public sector. Gradually and quietly, employees and workers in a number of industries have come to play a significant role in enterprise decision making concerning wages, working conditions, investment, and similar matters. In cooperation with capital or under a system of self-management, they aim at stimulating incentives and improving productivity and welfare. Although they grow at the expense of the traditional labor unions, which presently behave like tame dogs, they do not seem to raise questions of replacing the authority of property owners or the state. From the point of view of public finance, such a trend unloads the government from subsidy expenditures to moribund enterprises and other undesirable controls.

In a number of instances private companies encourage labor representation in enterprise decision making so that strikes and other disturbances may be avoided as workers become responsible for decisions affecting them. Moreover, when enterprises, public or private, are not profitable or approach bankruptcy, employees are asked and frequently accept to take over management in order to keep the firm in operation and preserve their jobs. In such cases, the government, or any other responsible authority, is not required to finance and rescue weak and bankrupt firms.

Incentives to participate in a democratized workplace may somehow be able to replace conventional incentives (pay, promotion, or discharge, for example). Industrial democracy may strengthen and stimulate production. This is important in modern societies because of growing specialization, which according to Adam Smith makes the individual naive and ignorant and increases nervousness and rivalry among workmates.[9] Incentive and accomplishment, affection, relief, and happiness in the workplace may require replacement of hierarchical and authoritarian structures in enterprises, whether private or public.

Along these lines, John Stuart Mill believed that collective decisions and participatory democracies advance human intellect, reduce bureaucracy, and increase efficiency.[10] However, through employee training, care should be taken to make participation workable and practical; otherwise there is the danger of frustration and inefficiency. A frantic participation or apathy and too great a public preoccupation with politics may make the system unworkable and inefficient, or it may lead to the creation of a professional elite in place of an old bureaucracy.

Years ago Joseph Schumpeter suggested that a new economic system, known as people's capitalism, could combine the advantages of both private sector capitalism and public sector socialism. Some successful lessons in that direction have been observed recently in the United States, Japan, and Western Europe through the spread of ownership. As the arguments go, partial or total employee ownership and self-management might be the answer to the problems of a growing public sector rife with bureaucracy and inefficiency. This would result from the expansion of democratic ideals and widespread educational improvement. People would learn to release their talents and combine their efforts in decision making and productive cooperation for the betterment of themselves and of society.[11] They would stop worshipping the state or being directed in their activities. Self-management or the labor-capital cosharing system, wisely managed, can probably be made more efficient for attaining economic ends than any alternative yet in sight. The main problem is to work out a system that will be efficient in achieving the best results with the least possible costs without offending people's notions of freedom and a satisfatory way of life.

Thus, the main question is how to attain acceptable material goals while preserving freedom and moral values. Rapid economic development and removal of market imperfections and state bureaucracies call for a new form of management organization. Moreover, efficient allocation of resources and exploitation of external economies may require departure from the structures of the competitive market or state controls.

A proper measure to stimulate productivity and keep production costs relatively low might be to pay part of wages in the form of bonuses, depending on the efficiency or profitability of each private or public enterprise. This flexible system of remuneration, which has been successfully introduced in Japan, has the advantage of reducing the fixed labor cost significantly. In addition, paying part or all of workers' compensation in the form of periodic bonuses has the financial advantage of providing the enterprise with working capital for several months.

Part of these bonuses may remain with a special fund for additional pension or for extra payment after a number of years of work.

Different schemes of employee participation in decision making, revenue, and ownership have been developed in a number of countries, including the United States. In the system of revenue sharing, employees would receive a certain percentage of revenue instead of fixed wages.[12] As an alternative, employee stock ownership plans, or ESOPs, have spread rapidly in the United States. More than 6,000 plants with 9.6 million workers, compared to about half a million in 1976, are under such plans, according to the National Center for Employee Ownership. They include such companies as Phillips Petroleum, Healthtrust Corporation, Weirton Steel, Dan River, Eastern Airlines, U.S. Sugar Corporation, Cone Mills Corporation, and Rath Packing. Today the employee-owned companies represent as much as 8 percent of the U.S. workforce and in some 15 years are expected to increase to 18 percent, equal to the present number of labor unions.

A number of companies offer these plans as substitutes for pension funds and profit sharing while others use leverage ESOPs to avoid unwanted takeovers. Employees and workers agree to buy the firms in which they work and offer concessions to avoid buyouts by other firms. Tax deductions, up to 25 percent of the annual payroll of the company's contributions to ESOP plans, and other incentives are offered by the U.S. federal government to encourage employee ownership. Also, lenders to ESOPs do not have to pay income on half the interest they collect. Such tax breaks are estimated to be $2 to $3 billion each year.

Moreover, loans and other support measures are provided by the state to problematic and moribund firms. As long as the state preserves complete or partial control of such firms, these rescue operations tend to be institutionalized and introduce a modern form of undesirable fiscal activity. However, with the introduction of a share economy and employee ownership of enterprises, such government interventions and undesirable controls can be reduced or eliminated.

In contrast, other countries such as Britain and France have resorted to the process of denationalization or "privatization" of state or semi-state enterprises. Thus, British Telecom (the state-owned telephone monopoly), Ferranti (the industrial electronics firm), Britoil, British Sugar, Jaguar (the luxury car maker), British Petroleum, Cable and Wireless, and British Airways, which were totally or partially owned by the state, have been or are in the process of total or partial denationalization (this is called Thatcherism), or have been taken to the market, with expectations of employee participation. Along these lines, France embraces "popular capitalism" and is in the process of selling off government-owned industry to employees and private investors. The campaign of denationalizing some 65 public enterprises, a number of which had been nationalized by Charles de Gaulle, has been warmly received by employee-investors and domestic and foreign financiers, who include such companies as Paribas, Saint-Gobain, Agency Havas, Compagnie Générale d'Electricité, and three major commercial banks. In Western Europe as a whole, a total of about 2,000 state enterprises worth of some $130 billion are expected to be sold by 1991. The main reason for this denationalization is to encourage competition, increase efficiency, and remove government subsidies.

PUBLIC SECTOR CONTROLS AND REGULATIONS

To discourage monopolization of the market, special laws and regulations have already been introduced. They aim to protect consumers from adulteration, pollution, resource depletion, and misrepresentation of quality and prices. In the United States such laws include the Sherman Act (1890), prohibiting activities that restrain trade and monopolize the market; the Clayton Act (1914), forbidding price discrimination and elimination of competition between corporations through interlocking directorates and other devices; the Trade Commission Act (1914), prohibiting unfair methods of competition; the Robinson-Patman Act (1936), making it illegal to try to eliminate smaller rivals by charging unreasonably low prices and using other supply discrimination techniques; the Celler Merger Act (1950); and other laws and regulations enacted later to achieve these goals, that is, to restrict monopoly and maintain competition. Such pieces of legislation extended the powers of the government in order to protect the public from unfair practices by monopolies and trusts.

However, in spite of all these pieces of legislation and the accompanying judges and lawyers to implement them, monopolization and oligopolization of the U.S. market continues to grow. This may be due to the economies of scale that large firms can achieve through concentration of capital and modern technology. As long as large monopolistic or oligopolistic firms can utilize mass production methods and reduce cost per unit, it is difficult to discourage their formation and operation through controls and regulations in the economy. The dilemma, therefore, is how to encourage competition and entrepreneurial intuition without hurting efficiency and economic progress.

Antitrust legislation may thus to a large extent be considered as unrealistic, just as are the models of competition it aims to protect. Breaking down large enterprises or prohibiting mergers and other monopolistic formations do not seem to accomplish much from the viewpoint of optimal resource allocation and entrepreneurial innovations. The problems that antitrust laws face today resemble the heads of the mythological Lernaean Hydra, for in the place of every problem solved two others appear.

Consolidations and mergers may lead to better organization and research and lower unit costs. To break or discourage such efficient formations is to punish efficiency and success. Antitrust laws and related restrictions should probably discourage price fixing and employment malpractices rather than obstruct mergers that can improve quality and reduce the cost of production. One could argue in favor of replacing all antitrust laws with modern and simplified pieces of legislation that would recognize the present real conditions of the oligopolistic and monopolistic structure of the domestic and international markets.

Public regulations and public enterprises have appeared as an alternative to the shortcomings of the antitrust legislation. The responsibility of public utility regulations is mostly entrusted to state and local agencies. However, federal government commissions have also been introduced to reinforce local and state controls, mainly during and after the Great Depression. They include the Federal Power Commission (FPC), regulating gas and electricity; the Securities and Exchange Commission (SEC), regulating stock and security markets; the Federal Communications Commission (FCC), controlling telephone and telegram as well as radio and TV services; the Interstate Commerce Commission (ICC), regulating interstate and foreign trade movements; the Federal Aviation Agency (FAA); and the Civil Aeronautics Board (CAB), responsible for enforcing airlines safety rules and economic aviation regulations, respectively. However, the CAB was abolished at the end of 1984, after 46 years in operation, and the Department of Transportation assumed some of its remaining functions.

In spite of all these regulations and controls, some commissions, especially the FCC, proved on many occasions to be helpless or indifferent. Two or more regulated industries may compete through offering services that can be substituted for each other. Such industries include telephone and telegram; AM and FM radio and TV; electricity and gas; and transport by air, highway, railway, and waterway. However, regulations have not proved to be adequate to reduce costs, check discrimination, induce technological progress, control excessive profits, or encourage competition. Although it is diffiuclt or impossible to measure the results of regulations, there seems to be a need to keep and vigorously enforce some of them in order to protect the consumer so as to avoid environmental deterioration and prevent monopolization of the market and the charging of unjustifiably high prices.

Excessive governmental interventions into the market processes through regulations and controls may alter entrepreneurial investment decisions and, all else being equal, may retard growth.[13] Thus, environment and health and safety regulations may require investment that might otherwise be made in plant and equipment. They may also require sufficient workforce to operate needed control equipment and administer legal activities and office work without adding to salable outputs. Nonetheless, public regulations are expected to yield contributions to total welfare, such as improvement in health and safety, that is difficult to measure and cannot be fully reflected in reported output. Thus, further research is needed into more efficient measurement of the economic impacts of public regulations on a society to determine if their total beneficial effects overpass their detrimental effects on productivity. For in general, U.S. antitrust regulations have indirect and modest influences on private sector allocations and free market operations.

Recent efforts to remove excessively burdensome regulations from the U.S. economy have fallen short of the political rhetoric, and limited goals have been achieved. The bulk of deregulations concerns transportation, financial services, environment, energy, and communications. The implementation of deregulations, though, have given more freedom to airlines and railroads to set prices as well as to commercial banks to set deposit interest rates freely after the elimination of ceilings on such rates. However, the breakup of the American Telephone and Telegraph Company and the congressional moratoriums on off-shore-acreage oil exploration present problems of the efficient operation and utilization of technological innovations.

Government regulation of airlines, for example, had been responsible for high labor costs and low efficiency. Since 1978, however, when the government's sheltering regulations of airlines was ended, increased competition suppressed operation costs including wages, which were reduced in a number of cases. Thus American West Airlines pilots receive $32,500 per year, compared to the industry average of about $100,000. Other examples of low labor cost and more competition are those of United Airlines and Eastern Airlines. The beneficiaries of increased competition from deregulation are the consumers, who get lower prices and more efficient performance. But, there is the danger that smaller companies are swallowed up by large ones, which eventually may control the market and charge higher prices. Also, problems of proper maintenance and dangers of air accidents may appear.

In recent years worldwide expansion of trade and investment as well as the introduction of floating currency rates has necessitated a new consideration of antitrust laws. Up to now, the main purpose of the antitrust laws has been to promote primarily domestic competition. The increasing importance of global competition, though, suggests a change in antitrust treatment and regulatory developments. Thus, the U.S. Justice Department and the Federal Trade Commission (FTC) look favorably on joint international ventures such as that of the General Motors Corporation of the United States and the Toyota Motor Corporation of Japan. Also, because of strong competition from Europe and Japan, a new look at steel and car industries has been taken by the antitrust regulatory authorities in order to effect investment and technological development.

Deregulation in air and surface transportation, financial markets and communications, oil prices, and stock exchange brokerage have intensified price competition and spurred efficiency in those industries. Moreover, proposals for regulatory reforms have been made for further deregulations in banking and natural gas prices, deposit insurance and private pensions, nuclear licensing, trucking and railroads, and environmental restrictions. In some cases, however, deregulation has led to overlapping markets, turbulent entry of new firms, and maneuvers toward price discrimination.

Regarding foreign trade deregulation, restrictions on color television sets and nonrubber footwear, mainly from South Korea, Taiwan, and Brazil, were lifted and quotas on copper were not imposed in spite of the cries of domestic industries for protection. Whereas for a number of products such as steel, cars, and cloth, voluntary quotas or the other limitations were introduced to reduce imports. Such quotas, though, may be considered detrimental to international competition and universal free trade. They seem to be worse than tariffs because they make it difficult for foreign competitors to increase sales and reduce prices. As a result, the U.S. trade policy seems to be moving gradually in a protectionalist direction, despite the cries for deregulation and the support of the free market mechanism in international transactions.

Supporters of legislative intervention argue that in order to ease the imbalance and reverse the trend of U.S. companies that move their facilities overseas and export jobs, the government should adopt protective measures and take steps to direct trade with other countries. This is so especially for manufacturing products such as textiles and shoes (three-fourths of which are imported). To avoid further self-inflicting wounds, they suggest that the U.S. government set a fixed ratio between exports and imports, particularly on nations with a history of excessive trade surpluses. Also, limitations on the percentages of import-increases are considered.

PUBLIC ENTERPRISES

The public sector sometimes operates public utility and other enterprises involved in the provision of marketable goods, primarily in the field of electricity, water, telephones, and transportation. This takes place because the private sector may not provide the optimal amount of goods or services, or for the protection of consumers. There are industries that are natural monopolies because it is difficult or impossible to have a large number of firms competing in the market. By nature, you cannot have many firms providing electricity or telephones or water in the same house and yet compete in prices and quantity.

Such monopolies can set prices above marginal cost, producing less than optimum output. When such firms exhibit increasing returns to scale and realize declining marginal cost, however, average cost is more than marginal cost by the amount of average fixed cost. In such cases, setting a price at the point where average revenue (the demand curve) equals marginal cost would result in losses for the firm, which may be covered by government tax revenue (that is, a subsidy). To break even, the firm must charge a price equal to average cost.

In many instances, the government uses regulations to restrict the pricing policy of natural monopoly firms to that which covers average cost or else sets up its own public enterprises or nationalizes monopolistic industries.

From the standpoint of efficiency, it is difficult for the state to decide whether it is better to establish a public enterprise or to rely on a regulated private natural monopoly.

In the first case, larger outputs and lower prices (equal to marginal costs) would be the outcome, but it should be desirable by society to pay for the losses incurred. In the second case of the regulated monopoly, the prevailing principle of profit maximization or cost minimization would increase efficiency compared to public enterprises, which usually run with less efficiency (X-efficiency), but prices would be set at the point where the price is equal to average cost. Moreover,

Figure 3.1
Optimal Social Allocation in an Imperfect Market

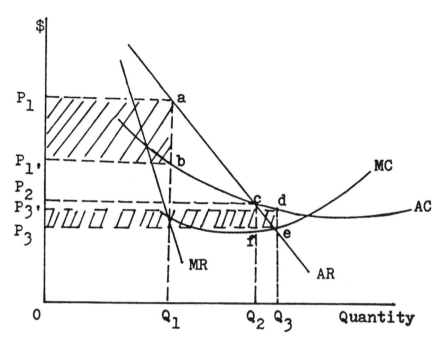

the existence of significant external benefits may be another reason for establishing public enterprises.

If the capacity limit of a public or a regulated enterprise is fixed, then part or the whole amount of output may be rationed or bought by a public institution at a determined price, while storing any remaining output for sale at a later period. However, the capacity may be expanded at discrete steps or it may fluctuate. When the capacity is fully used, we have peak periods. When it is not, then capacity is at off-peak periods. Therefore, investment decisions of public or regulated enterprises should consider the problem of capacity related to demand for the products in question.

Figure 3.1 shows that at point c, a firm is producing quantity Q_2 at a price P_2, which is equal to average cost, leaving no losses. At this break-even point, imposed probably by a public utility regulation, the firm may realize a small "normal" economic profit, which is included into average cost, perhaps as an insurance premium against losses. This is the proper size of an enterprise, public or private, to achieve the highest possible output at the lowest possible price without any losses. However, profit maximization is achieved at point a, where marginal cost is equal to marginal revenue, with price P_1 and output limited to Q_1. At this point, total profit is shown by the area a b P_1 and P_1' (or $ab \times aP_1$). This profit maximization model is normally used by private enterprises.

In contrast, for public enterprises or public policy aiming at the highest possible output and employment, point e, where marginal cost is equal to average revenue, is the point of optimal social allocation with price P_3 and output expanded to Q_3. At this optimal social output Q_3, there is a loss $e\ d\ P_3\ P_3'$ (or $ed \times OQ_3$). For the production of this good to continue at Q_3, the government should subsidize the losses of the producing enterprise. On the contrary, a public enterprise producing at point a and charging a price OP_1 is like the government imposing an excise tax on the product, a tax collected by that public enterprise.

The loss in total benefits to consumers from consuming Q_1 rather than Q_3 is the area under the demand curve Q_1aeQ_3. However, the saving in resource costs from reduction in output from Q_3 to Q_1 is the area under the marginal cost curve. The net cost to society is the difference between these two areas. In other terms, the net loss to society is the consumers' loss less the producer's gain. On the other hand, the net loss to society from average cost pricing at point c (in a regulated firm) and a pricing at marginal cost at point e (in a public-owned enterprise) would be the area cfe.

In the event of declining marginal and average costs, that is, continuing economies of scale, as the majority of empirical cases have proven to be, the market seems to fail in its allocative mechanism, producing limited output at $MC = MR$. This is so because of the higher production concentration and monopolization, which is justified in this case on the grounds of declining per-unit costs in larger firms.

Figure 3.2 shows that an enterprise, private or public, would produce quantity Q_2 at price P_2 equal to cost per unit ($AR = AC$). At this break-even production point three would be no profits—and no losses either. At Q_3, however, there is a loss equal to the difference of AC and MC per unit, that is, equal to the average fixed cost (AFC). This loss can be covered by subsidy from the public sector if it is desirable to produce large quantities of output at Q_3. On the other hand, implementation of the profit maximization principle would mean production of output OQ_1, which is far less than OQ_2, and at price P_1, which is far higher than P_2 at the break-even point.

Figure 3.3 also shows government subsidization (PP') per unit of a commodity to keep the low price (P) and the same quantity produced (Q) by a nationalized firm. In this case, the firm can produce and sell a quantity (Q) where the marginal social benefit, indicated by D', equals the marginal cost. It can sell at price P and receive a subsidy by the government (PP') per unit to cover its costs. Although government subsidies are usually extended to public enterprises, private firms have also been bailed out by public funds and government loans, as has happened with Lockheed and Chrysler.

Public ownership and public controls and subsidies in some cases may serve as an effective means of controlling market power, yet they do not constitute a panacea. Problems of scarcity and adjustment of revenues and expenditures are present in nationalized firms, as they are in private firms. Such problems should be solved and control decisions should be taken on the basis of costs and benefits

Figure 3.2
Social Allocation with Declining Costs

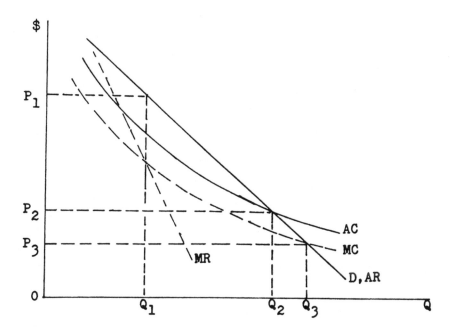

Figure 3.3
Subsidization of a Nationalized Firm

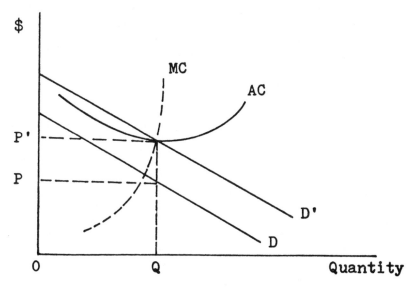

or efficiency, not on grounds of ideology and prejudice. Public firms should not become part of the political patronage system: Industries or regions should not receive or lose services as a form of political reward or punishment.

Usually prices are regulated to allow private firms to earn a certain rate of return on capital over and above the average cost of production. As long as the rate of return is competitive, such regulated firms may expand their capital stock and use excessive capital relative to labor in order to increase total return. Such regulations, which encourage capital-intensive methods, increase output but may raise costs and unemployment, thereby introducing one efficiency to eliminate another.

When a public enterprise follows a marginal cost pri., the losses that may occur may be made up by price discrimination, for example, by charging a fixed license fee (as for telephones) or different prices for groups of consumers, depending on demand elasticity (residential versus industrial users and so on). Another method is to levy lump-sum taxes (head or poll taxes). They are non-distortionary, but they are not preferable from the point of view of equity and income redistribution because they are not progressive.

When a public enterprise determines prices under conditions of efficiency (at marginal cost) similar to those in every other industry, then we have the case of "first best," or Pareto optimum. But if distortions exist elsewhere, except in the controllable sectors of the economy, then we have the case of "second best." In the second-best theory, a public enterprise establishes prices equal to marginal costs, but in other sectors of the economy this does not occur, probably because of taxes, externalities, or monopolies.

For public enterprises, evaluation of projects regarding net social benefits requires cost-benefit analysis different from the profit maximization principle of the private sector. This is so mainly because of the associated extensive externalities, that is, the indirect effects elsewhere in the economy. Public expenditures in irrigation projects, roads, education, research, health, and similar programs are not guided by competitive market prices that reflect marginal values. In such cases, a set of prices reflecting opportunity costs of the foregone use of resources (shadow prices) can be used to calculate marginal social benefits and costs and determine social profitability of the projects considered. More details on cost-benefit analysis are presented in a later section in this chapter.

Although in the United States direct productive operations belong primarily to the private sector, there are certain activities of a mainly public utility nature that are regulated or owned by the public sector. They include the Tennessee Valley Authority, the Bonneville Dam in the Northwest, the Hoover Dam in the Southwest, rural electrification, the space program, and some direct or indirect projects on atomic power. Also, a number of activities and operations on the local level belong to the public sector, for example, airports, subways, and buses. As a result, some people talk about creeping public sector trends in the United States. Yet in Western countries such as Canada, Britain, Sweden, and France a number of other enterprises belong to the public sector. They include coal mines, railroads, steel mills, airlines, radio and TV broadcasting, and even car industries that are totally or partially owned by the state.

Private-public ventures might be considered as another way of using the advantages of both sectors for effective enterprising. Utilizing private management techniques in public or collective ownership might prove to be beneficial in productive capital investment and employment creation.

However, it seems that certain governmental controls and policies tend to cripple growth rates by checking private investment and real growth. As a result of such policies, work incentives tend to decline and inflationary pressures to rise. Moreover, central and local governments tend to waste resources because their outlays are not subject to the disciplines of the market. From that point of view, public spending has been tapering off in recent years as it approaches its economic and political limits.

FISCAL CHOICES IN A DEMOCRATIC PROCESS

In small groups of individuals, preferences on public goods can be expressed and implemented through negotiations and bargaining. However, in cities, regions, and nations with large numbers of people involved, preferences on social goods and fiscal matters are expressed by voting. Each citizen delegates authority to political parties or leaders by voting for them or their representatives. For some fiscal issues concerning city, state, or federal matters, though, direct referendums take place. Such matters may refer to public sector revenue or spending for some projects or borrowing money for certain government activities. For most of the public sector services and major fiscal issues in Western types of democracies, decisions are taken and implemented through political representatives and leaders who have been elected by the majority of individuals in such public offices as congresses or parliaments.

Although the rule of *simple majority* (50 percent plus 1) is normally used, especially on fiscal (that is, tax and expenditure) decisions, *qualified majorities* of, say, two-thirds or three-fourths are sometimes used in such important matters as constitutional changes, impeachments, or over-riding presidential vetos. If more than two alternatives are involved, *plurality voting* may be used, where the voter can rank issues in numerical order. Moreover, *point voting* may be used where the voter can distribute a number of given points among different alternatives.

In modern democracies each person has one vote of equal weight and, as a rule, the simple majority wins in political decision making.[14] However, in economics a nonegalitarian standard exists wherein the distribution of dollar votes is not equal, as are the political votes.

Partial market failure in the allocation process in some goods may lead to public sector allocations intervention, which may result in similar or different kinds of inefficiencies. As noted, welfare economics aims at the attainment of Pareto's optimality as the ultimate allocational objective. In contrast, positive economics deals with reality and is concerned with political or institutional decision making regardless of whether the welfare goals are fully attained. However, a democratic political process may, through voting, improve the revelation of social preferences for public goods.

Although people in their natural state are free, they form governments to protect their lives and property. As John Locke has opined, people put a piece of their freedom into a common pot to buy a little order that will enable them to combine their labor with other factors around them and create property that they use for their livelihood. For government protection of life, liberty, and property, people pay a price in the form of taxation. The question is: How much personal freedom or civil rights should be given away for public order? And how many property rights or tax payments should be turned to the government or the public sector? One of the objectives of public finance is to try to strike a balance between these two factors, that is, to combine or compromise the rights of civil liberty and property liberty.

Representative democracy may delegate and thus alienate the political will of the people it purports to serve, and as Rousseau once said, "Once a people permits itself to be represented, it is no longer free." However, a system of unmediated self-government by an engaged citizenry and people's assemblies, similar to those in the Greek polis, the Swiss canton, the New England town meeting, and the Jeffersonian ward system, is nonpractical in modern societies with mounting fiscal and social problems that require swift and decisive actions. Direct participation by an informed public seems to be ideal, but in large communities this system is difficult to work and such assemblies may be transformed into an unruly mass. Although electing politicians to public offices may be inferior to the democratic ideal of direct participation by the individual, parliamentary representation and the process of moving from public speaking to public office seems to be more effective, in spite of the passivity, manipulation, and privatism associated with representation. Even an informal neighborhood assembly needs an organizing committee to represent its interests.

Knut Wicksell (1851–1926), the Swedish economist, argued that perfect competition will produce a collective maximum of ophelimity or utility to achieve neutrality and efficiency. Some public services are provided at less than optimum levels while others are overextended. However, public expenditures are normally determined first and then the means for their financing are projected.

As noted earlier, under democratic individualism decisions are based primarily on a simple majority vote of 50 percent plus one. According to Wicksell, however, 100 percent approval, that is, unanimity, should be required so that no individual would be forced to pay for goods and services he or she does not like, in a way similar to the preference in a free market. But he recognized the extreme limitations of this principle and suggested a rule of relative unanimity of some qualified majority of perhaps three-fourths as a next-best solution, although this creates a "tyranny of the minority" by the remaining 25 percent of the voters.[15]

Budget formulation and approval involves fiscal politics. The determination of government expenditures and taxation involves an economic and primarily a political process. Thus, political systems, social classes, party structures, and interest groups play a significant role in deriving budgetary decisions, determining the size of the public sector, and shaping sociopolitical trends in each country.

There are political systems based on one or another form of democratic majority rule where the voters, through their elected representatives, influence government decisions and directly or indirectly determine economic policies. In other systems, an oligarchic group, composed predominately of army officers and landlords or other wealthy individuals, controls economic policies and the state apparatus through open or hidden dictatorships. Finally, in a number of countries a political party, primarily the communist party, exercises complete control over all the economic and sociopolitical aspects of the state. In such command economies, the relationship between politics and fiscal functions or social choices is different from those in plural democracies.

In the democracies of the market economies, notably that of the United States, there is growing concern that special interest groups and political action committees (PACs) largely influence the political process. Labor unions, trade associations, lobbying groups, and a host of special interest PACs pour money into the coffers of congressional or parliamentary candidates and affect the democratic process. In that way, laws and regulations, as well as public money appropriations, are turned in favor of these pressure groups. However, the people have to govern, not money and cliques: That is what democracy is all about.

Candidates for public office have to find a rich partner, a friend, or neighbor to finance their campaigns and then to declare their candidacy, unless they have been born into a rich family, or "the right" one. Such friends or neighbors or interest groups form PACs and collect money to contribute to political candidates for advertisement, traveling expenses, or even vote buying. Thus, PACs contributed more than $100 million to congressional candidates in 1984, compared to $12.5 million in 1974 and $83.6 million in 1982, while the number of PACs increased from 608 in 1974 to 4,000 in 1984.[16] To break the link between contributions and expected favors by special interests and to put a cap on PAC influence, new legislation has been suggested to set an alternative system of political campaign financing by small contributions. In such a system, big money contributors and special interest PACs would be less influential, and so popular vote as the basis of democracy could be restored. That is why there are limitations on contributions to the candidates for public office. As a result, contributions to presidential candidates cannot be more than $1,000, while up to $250 can be matched by the federal government. Similar limitations prevail at the local level, as for example in New York City for mayoral candidates.

VOTING RULES AND PUBLIC CHOICE

The Median Solution in Simple Majority Voting

Ordinary citizen-voters are not expected to be fully informed because the procedure is too expensive. This is one of the reasons why citizens leave many issues to elected politicians, who in turn authorize government agencies and expert bureaucrats to administer approved programs. Elected politicians are frequently provided with low-cost information and are affected by special interest groups. Lobbying activities by such groups as unions, trade associations, and PACs in general aim at providing benefits to special groups while the related costs are spread indirectly to large groups of taxpayers. From the viewpoint of public choice, however, such activities may lead to conflicts of interest and doubt regarding the long-run implications of decisions on various public projects.[17]

Collective decision making, or the theory of public choice, has acquired great importance in recent years. The complexities of political structures with many participants in decision making present new problems that may be different from the economist's normative principles. The right of citizens to vote on fiscal matters, directly or indirectly, plays a significant role in public sector expenditures and taxation, as well as on government controls and regulations in the economy. The rule of majority vote is the most popular in the democratic political process and the "moderate" or median solution seems to be effective and efficient in translating people's preferences.

Thus, if three persons are to vote for expenditures in a public project, such as a road, an airport, a hospital, a lighthouse, an old-age home, or a school budget, they can rank their preferences in a single-peaked or well-ordered fashion. For example, the first choice of one person is the most expensive project, and if the person cannot get it, he or she will vote for the less expensive ones. The second person's first choice is a median-expenditure project, while the third person's first choice is the least expensive project. However, the first and the third persons would prefer the middle solution as a second choice instead of choosing the two other extreme solutions, and the majority voting will reflect the median preference.[18]

Figure 3.4 shows the demand curve of an individual for a public good. At price P the individual would choose to consume quantity Q which maximizes his or her consumer surplus (DPa). An alternative choice Q' or Q'' is inferior to Q because the consumer surplus is less than the maximum by the area abc (equal to ade). This is the individual's middle-size preference or single-peaked ranking of the quantity of the public good in question.

Figure 3.5 shows the principle of minimum differentiation in a political equi-

Figure 3.4
Demand for a Public Good

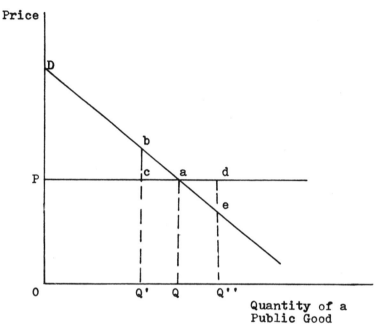

Price

D

b

P ———— c   a   d

e

0   Q'   Q   Q''

Quantity of a
Public Good

Figure 3.5
The Median in a Political Equilibrium

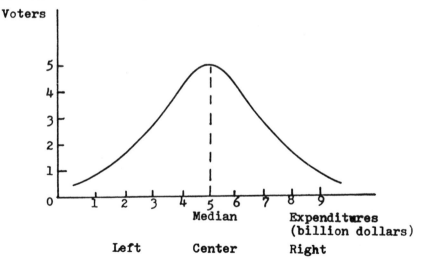

Voters

5

4

3

2

1

0   1   2   3   4   5   6   7   8   9

Median

Expenditures
(billion dollars)

Left   Center   Right

librium. Voters have different preferences regarding a government expenditure or any other public activity. Thus, in an election, for example, one voter or a group of voters is willing to vote for $1 billion for a government activity or the production of a public good. All the other voters are willing to vote for higher amounts, but voter 1 is rejecting any proposed activity that would cost more than $1 billion. At $4 billion, all but the previous voters would prefer to move to $5 billion. Once at $5 billion, no majority would agree to change. A move to $6 billion would be supported by less voters ($4 + 3 + 2 + 1 = 10$), but it would be opposed by more voters ($1 + 2 + 3 + 4 + 5 = 15$). The preferences at $5 billion, the median, would prevail and the allocation of the public good, attained under majority rule, would be optimal.

Therefore, for a simple-issue election, simple majority rule is capable of achieving a unique political equilibrium at the median peak of the voters. The median voters are fortunate to have the political equilibrium coincide with their individual equilibrium and the tax share per unit to be equal to the market price of the public good, if available. The other voters consume either less or more of the public good than they prefer. This analysis, credited primarily to Duncan Black, suggests that political parties should move toward the median peak, or the middle, to win elections.[19] This principle is in agreement with the Aristotelian mean, or the avoidance of extreme solutions.

Political Logrolling

If preferences were distributed, not normally, but according to income, the mean would be higher than the median in a positively skewed distribution. The principle of majority voting, though, prevents the production of too small or too large an output of the public good, which would result if preferences were allocated in a way similar to income. This principle is of great importance to the theory of public choice.

Voters normally vote for solutions and alternatives closest to their most-preferred outcome, which is the median peak in a single-majority direct-democracy system. When there are issues with different preferences, there may be incentives to trade votes in favor of the most favorable issues for groups of voters. This process is called political logrolling. Such an explicit or implicit trading of votes affects the formation of political platforms and public sector decisions. It also enhances the importance of income redistribution in collective decision making, as well as public sector expenditures where benefits are more indirect and undervalued than cost or taxes.

In a democratic society logrolling may be considered as a safety value for avoiding social instabilities and revolutions by minorities that have no other outlet for venting their preferences. A combined package of two or more issues may succeed in a simple-majority voting as each minority is expected to support the deal to get its own favored program passed, instead of seeing it defeated under a separate voting.

COST-BENEFIT ANALYSIS

Cost-benefit analysis is the process of weighting costs and benefits of government programs in order to rank them according to their merits. Because of their intangible and largely nonmonetary nature, public projects or programs are difficult to evaluate in practice. As a result, social benefits from reduction in pollution, betterment in literacy, avoidance of accidents, and improvements in health from investment in hospitals, sewage, and other facilities are difficult to assess.

As far as collective choices are concerned, the rational citizen will favor government expenditures in a public project when the expected cost or the tax share is lower than the expected personal benefit. If the marginal or additional cost is higher than the marginal or additional benefit, the individual voter will not support such a project. If the marginal cost or the tax share is equal to the marginal benefit, the voter might be indifferent and not bother to vote. Thus, politicians can be expected to approve public activities that offer net benefits to their constituency and thereby gain votes.

In the real world decisionmakers face problems different than those of Pareto's optimality, that is, of improving the position of an individual without harming that of somebody else. The principle of nonexclusivity or the sharing of benefits by all people in public goods regardless of whether they pay for them or not prevents the market mechanism from determining individual preferences. Consequently, all rationally behaving citizens are expected to be free riders in the sense that they enjoy external benefits produced by others with no cost to themselves. If all citizens choose such a free-rider strategy, though, there would be no production of a public good and benefits would be forgone. In that respect, individual independent actions would result in a limited amount of production of a public good, but not to an optimum amount, where the sum of marginal benefits equals marginal costs.

Cost-benefit analysis, which is used to make comparisons of costs and benefits of public projects over time, aims at maximizing the community's welfare. This can be achieved by improving the welfare of some people without reducing the welfare of others.[20] However, interpersonal utility measurements are difficult and largely impractical, since consumers will not rationally reveal their true preference for a public good. Here, the compensation principle can be considered more applicable than Pareto's optimality. According to this principle, if the individuals who gain from a public project could compensate those who lose and still be better off, then the welfare of the community would be improved.

Present-Value Analysis

For the determination of the present value of the costs and benefits of a project, the discounting principle is employed. When the benefits of a public project are difficult to evaluate, then the cost-effectiveness analysis is used as an alternative procedure. In this case, the objective is given and the associated different costs for achieving that or a similar objective are evaluated. Thus, using ear plugs in a workplace where there is severe noise pollution may cost less than drastically changing the equipment employed to achieve the same level of hearing protection. The same analysis may be applied for the protection of workers from contamination in an atomic plant.

However, costs and benefits normally accrue over time and should be discounted to present values. The basic premise is that future benefits are less valuable than present ones. A dollar of today is worth more than a dollar of tomorrow. This is so mainly because of consumer preference for present consumption versus future consumption. The discount rate, then, reflects the sacrifice of the community to forgo current consumption in exchange for future consumption or enjoyment. Also, it reflects the productivity of capital, which is possible because of what Böhn Bawerk, the Austrian economist, called the more efficient, roundabout method of production, through capital accumulation. The discount rate is affected by other factors as well, factors such as uncertainty, risk, market imperfections, maturity of securities, taxes on capital income, and expected inflation.

Thus, if the interest rate is 10 percent per year, the present value of a dollar one year from today is $0.909, that is, $1/(1 + 0.1)$, and only $0.621 five years from today, that is, $1/(1 + 0.1)^5$. Compared to private profit-making projects, public projects should also consider indirect social costs and benefits or by-products in the discounting process. Thus, for example, a school building may be used for voting on election days or for evening activities for senior citizens, in addition to educational services.

In cost-benefit analysis used in the fiscal decision process, projects can be ranked according to the difference of the present value of the stream of benefits (B) minus the present value of the stream of costs (C), that is, (B − C).

The present value of a benefit stream B_1, B_2, ..., B_n for n years, discounted at the rate of discount, or the time preference rate, r, is:

$$B = \frac{B_1}{1 + r} + \frac{B_2}{(1 + r)^2} + \frac{B_3}{(1 + r)^3} + \ldots + \frac{B_n}{(1 + r)^n}$$

The same holds true for the stream of costs.

The present value of a project is equal to the stream of benefits minus the stream of costs, discounted, as follows:

$$V = \sum_{t=1}^{n} \frac{B_t - C_t}{(1 + r)^t}$$

A project that gives a positive present value (V) can be expected to be approved. If it gives a negative present value, it should be rejected.

Figure 3.6
Project Evaluation

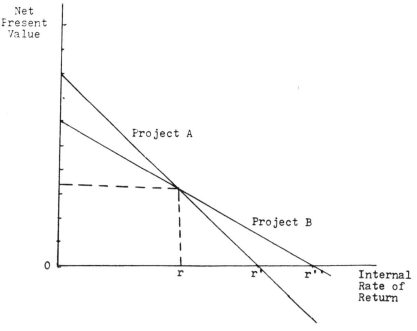

Also, the ranking of projects can be determined according to the ratios of their discounted benefits over their discounted costs, that is,

$$\frac{B}{C} = \frac{\sum_{t=1}^{n} B_t/(1 + r)^t}{\sum_{t=1}^{n} C_t/(1 + r)^t}$$

Where B_t and C_t are benefits and costs in year t, respectively, n is the life of the project, and r is the rate of discount. Projects with benefit-cost ratios greater than one are expected to improve social welfare and deserve approval, while projects with less than a one ratio should be abandoned. Such projects may include irrigation and other water works, transportation, health, and educational programs.

In Figure 3.6, the net present value of project A, which is assumed to have the same cost as B, is higher than that of project B at discount rates lower than at point *r*. At *r*, the two projects intersect and it would be indifferent as to which project would be selected. At rates above *r*, project B would give higher net present value and would be preferred over A. At rates higher than *r′*, project A gives negative net present values, as does project B at rates higher than *r″*. The discount rate r can generally be referred to as the internal rate of return or the productivity of an asset and should be compared with the opportunity cost or the market interest rate.

Government projects with benefit-cost ratios below specified magnitudes may be considered wasteful. If the cost of an additional dollar of revenue is high, the related project should not be pursued. Along these lines, it is estimated that a dollar of public funds was efficiently spent only if it generated social benefits of at least $1.09 to $1.16.[21] On the other hand, when fiscal measures are used to encourage production of certain goods and services, practical-minded officials usually prefer subsidized prices to direct transfer payments because of the lower cost and simplicity involved.

The Use of Efficient Technology

In many instances, a good part of economic activities is performed by public and semipublic or parastatal enterprises, mainly in the field of transportation, electricity, water works, sewage, and other utilities. Public enterprises, such as the Metropolitan Transportation Authority (MTA) of New York, are, to a large extent, subsidized by government, and taxpayers have to bear the brunt of additional expenses to cover the cost-revenue difference. Despite privileges in taxes and interest subsidies, which public enterprises enjoy in competing for scarce capital and materials, such entities are frequently under political pressures and the weight of governmental bureaucracy, which restrict work incentives and tend to reduce efficiency. More often than not, bureaucrats and politicians try to serve themselves instead of the public. Nevertheless, public or semipublic enterprises perform an important role in infrastructural and industrial investment where the private sector may be unable to provide the necessary finance and organization required.

In order to accommodate unemployed workers during periods of recession, bureaucrats and politicians have stuffed the offices of such enterprises with superfluous personnel. As a result, operational cost is high relative to revenue and excessive budgetary deficits appear year after year. The main reasons for such deficits are high labor cost, low productivity, and bureaucratic inertia. In many cases laying off employees is difficult or impossible in these enterprises. What remains to be explored is the introduction of new technology for high productivity and discipline of labor cost to related product prices and revenues.

Distortions in labor cost and wage rates, especially in urban public utilities, imply the need for the use of shadow labor prices, in which are considered the weighted averages of the different wage rates in proprotion to labor used. Similar shadow prices reflecting forgone alternative use of resources can be used in foreign exchange markets for imports and exports as long as such markets are distorted because of currency restrictions, tariffs, quotas, and other controls.

New technology is primarily embodied in new investment. The use of new investment may result in proportionately more capital per unit of output (capital-deepening or labor-shallowing technology) or more labor per unit of output

Figure 3.7
Technological Change and Project Selection

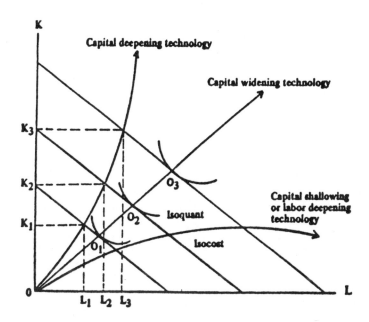

(labor-deepening technology) or in equiproportional change in capital and labor per unit of output (capital-widening technology). In periods of high unemployment, politicians and economists may argue in favor of labor-using technology in public projects. In such cases, depending on factor endowment and skills available, governments can encourage labor-deepening technology, which is using more labor (L) and less capital (K) per unit of output (O). This can be done through subsidies and taxes or other fiscal measures. Also, projects with capital-widening technology can be selected. In that case, the capital-labor ratio remains the same along the expansion line (O, O_1, O_2, O_3) as output moves up the hill to higher levels of production (isoquant curves), as Figure 3.7 shows.

Depending on the availability of factors of production and the relative prices of the services of labor (w) and capital (r), substitution of one factor for the other may take place in the production function. The elasticity of substitution of capital (K) for (L), E_{KL}, in differential terms can be expressed as follows:

$$E_{KL} = - \frac{d(K/L)}{K/L} \div \frac{d(r/w)}{r/w}$$

Thus, if the percentage change in capital-labor ratio, d(K/L)/(K/L), is 20 percent and the percentage change in the rental-wage ratio, $d(r/w)/(r/w)$, is 10 percent, then the elasticity of substitution, E_{KL}, is -2; that is,

$$E_{KL} = -\frac{0.20}{0.10} = -2$$

Or, for each change in rental-wage ratio there is a double change in the capital-labor ratio.

4

Government Expenditures

This chapter deals with government expenditures and their changes over time. General governmental expenditures include federal, state, and local government spending. United States federalism establishes a division of powers between the national and the state governments, in contrast to other nonfederal countries such as Britain, France, Italy, and other European and third world nations. Governmental spending involves payments for goods and services and other transfer and intergovernmental activities. A distinction among general, federal, and state and local government expenditures is made in the sections that follow to reveal relative sizes and trends.

GENERAL GOVERNMENT EXPENDITURES

Postwar Trends

The U.S. federal system of government, that is, the system of a national government and a number of independent state governments, provides for regional diversity and preserves liberty. However, there are complaints that the national, or federal, government has become more intrusive and more pervasive through time and weakens the autonomy of the states.

To observe changes and trends in all forms of government expenditures (G) as related to national income (Y), the average propensity to spend (APG), the marginal propensity to spend (MPG), and the income elasticity of governmental spending (Eg) can be calculated as follows:

$$APG = \frac{G}{Y}$$

$$MPG = \frac{\Delta G}{\Delta Y}$$

$$Eg = \frac{\Delta G/G}{\Delta Y/Y}$$

The U.S. public sector has grown proportionately at a faster rate than the overall economy in the long run. As Figure 4.1 shows, general government expenditures increased from 23 percent of national income in 1950 to 28 percent in 1960, 33 percent in 1970, 36 percent in 1980, and 40 percent in 1985.[1] The expansion of the public sector, or the growing APG, is the result of the ever-increasing demand for governmental services (including those of regional and local units of government), which in turn lead to high elasticities of government expenditures with respect to national income (1.4 in 1950–60 and 1960–70, 1.2 in 1970–80, and 1.3 in 1980–85).

On the other hand, the marginal propensity to spend (MPG), $\Delta G/\Delta Y$, increased from 0.37 (or 37 percent) in the 1960s to 0.39 in the 1970s and 0.47 in 1980–85. Federal government accounted for a constant or declining spending of a proportion of total governmental expenditures; state and local government spending changed from 37 percent of general government disbursement in 1950 to 41 percent in 1980 and 37 percent in 1985.

Regarding the mixture of public spending in consumer versus capital goods at the early stages of development, large expenditures are needed for the creation of such capital goods as highways, railways, seaports, airports, schools, hospitals, power installations and similar projects that offer external benefits to private industries. As development proceeds, public expenditures on consumer goods and services such as external and internal security, sanitation, fire fighting, education, parks and environmental protection, and health increase more than do expenditures on capital goods.[2] However, high stages of development create urban and social problems that may require public investment to counter private sector diseconomies.

Cross-Sectional Comparisons

Since different countries operate under different social and political conditions, the relationship between per capita income and the public sector share seems to be complex, especially in low-income countries. However, as Figure 4.2 indicates, there is a positive correlation of per capita GNP and general government expenditures as percentages of gross domestic product (GDP). As countries move to higher levels of development with higher per capita GNP, government expenditures increase proportionally more than national product or income. This trend verifies the "law of rising public expenditures" of Adolph Wagner, mentioned earlier.

Figure 4.1
The Growing Public Sector in the United States (General Government Expenditures over National Income)

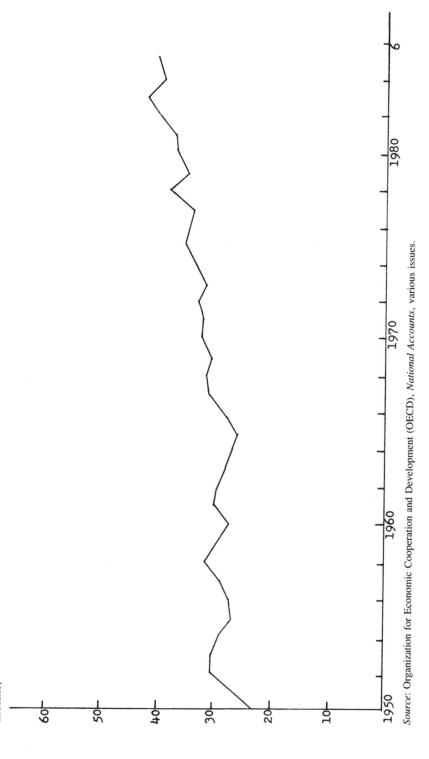

Source: Organization for Economic Cooperation and Development (OECD), *National Accounts*, various issues.

Figure 4.2

Relationship of Per Capita GNP and General Government Expenditures as Percentages of GDP (1985)

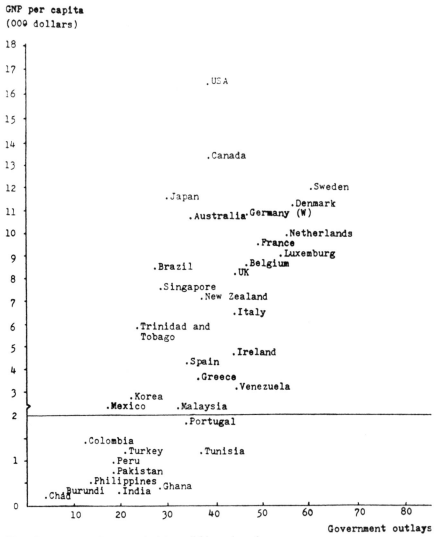

Note: In some cases closest year's data available were used.

Source: World Bank, *World Development Report*; OECD, *National Accounts*; United Nations, *Statistical Yearbook*, all various issues.

From the developed market economies Sweden, with 57 percent of GDP absorbed by general government (central, state, and local), has the largest public sector. Japan, with 27 percent of GDP absorbed by the general government, has the smaller public sector, while the United States and the European Economic Community (EEC) are in between. Israel, with a public sector more than 70 percent of national income is an exception.

In contrast, developing countries with low per capita GDP have a small public sector, varying from 4 percent of GDP for Chad to 8 percent for Burundi, 12 percent for Colombia, 13 percent for the Philippines, 18 percent for Peru and Pakistan, 19 percent for India, and 20 percent for Turkey.

Centrally planned economies have large public sectors. The proportion of net material product (NMP) absorbed by the central government varies from 53 percent for Rumania to 63 percent for the Soviet Union and 73 percent for Hungary. However, Yugoslavia has only 17 percent of national income absorbed by the central government, primarily because of the self-management system and the extensive measures of decentralization implemented in the post-World War II years.[3]

BUDGET PROCEDURE

Modern Incremental Budgeting

The modern U.S. federal budget, which started with the Budget and Accounting Act of 1921 (some 100 years after the United Kingdom instituted a similar one), follows a complex procedure in its preparation by the executive, approval by Congress, implementation by the executive, and audit by the General Accounting Office. The Budget Act of 1974 strengthens the power of Congress in the budget procedure. In addition to the presentation of budget outlays by agencies, budget outlays by functions are also presented. The last presentation is related to the planning-programming-budgeting (PPB) procedure, introduced under Presidents Kennedy and Johnson, according to which entire program areas rather than appropriations for particular departments are to be evaluated on a cost-benefit basis. However, this PPB procedure and the zero-base budgeting, to be explained later in this chapter, are largely impractical.

The prevailing budget procedure in the United States and Western European and other countries is incremental budgeting. It is an administrative approach according to which the budget process accepts the previous year's budget outlays and concentrates on marginal or incremental changes. It is very difficult to formulate each year's budget from scratch, and so limited increases or decreases are made. Although incrementalism has been criticized as irrational and mindless, it is an inevitable part of the complex process of resource allocation in the public sector. Perhaps a rotating process of subjecting particular departments or programs to scrutiny every two or five years is more practical and efficient for controlling excessive outlays.

The federal budget is prepared by the executive and is submitted to the legislation branch of government for review. Some 20 months before the budget goes into effect, the federal agencies prepare their estimated expenses for the fiscal year, which begins on October 1. Within a period of 3 months, or 17 months before the end of the fiscal year, the federal agencies submit their estimates to the Office of Management and Budget (OMB).

After the review of these estimates, the OMB returns them in three or four months to the agencies with suggestions about changes in accordance with policy directions of the administration. Such policy is formulated by the president in consultation with the secretary of the treasury, the OMB and the Council of Economic Advisors. The Treasury Department is responsible for revenue estimates and tax issues. The revised estimates, resubmitted to OMB about a year before the budget goes into effect, are finally submitted to Congress in January of the same year in which the fiscal year begins.

In Congress the budget is referred to the Appropriations Committee and hearings are conducted by its various subcommittees. Finally it is submitted to the floor of the House for approval. A similar procedure is followed by the Senate Appropriations Committee until the budget reaches the president. After approving the budget, the president, is responsible, through the OMB and other agencies, for the implementation of the budget, while the General Accounting Office audits it and reports directly to Congress.

Zero-Base Budgeting

Contrary to incremental budgeting, which is based on last year's budget for relative changes, zero-base budgeting (ZBB) requires periodic justification and reaffirmation of the programs considered. Alternative levels of spending for each program are proposed and ranked by the administrators and approved by decisionmakers. The objective of ZBB, as suggested by the Carter administration, is to avoid the yoke of previous years' budgets and reduce excessive spending. However, it requires large amounts of paperwork and timing for preparation and review. Otherwise trimming unnecessary items and even closing particular inefficient programs can be achieved also through the incremental budgeting.

Capital Budget

A number of countries, including Sweden, Britain and Canada, as well as some U.S. states and municipalities explicitly or implicitly use capital budgets in addition to operational or recurring government expenditures. Such capital budgets include expenditures on long-term investment and other durable assets and frequently have a countercyclical function. Although their financing should be related to borrowing, surplus revenue may be available during upswing economic stages for investment use in downswing economic stages. Thus, stabilization policies aimed toward full employment can be pursued with government investment as a supplement to private sector investment. However, the use of significant amounts of government spending for capital projects and assets acquisitions may present problems of transferring resources from other social programs and lead to unwise fiscal actions. For reasons of intergeneration equity, though, separate capital budgets may be used, particularly by local governments.

FEDERAL GOVERNMENT OUTLAYS

Federal Budget Expenditures

Since 1790, when the number of states was 13 and the U.S. population 3.9 million, federal government outlays increased dramatically. From $5.1 million in 1792 they increased to $10.8 million in 1800, $39.5 million in 1850 with 31 states and a population of 23.2 million, $520.9 million in 1900 with 45 states and a population of 76 million, $42.6 billion in 1950 with 48 states and 152.3 million people, and $989.8 billion in 1986 with 50 states and 240.5 million people. As expected, in periods of war government outlays increased far more. Thus, in 1864 (Civil War) they reached $600.7 million; in 1918 (World War I), $12.7 billion; and in 1944 (World War II), $91.3 billion. As a percentage of GNP, federal government expenditures increased from 2.8 percent in 1900 to 14.9 percent in 1950, 22.1 percent in 1980, and 23.8 percent in 1986; whereas, on a per capita basis these expenditures increased from $7 in 1900 to $286 in 1950 and $4,116 in 1986.[4]

The largest part of federal expenditures goes to direct benefit payments to individuals, followed by military spending and interest payments to service the federal debt. As Figure 4.3 shows, social security payments absorb about 25 percent of total expenditures, military outlays 28 percent, and interest payments 14 percent. The rest goes to state and local grants (10 percent) and other administrative operations (5 percent).

Table 4.1 presents detailed figures on budget outlays for selective postwar years. Defense and social security (including Medicare) absorb the largest parts of budgetary expenditures. Interest payments and income security are the next two largest items of federal outlays, followed by health, education and social services, transportation, and veteran benefits and services. All these items have grown rapidly during the postwar years and many of them are expected to continue growing in the forthcoming years. This is especially so for interest payments because of the rapidly growing federal debt, which was more than $2.5 trillion in 1987.

To establish justice, insure domestic tranquility and liberty, and promote the general welfare, as the U.S. Constitution provides, equity in sharing costs and benefits should be pursued. This requires proper budgetary appropriations for security, education, housing, and health care. To achieve these goals, upper and lower limits of government spending for such programs should be set, determined by social considerations.

Figure 4.3

Federal Government Expenditure for Major Financial Sectors: 1984–85

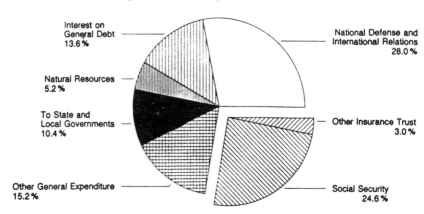

Interest on
General Debt
13.6%

National Defense and
International Relations
28.0%

Natural Resources
5.2%

To State and
Local Governments
10.4%

Other Insurance Trust
3.0%

Other General Expenditure
15.2%

Social Security
24.6%

Source: U.S. Department of Commerce, Bureau of the Census, *Governmental Finances, 1984–85,*
   GF, no. 5, p. xix.

Defense and Civilian Expenditures

Federal expenditures for defense in absolute dollars has risen substantially
since 1950. However, as proportions of total federal spending, they changed
from 54.0 percent in 1950 to 49.8 percent in 1960, 40.0 percent in 1970, 23.4
percent in 1980, and 29.0 percent (estimated) in 1988. Disregarding a few peak
years of cold or hot war, these proportions declined until 1980 and then started
rising again.

Nondefense or civilian expenditures also followed an increasing path after
World War II, as they did before the war. Their significant increase in the late
1960s and during the 1970s was primarily the result of the Great Society and
the "war on poverty" introduced by President Johnson in the mid–1960s. The
rise in civilian expenditures has been due mainly to social welfare payments,
particularly social security, including Medicare, income security, interest payment for debt, health, education, transportation, international affairs, environmental protection, subsidies to the agricultural sector, and some other smaller
expenditures that show an increasing or fluctuating pattern.[5]

Increasingly since the 1950s the federal government has accepted responsibility
for a higher share in expenditures to construct highways, schools, hospitals, and
other public works, which traditionally are state and local activities. These forms
of federal grants and the large transfer payments increase budget expenditures
significantly and intensify the problem of outstanding debt. In addition to social
security and unemployment benefits, large amounts of federal transfer payments
are absorbed by interest payment, grants-in-aid to state and local governments,
and subsidies of government enterprises.[6]

Table 4.1
Federal Budget Outlays (billions of dollars: fiscal years)

DESPCRIPTION	1950	1960	1970	1980	1987	1989*
TOTAL BUDGET OUTLAYS	43.1	92.2	196.6	590.9	1,004.6	1,094.2
National defense	13.1	45.9	78.6	134.0	282.0	294.0
International affairs	4.8	3.1	4.3	12.7	11.6	13.3
General science, space and technology	0.1	0.4	4.5	5.8	9.2	13.1
Energy			1.0	10.2	4.1	3.1
National resources and environment	1.2	1.0	3.1	13.9	13.4	16.0
Agriculture	2.8	3.3	5.2	8.8	27.4	21.7
Commerce and housing credit			2.1	9.4	6.2	7.9
Transportation	1.6	4.8	7.0	21.3	26.2	27.3
Community and regional development	0.2	1.0	2.4	11.3	5.1	5.9
Education, training, employment and social services	0.2	1.3	8.6	31.8	29.7	37.4
Health	0.3	.8	13.1	23.2	40.0	47.8
Medicare				32.1	75.1	84.0
Income security	4.7	18.0	43.1	86.5	123.2	135.6
Social Security				118.5	207.4	233.8
Veteran benefits and services	8.8	5.4	8.7	21.2	26.8	29.6
Administration of justice			1.0	4.6	7.5	9.9
General Government	1.2	1.3	2.4	13.0	7.6	9.5
Net Interest	5.7	8.3	18.3	52.5	138.6	151.8
Undistributed offsetting receipts	- 1.2	-2.3	- 6.6	-19.9	-36.5	-41.0

*Estimated

Note: Medicare was in Health and Social Security in Income Security in 1950, 1960, and 1970. Commerce and housing credit was in Transportation; and Administration of Justice was in General Goverment in 1950 and 1960. On-budget interest in 1989 was estimated at $161.9 billion and off-budget interest was − $10.1 billion.

Source: Economic Report of the President, various issues; and U.S. Department of Commerce, Bureau of the Census, *Historical Statistics of the United States, 1975*, p. 1116.

Defense absorbs large amounts of expenditures and has become a serious problem for budget deficits. Spending for MX missiles, B–1 bombers, Maverick missiles, Aegis cruisers, F–18 fighters, M–2 fighting vehicles, DDG–51 destroyers, among many others, and the planned Star Wars initiative has driven the defense budget high up in recent years and will loom even larger in the future.

Specialists suggest that numerous new weapons programs are duplicative or simply excessive and as such could be eliminated with no cost to the nation's security. However, for some weapons programs cancellation is highly unlikely because related contracts and subcontracts are spread in many states and districts and it becomes politically difficult to reduce or eliminate them. For the B–1 bomber, for example, there are contracts or subcontracts in 48 states.[7] Also, the military pension program, which costs some $18 billion, up from $7.3 billion in 1976, is difficult to reduce or even to stabilize.

Spending for production of military goods drains private investment funds and transfers resources from nonmilitary production, reducing their supply in the market. Yet military hardware in the form of guns, tanks, rockets and the like is piled up in stores and does not enter the market to increase supply and suppress prices, as do other consumer and capital goods. However, they are considered as investment goods needed for the defense of the country.

Regarding arguments that military spending creates jobs, Keynesian reasoning suggests that although political leaders easily support military spending for employment, from an economic standpoint nonmilitary expenditures perform equally well or better in creating jobs even in projects of doubtful usefulness. That is so if spending is directed to labor-intensive projects particularly in services and other sectors requiring low skills, as well as to capital goods to be used for further production (input for input) in the form of factories and equipment.

Future expenditure cuts are being considered in such items as housing and urban development, agricultural subsidies, revenue sharing, education, and interior outlays. Small changes are expected in social security and health and human services. Specifically, freezes and program reforms are expected to Medicaid and Medicare, student aid, veteran Medicare and civil service, retirement, child nutrition, farm price support and credit programs, housing, postal services, and rural electric and telephone services. Further, major program eliminations are being considered in job corps, general revenue sharing, Amtrak subsidies, small business administration, urban development grants and mass transit assistance, direct loans for the Export-Import Bank, and air carrier subsidies.

INTERGOVERNMENTAL FISCAL OPERATIONS

Local government administration, a neglected corner of public finance, needs a deeper review and a thorough revision. Local government fiscal policies are affected largely by central governments as to the levels and directions of local public expenditures and revenue. Although it is difficult to unravel the complexities of the interrelationships between local and central governments, a clear distinction and separation of related functions and their financing will help the proper allocation of responsibilities and increase productivity in the public sector as a whole.

Adam Smith suggested that public works of a local nature should be maintained and financed by local authorities. According to Smith, "Public works . . . confined to some particular place or district, are always better maintained by a local or provincial revenue, under the management of a local and provincial administration, than by the general revenue of the state."[8] Moreover, he argued that the abuses which sometimes creep into local and provincial administrations are smaller than those of the central or state authorities.

Because many colonists had come to America to avoid government oppression in Europe, they disliked government controls. That is why the Articles of Confederation (1776) gave the federal government no power to collect taxes, to regulate trade, or exercise controls over the states or their citizens.

However, for purposes of unifying the states and strengthening the new nation, the United States Constitution of 1788 gave the federal government the power to create money, to collect taxes, to regulate trade, and to conduct wars. All other powers and controls were left with the individual states, which drew their own constitutions and established their own rules for tax collection, chartering local governments, and exercising other policies and controls.

To encourage regional specialization and permit economies of scale and lower production costs, some restrictions on state governments were introduced regarding freedom of trade across state lines. With no regional barriers, resources and goods would move to markets of greatest demand, competition would be enhanced, and output and employment would increase. This policy not only promoted positive externalities and diffusion of technologies among regions but helped the national government to ensure fairness, or equity, in income distribution. However, the critical question that still remains to the answered is: How to achieve the proper balance of power between local and central governments preserving, at the same time, efficiency and a fair wealth and resource allocation?

Federations such as that of the United States seem to be economically more efficient than separate state-nations similar to the divided city-states of ancient Greece. Such federal systems include, apart from the United States, Australia, Canada, India, Yugoslavia, and to some extent the Soviet Union. Yet problems of fiscal coordination may appear in such federations, which feed instability and possibly conflicting policies regarding vertical or horizontal intergovernmental relations. In the case of instability, questions may appear as to the degree of decentralization and the specific fiscal functions between the central government and the republics or other public authorities in the federation. In the case of conflicting policies, variations and fiscal imbalances between horizontal units of government may appear as to expenditures realized and revenue collected per person. To preserve federation over separation in different sovereignties (similar to the Balkan nations), equalization and stabilization policies may be pursued by the federal government.

On many occasions, the fiscal actions of one governmental unit affect the residents of another unit of government either by harming or benefiting them; these are negative or positive externalities or spillover effects. Examples of negative externalities are air pollution or chemical spray from unsound health policies of one city that may affect other cities or the dumping of raw sewage in a river, a seashore, or a lake shared by two or more communities. Examples of positive externalities are fiscal measures to improve air or water quality or to establish employment-creating economic units in a community that may have beneficial effects on other communities. With growing industrialization and urbanization in the United States and in other countries, such spillover effects become important, so that more cooperation and coordination in fiscal activities are needed.

There is a trend, primarily in state and local levels, toward shifting decisions from the legislative and executive branches of government to the judicial branch. This process seems to upset the traditional balance of power and burdens the courts with solving many problems that should be solved by other branches of government. As a result, the vacuum is filled by a growing number of lawsuits and a greater influence of courts on such issues as environmental protection, prison conditions, care for the homeless, civil rights, employment, and welfare programs that could be dealt with by legislation or governmental administrative acts. This practice makes courts determine public policy and mandates expensive programs for local governments regardless of the difficulties of their financing. It is obvious from an economic standpoint that state and local politicians and government officials should take their responsibilities seriously and pass related laws instead of dumping important and complex decisions on the courts.

The budgetary process in the state and local governments may be similar to that of the federal government; that is, the executive chief (governor or mayor) prepares the budget and presents it to the legislature, or it may be undertaken by a representative committee (decentralized administration), or by a legislative agency (in small local units of government). Although it is difficult to implement cost-benefit analysis in public sector budgetary decisions, comparisons of alternative projects and programs according to their economic merits would improve resource allocation and increase the efficiency of government services. Such comparisons may refer to intrapublic sector allocation or the government versus the private sector projects. In the last case, the marginal cost ratios of a government sector project (MCg) over the marginal cost of a private sector project (MCp) must be equal to their marginal benfits (MB) ratios; that is, $MCg/MCp = MBg/MBp$.

GROWING STATE AND LOCAL GOVERNMENT EXPENDITURES

Great centralization in government authority involves, among other things, great inefficiency and waste of valuable resources. The slow-moving central government bureaucracy is usually unable to conceive and implement efficiency projects of local importance. Most of the time dead hand of the central government acts as a drawback to the development efforts of those immediately involved at the local level. More often than not, the central bureaucrats fail to see and understand the real need of specific regions and communities. This explains to a great extent their propensity to embark sometimes on projects that have little to do with the real needs and aspirations of the people. It seems, therefore, that inefficiency goes hand in hand with government centralization. Moreover, centralization leads to the suffocation of individual and collective initiative at the regional and local levels and encourages corruption at high levels of government.

However, there are certain public or collective activities, such as defense, that the central government can provide more efficiently than local governments. Also, a number of public or quasi-national goods of social importance can be efficiently allocated by higher level governments. At the same time, stabilization and redistributional policies, as well as economies of scale in tax administration, can be better achieved by central, rather than state and local, government. Nevertheless, for a large spectrum of public services subnational authorities can make more efficient decisions for their regions than those made by centralized authorities, since local representatives are under greater pressure to relate tax costs and public benefits on a regional level rather than on a central bureaucratic basis.

Decentralization in government authority allows for a more direct participation of the local population in cultural, economic, and political decision making. People in cities, towns, and villages are much more interested in solving their own regional problems rather than in involving a remote and impersonal bureaucracy to find solutions. The greater the decentralization of the public sector, therefore, the greater the amplitude of participation of citizenry in the decision-making process and the greater the efficiency in solving regional and local problems. However, in order for local authorities to perform such functions effectively, they need the required financial resources.

Certain functions performed by the central government could easily be delegated to local authorities. This would facilitate the process of decentralization, reduce central government bureaucracy, and provide for a source of revenue for the local authorities. Authorization for municipalities and communities to issue housing permits or to deal with education, police protection, administration of justice, traffic accident reports, marriage licenses, construction or expansion of roads in remote areas, and licenses for water lines exemplifies such a decentralization policy.

Economic activity shifting from region to region tends to equalize average personal income and bring about regional convergence in such a way that different state and local governments become more alike in their taxable capacity. Thus, the difference in per capita personal income among the U.S. states is not much. In 1981, for example, it varied from $7,408 for South Carolina to $9,410 for Montana, $10,370 for Pennsylvania, $10,729 for Texas, $11,466 for New York, $11,923 for California, and $12,127 for New Jersey.

Table 4.2 shows the rapid growth of expenditures of the state and local governments since 1927; especially during recent years. Whereas Figure 4.4 shows such expenditures for major financial sectors. As will be analyzed later, in addition to central government grants, the main sources of financing such

Table 4.2
State and Local Government Expenditures, Selected Years, 1927–86 (millions of dollars)

Fiscal Year	Total	Education	Highways	Public Welfare	All Others *
1927	7,210	2,235	1,809	151	3,015
1932	7,765	2,311	1,741	444	3,269
1940	9,229	2,638	1,573	1,156	3,862
1950	22,787	7,177	3,803	2,940	8,867
1955	33,724	11,907	6,452	3,168	12,197
1960	51,876	18,719	9,428	4,404	19,325
1965-66	82,842	33,287	12,770	6,757	30,029
1970-71	150,674	59,413	18,095	18,226	54,940
1975-76	256,731	97,216	23,907	32,604	103,004
1980-81	407,449	145,784	34,603	54,121	172,941
1981-82	436,896	154,282	34,520	57,996	190,098
1982-83	466,421	163,876	36,655	60,484	205,405
1983-84	505,006	176,108	39,516	66,414	222,969
1984-85	554,161	192,686	45,002	71,532	244,921
1985-86	605,789	210,819	49,368	75,958	269,644

* Includes expenditures for hospitals, health, social insurance administration, veterans' services, air transportation, watertransport and terminals, parking facilities, police protection, fire protection, correction, protective inspection and regulations, sewerage, natural resources, parks and recreation, community development, sanitation other than sewerage, general control, financial administration, general public building, interest on general debt and unallocable items.

Note: Data for fiscal years listed from 1965–66 to 1985–86 are the aggregations of data for government fiscal years which ended in the twelve-month period from July 1 to June 30 of those years. Data for earlier years include data for government fiscal years ending during that particular calendar year.

Source: U.S. Department of Commerce, Bureau of the Census.

expenditures are property, income, and sales taxes. Expenditures are directed primarily to education, welfare, highways, and other social programs. Contrary to the large federal budget deficits, state and local government budgets present mostly comfortable surpluses. Because of the surpluses, state tax reduction, similar to the recent federal tax cuts, especially in heavily taxes states such as New York, is suggested.

The bulk of expenditures goes to purchases of goods and services, primarily for compensation of employees, followed by transfer payments to persons, for both state and local governments. However, states spend sizable amounts of

Figure 4.4

State and Local Government Expenditure for Major Financial Sectors: 1984–85

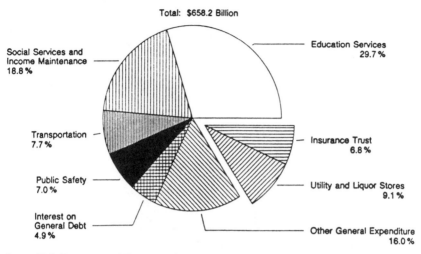

Total: $658.2 Billion

Social Services and Income Maintenance 18.8%

Transportation 7.7%

Public Safety 7.0%

Interest on General Debt 4.9%

Education Services 29.7%

Insurance Trust 6.8%

Utility and Liquor Stores 9.1%

Other General Expenditure 16.0%

Source: U.S. Department of Commerce, Bureau of the Census, *State Governmental Finances, 1986*, GF 86, no. 3, p. viii.

money for grants to local governments. Net interest paid is negative because of the larger amounts received by these governments.

State governments spend more than local governments on public welfare, insurance trust, and natural resources; whereas local governments spend more on education and libraries, public safety (fire, police, correction), sewerage and sanitation, parks and recreation, and housing and urban renewal. Both levels of government use about the same proportions of general government expenditures for health and hospitals, transportation, and administration.

Table 4.3 demonstrates state and local government expenditures per state. On a per capita basis, Alaska is the first state with high expenditures, followed by Wyoming, New York, and Minnesota; Arizona is the last one, followed by Tennessee and Missouri. State government expenditures, as percentages of GNP, increased from 3.5 percent in 1954 to 9.0 percent in 1986, and for the local governments from 4.0 percent to 5.8 percent respectively. The proportion of total intergovernmental transfers to the local governments was far larger than that to the state governments.

State and local government spendings vary from state to state and locality to locality, and both levels of government supplement payments made by the federal government, mainly for public assistance. Most state government spending is directed to education, notably colleges and universities, and public welfare, as Figure 4.5 indicates. Social insurance such as unemployment programs and public employee retirement programs account for around 15 percent, while spending for transportation, mainly state highways and toll roads and bridges, and

Table 4.3
Population (July 1, 1986) and State and Local Government Expenditures (1970, 1980, and by state 1984–85 fiscal year, million dollars)

	POPULATION (000's)	TOTAL	EXPENDITURES EDUCATION	HIGHWAYS	PUBLIC WELFARE
1970		131,332	52,718	16,427	14,679
1980		367,340	133,211	33,311	45,552
1984-5	240,451	658,152	192,686	45,022	71,532
Alabama	4,053	9,400	2,928,623	815	669,101
Alaska	534	5,634	1,233,974	550	210,393
Arizona	3,317	8,967	2,778,858	774	577,198
Arkansas	2,732	4,463	1,704,218	413	467,017
California	26,981	84,122	22,270,812	3,271	11,292,792
Colorado	3,267	9,409	2,865,965	706	699,774
Connecticut	3,189	8,428	2,346,202	617	1,004,663
Delaware	633	1,856	635,952	156	117,953
Florida	11,675	26,201	7,607,107	1,681	1,673,864
Georgia	6,104	14,538	4,061,627	1,143	1,033,398
Hawaii	1,062	3,201	730,269	134	292,517
Idaho	1,003	2,125	712,109	242	147,186
Illinois	11,553	29,032	8,371,324	2,403	3,613,769
Indiana	5,504	11,553	4,113,210	851	1,165,688
Iowa	2,851	7,527	2,580,805	936	794,048
Kansas	2,461	6,166	2,143,831	703	468,393
Kentucky	3,728	7,685	2,412,669	720	879,107
Louisiana	4,501	11,580	3,280,010	1,026	1,123,913
Maine	1,174	2,750	836,696	267	440,518
Maryland	4,463	11,711	3,578,261	939	1,215,796
Massachusetts	5,832	17,319	4,232,712	752	2,497,658
Michigan	19,145	25,777	8,179,915	1,417	4,011,958

Minnesota	4,214	13,618	3,925,852	1,222	1,806,674
Mississippi	2,625	5,338	1,645,963	554	494,619
Missouri	5,066	10,076	3,268,431	922	947,942
Montana	819	2,437	798,344	304	197,287
Nebraska	1,598	5,200	1,424,808	489	337,728
Nevada	963	2,762	605,580	260	133,556
New Hampshire	1,027	2,029	605,293	226	209,181
New Jersey	7,620	21,349	6,344,768	1,370	2,261,816
New Mexico	1,479	4,022	1,444,806	407	260,103
New York	17,772	71,448	16,926,126	3,255	10,811,524
North Carolina	6,331	13,899	4,780,395	937	1,003,864
North Dakota	679	1,990	682,838	271	183,391
Ohio	10,752	27,402	8,491,823	1,718	3,490,972
Oklahoma	3,305	7,886	2,637,635	638	693,125
Oregon	2,698	8,084	2,468,712	554	519,268
Pennsylvania	11,889	29,086	8,348,628	2,132	3,936,402
Rhode Island	975	2,743	763,152	155	431,830
South Carolina	3,378	7,178	2,453,370	422	516,586
South Dakota	708	1,778	524,518	263	130,974
Tennessee	4,803	11,701	2,915,459	861	893,259
Texas	16,682	39,027	14,107,315	2,652	2,226,306
Utah	1,665	5,720	1,585,386	462	311,580
Vermont	541	1,462	482,275	160	171,726
Virginia	5,787	12,653	4,553,836	1,153	1,035,143
Washington	4,463	15,276	3,934,103	1,159	1,201,292
West Virginia	1,119	4,502	1,554,119	460	356,075
Wisconsin	4,785	13,533	4,533,118	1,067	1,995,585
Wyoming	507	2,335	801,065	344	91,542
District of Columbia	617	3,803	473,098	90	486,212

Source: U.S. Department of Commerce, Bureau of the Census, *Governmental Finances, 1986*, GF, no. 5.

Figure 4.5
General Expenditure of State Governments by Function: 1986
Total: $376.5 Billion

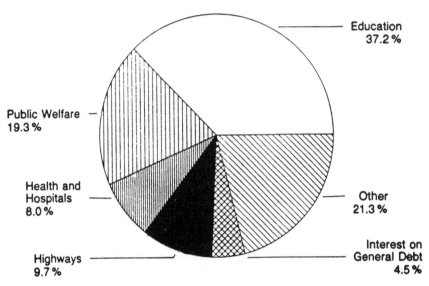

Source: U.S. Department of Commerce, Bureau of the Census, *Governmental Finances, 1986*, GF
86, no. 3, p. viii.

health outlays, primarily hospitals, account for about 10 percent each. Other
state expenditures include state police and prison operations as well as parks and
recreational facilities. Figure 4.6 shows state government expenditures per
$1,000 of personal income. It excludes Alaska, the highest-ranked state ($410
per $1,000 of personal income).

About 35 percent of local government spending goes to education, primarily
elementary and secondary schools; 15 percent, to police and fire protection,
sanitation and sewerage; and about 10 percent, to health, public welfare, and
transportation. The rest goes into other public services such as public libraries,
interest on debt, parks, urban transit and roads, and housing and urban renewals.

Concerning subsidies at public universities, there are complaints that the cities
and states support rich students with taxpayers' money, whereas in private universities subsidies are paid by alumni and endowment. In addition, the complaint
goes, tuition payments by the students in many private universities are high
(more than $10,000 annually in Ivy League universities, not counting room,
board, and other costs), but in public universities tuition is comparatively low
(around $1,500 to $2,000 a year) even though cost is as high as in private
universities. The difference is covered by the public purse—that is, by federal,
state, and city governments or the taxpayers in general—regardless of the income

Figure 4.6
General Expenditure of State Governments per $1,000 of Personal Income by States: 1986

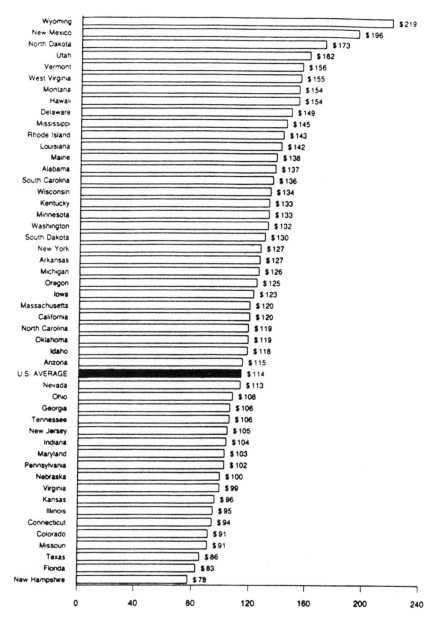

Source: U.S. Department of Commerce, Bureau of the Census, *Governmental Finances, 1986*, GF 86, no. 3, p. x.

81

of the student's family. As a result, public colleges and universities undergo a continuous expansion while their independent or private counterparts confront the harsh realities of quantitative and qualitative decline. With the sharp reduction in student loans and the gradual nationwide decline in the U.S. student population, private schools work hard to attract students and in many cases are threatened with extinction, whereas public schools are overcrowded and thus becoming more selective. They may attract sons and daughters of white-collar families with superior academic backgrounds at the neglect of those of blue-collar workers. And all this with public subsidization—that is, with taxpayers' money.

A rapidly growing expense of local governments is that of Medicaid and hospital services. As a result of this expense, balancing the budget has become more and more painful and now requires significant tightening of state and local spending for other projects and services. To add to the squeeze serious mismanagement and sloppy shopping can occasionally be observed in local-level spending.[9]

FISCAL PROBLEMS OF STATE AND LOCAL GOVERNMENTS

State and local fiscal problems have been largely neglected in the United States as well as in other countries. Great changes and regional shifts create problems of housing, health, energy, education, pollution, and other urban disamenities. Despite the introduction of model cities, wars on poverty, safety nets, and similar political proclamations, many urban people live in poverty. Population shifts from the U.S. Northeast to the South are expected to invite dramatic changes and present new problems for state and local government financing. Demographic changes contribute to expenditure-revenue imbalances and create chronic fiscal problems in state and local governments, thereby increasing dependence on federal assistance. However, such changes make some central cities deteriorate while suburbs and provincial towns thrive. It should be recognized, though, that statistical data are limited and it is difficult to measure local changes in employment, migration, prices, and other economic variables affecting budgetary expenditures in recessions and recoveries.

According to the Census Bureau, locational changes in the population of the United States, which was 240.5 million in 1986, take place rapidly. Regionally, Alaska is the fastest growing state, followed by Nevada, Utah, Florida, Texas, Arizona, Colorado, New Mexico, Oklahoma, Wyoming, California, and Hawaii. Presently, New England's population presents a small growth or no change, while Ohio, Michigan, Iowa, and Washington, D.C., present a small decline. New York, New Jersey, and Pennsylvania show a more or less stable population. With changes in population, regional economic activities change and new intergovernmental fiscal measures are required. Figure 4.7 shows divisions of the United States in different regions and individual states.

Figure 4.7
Map of the United States, Showing Census Divisions and Regions

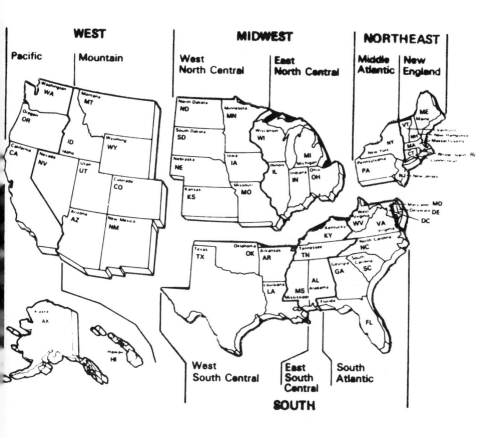

Source: U.S. Bureau of the Census

Welfare payments to the poor present serious problems in states and cities all over the United States. About 900,000 residents are on welfare in New York City alone. To enable escape from welfare dependency and reduce state and city expenditures, work and training programs have been introduced by a number of states; these programs enlist participants either on a voluntary basis or as a condition of receiving benefits. Such a workfare approach, to replace welfare, encourages recipients to participate in work programs and avoid dehumanizing welfare rolls. However, there are complaints, especially by labor unions, that government officials often use such work programs to dismiss regular public workers and pay less benefits provided by labor contracts.

Housing Problems

Reduced family size, rent controls, and high construction costs push housing prices to high levels and increase homelessness. In a number of cities one may see people sleeping in streets, hallways, and overflowing municipal shelters. The endlessly tormenting problem of housing is due primarily to rent controls and housing policies that are usually popular politically but unwise economically under the U.S. market economy. City public housing programs do not charge enough rent to pay for rehabilitation, and homeowners cannot cover the cost of maintenance. The result is building deterioration and in many cases abandonment of houses.

More than 200 cities, including Boston, Chicago, Los Angeles, New York, San Francisco, and Washington, D.C., have adopted rent controls. In fact, more than 10 percent of the rental housing in the United States is under rent controls. Such controls destroy incentives to invest in housing and lead to misallocation of resources. The resulting lower quantity and quality in housing lead to home shortages, high rents for noncontrolled apartments, and all kinds of illegal and black market arrangements. Thus, for example, tenants frequently leave apartments to their children or take bribes to get out of rent-controlled houses, and some landlords let their buildings deteriorate. Probably it would be better for cities to help low-income people buy houses and let the market reach its equilibrium.

Figure 4.8 shows that under a free housing market, with no rent or other controls, supply and demand would determine the point of equilibrium (E) at a price (rent) OP and quantity of apartment units OQ. The rent control price brings about an increase in the apartments demanded and a decrease in supply, creating a shortage AB. In restricting the amount of housing available, the new price would be OP_1, which is higher than that at equilibrium (OP). By eliminating rent control, the equilibrium price would be restored and the amount of housing offered would rise.

There is a strange phenomenon in states, and particularly in large cities that creates many financial and welfare problems. Large numbers of families are homeless although many buildings have been abandoned and remain vacant.

Figure 4.8
Housing Shortages from Rent Controls

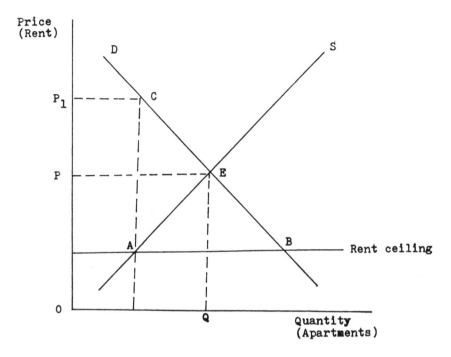

Some 540,000 families are on public assistance in New York State alone, many of which are under welfare rent allowance. Such allowance costs more than $200 million per year in the state of New York, one-third of which is paid by the federal government, another one-third by the state, and the rest by the individual cities. The city of New York alone pays around $50 million annually for that allowance, with a limit (in 1983) of $218 a month per family of four. This sharing in welfare rent allowance has, in many instances, inflamed relations among city, state, and federal governments, particularly when increases are required to match soaring rents in urban centers.

The cost of prison maintenance is also growing rapidly for the federal government and more so for the individual states and localities. The number of Americans behind bars has doubled to 663,000 in the last decade and billions of dollars are spent year after year on new prisons. It was estimated that the federal average annual cost per inmate was $14,400 in fiscal 1984, while that of the states varied from $7,000 for Texas to $18,500 for New York, $19,000 for California, and $36,500 for Alaska. In addition, the construction of prisons costs about $100,000 per cell. Because of the high cost of imprisonment, the public sector has increasingly considered the possibilities of turning over this growing industry to the private sector, which seeks to employ prisoners with pay and transform "warehouses" into factories within fences, thereby costing less to taxpayers and creating skills. However, there are serious questions as to the conflict between the private profit motive and the pursuit of corrections and criminal justice in general.

Cross-Sectional Trends

In contrast to what is happening in countries with growing central governments, decentralizing trends continue and local governments are strengthened in many countries, particularly in the United States, Australia, France, Greece, and Italy. Also, declines in central government and increases in state and local government shares can also be observed in Korea, Tunisia, and Zimbabwe.

Similar messages are conveyed when one considers the elasticity of state and local government expenditures with respect to general government expenditures. The elasticity for the countries moving toward more centralization was less than one during the postwar years. This is in sharp contrast to the countries moving toward more decentralization where the elasticity of local and state government expenditures with respect to general government was either very close to one or considerably greater than one.

The standard interpretation of these values for elasticity is clear and imply that, on the average, when general government expenditures were increased by 1 percent in the decentralized countries, the state and local government expenditures were increased by more than 1 percent. In the centralized countries, however, with an increase in the size of general government by 1 percent there was a corresponding increase of less than 1 percent in the size of state and local government.

Noted here that in many, mainly developed, countries a wide variety of additional services are offered by the local authorities. Those services include elementary, secondary, and in many cases higher education; police and fire protection; hospital care and mass transportation facilities; as well as court functions. From a sociopolitical standpoint, such extensive delegations of power to local authorities would defuse the decision-making power to more people and strengthen democratic institutions. Even in some socialist or centrally planned countries, including Yugoslavia and China, the trend is toward more decentralization in recent years. In many instances, however, it appears that appointing sound and skilled managers and introducing work incentives are important keys to making the public sector efficient, regardless of whether local, state, or central governments are considered. In such endeavors, overorganization and bureaucracy, as well as underorganization and managerial inefficiency associated with nepotism and favors, may be responsible for public sector failures, mostly in developing nations.

With a system of bottom-up decision making, in which initiatives would be derived from the general populace, manipulation of the state for private benefits and the paper power of the miniczars and the elite class of bureaucracy would be reduced or eliminated.

Development plans and related legislation in a number of countries provide for the gradual emancipation and financial independence of the provincial localities. However, since there are so few experts and organizations to implement decentralization, mass education programs are needed to make local people familiar with a more democratic way of making decisions. To avoid the vicious circle of "keep power to transfer power," incentives for population participation in community affairs and decisions are needed even at the cost of some initial disorganization.

Overcentralization and bureaucratization kill initiative and create unhealthy economic dependencies. In many cases, economies lack the necessary managerial skills to run decentralized collective activities. To use the services of well-trained bureaucrats and other managers to push for local self-administrations, that is, to use centralized means for decentralized ends, there is the risk of creating a new elite that may consolidate its power and allocate excessive benefits to its members.

Developed countries generally have larger proportions of state and local government expenditures than developing countries. Countries with decentralized public sector activities or federations have large state and local government expenditures as a portion of total government spendings. They vary from 56 percent for Canada to 46 percent for Australia, 43 percent for Sweden, 42 percent for Japan, 40 percent for the United States and West Germany, and 28 percent for the United Kingdom. However, for countries with relatively lower per capita income such as Portugal, Spain, and Greece, these expenditure ratios are low, varying from 4 percent to 10 percent. This indicates that high concentration of public authority to the central government and low decentralization can be observed in these last countries. Also Belgium and France have low levels of state and local government expenditures (11 percent and 13 percent, respectively) and therefore a high concentration of the public sector mainly because of their institutional structure.

Developing countries, except Honduras and India, have low proportions of state and local governments (varying from 2 percent for Venezuela to 7 percent for Turkey, and 17 percent for Colombia) and a high concentration of the public sector in central governments. It would seem, then, that on the average countries with a higher degree of decentralization and less central bureaucracy are performing better on matters of economic development and per capita income. However, the trends seem to be inconclusive, with many countries presenting a growing proportion of state and local government spending while others have a relatively constant or a declining ratio of local to the central government expenditures. One can surmise, though, that more decentralization is associated with higher degrees of democratization and more efficient economic performance.

SOCIAL SECURITY EXPENDITURES

Growing Government Spending for Social Insurance

The social security program was introduced by the Old-Age and Survivors Trust Fund during the depression (Social Security Act, 1935) to provide income for the elderly and their spouses. In Europe, it was introduced in the 1880s, first by Germany. Gradually, the social security benefits paid by the government have increased because the life expectancy of individuals has improved steadily. In 1900, for example, the average American could expect to live for 47.3 years. By 1985, according to World Bank statistics, life expectancy at birth had increased to 76 years (72 for males, 80 for females). In 1950, the over–65 population represented 8.2 percent of the total population, but in 1988 it increased to 11.2 percent. This trend, along with the declining birth rates, leads to what is known as the graying of America.

National health expenditures is about 11 percent of GNP, compared with 6 percent in 1965. About 42 percent of this amount is the contribution of government, compared to 26 percent in 1965. On a per capita basis, total health expenditures increased from $207 in 1965 to about $1,500 in 1988, with the government contributing more than $600. Social security, including Medicare, absorbs some 30 percent of the federal budget. Some 37 million Americans receive retirement benefits and about five million are on disability.

To mitigate the impact of inflation upon social security benefits, Congress has introduced annual cost-of-living raises to the recipients of such benefits according to the increases in the consumer price index (CPI). Such increases have raised the average monthly benefits from a little below $200 in 1975 to $464 in 1986. The maximum monthly benefit reached $999 in 1988. A minimum of 3 percent inflation is necessary to force a yearly adjustment in benefits. Table 4.4 shows the percentage increases in social security benefits since 1975.

For average annual covered earnings, $923 or less, the benefits used to be $122 and $61 for the spouse. No low limits exist at present. The maximum amounts of covered earnings upon which social security taxes were calculated increased from $3,600 in 1951 to $42,000 in 1986 and $45,000 in 1988. As will be explained in Chapter 6, social security outlays are smaller than contributions, leaving a large surplus annually. Low incomes receive excess benefits over contributions up to a point of the income scale; the reverse occurs for high incomes.

According to the Census Bureau, 35 million Americans lack any kind of health insurance. That is, 15 percent of the U.S. population, compared to 12 percent in the late 1970s, is not covered by any health insurance, including Medicare and Medicaid. Some 75 percent of the insured people have private health insurance, and 10 percent are covered by government insurance. Large proportions of people not covered by health insurance are in the South (about 19 percent), followed by those in the West (18), the Midwest (12) and the Northeast (10 percent). Close to 30 percent of uninsured Americans are Hispanic people; 22 percent, blacks; and 14 percent, whites. Some 70 percent of the people covered by Medicare also have private health insurance to fill the gap. But there are complaints that a number of companies have sold the elderly health insurance that they did not need because they already had coverage for the same insurance by other companies.

Table 4.4
Social Security Benefits Increase in Percentages

Years	Percentage Increases
1975	8.0
1976	6.4
1977	5.9
1978	6.5
1979	9.9
1980	14.3
1981	11.2
1982	7.4
1983	3.5
1984	3.5
1985	3.1
1986	1.3
1987	4.2

Note: Payroll tax will not rise again until 1990, when it rises to 7.65 percent compared to 7.51 percent in 1988. The highest amount of benefits in 1987 were $822.
Source: Social Security Administration.

It is indeed true that retiring people get more back per dollar contributed and that a transfer from the working young to retired old takes place. The monthly check and medical benefits in a similar private insurance would only be about a quarter the amount social security pays.

However, social security is not a private annuity, nor a straightforward welfare system, but a hybrid of annuity and welfare payments. It incorporates also the concept of income redistribution so that old, unprotected retirees and their spouses, as well as disabled members of society, can be provided with a limited amount of income for their survival. With this concept of the "social" security system in mind, some economists and sociologists suggest that the government transfer revenues from other sources to finance retirement benefits. This last approach of revenue transfer seems to be gaining political support not only in the United States. Such political support is due in part to the growing populations of voting retirees and those close to the retirement age. As the rate of population growth continues to decline and the number of younger people shrink, the transfer of funds from the relatively affluent to poorer beneficiaries may be urgent.

This social concept of retirement benefits incorporates the entitlement of pensions to the spouses of the working people regardless of whether or not they work. Thus, spouses of retired persons can collect half the monthly benefits of the retired working husbands or wives. This principle was passed into law in 1939. If the spouses themselves were employed and are entitled to social security payments, they can choose the larger benefit, theirs or that of their spouses, which is less when collection starts before the age of 65 (from 62 to 64). The spouse who outlives the retired worker would receive the full benefits of the predeceased retiree.

The payments of benefits to nonworking spouses have been criticized on the grounds that a single-earner couple can collect higher payments from social security than a dual-earner couple, although the payroll taxes have been the same for both couples. However, payments to the system by the working spouse who receives half benefits of the other spouse with higher earnings are not included.

Similar conditions can be observed with expenditures for veterans. As the number of elderly veterans is growing rapidly, larger amounts of budget appropriations will be needed in the future to finance related expenditures. There are now around 28 million veterans and the Veterans Administration runs close to 180 hospitals and more than 100 nursing homes and 200 outpatient clinics. Millions of World War II veterans are reaching retirement age year after year, and it is expected that the number of those veterans over 65 will increase from about three million annually now to nine million in the year 2000. To mitigate growing veterans' health care expenses, proposals have been made to subsidize care only to veterans with an annual income less than a specified amount, say less than $15,000, or to use alternatives to hospital care, such as home and adult day care and outpatient services. Also being considered is the idea of combining veteran's benefits with Medicare. However, disabled veterans, former prisoners of war, and persons exposed to atomic test radiation and to the herbicide agent orange would be exempted.

Through gradual improvements, elderly people are in a better position now than they were in earlier years. The higher the level of development of a country, the higher the financial security retired people enjoy. For example, in the United States average monthly social security benefits increased threefold in real terms since the 1950s, that is, twice as much as average wages (905 percent in nominal terms, compared to 451 percent for wages, with a price index of 312 percent in 1950–83). There are also preferential tax treatments, such as no payment of tax on capital gains from the sale of a residence for those over 55 years of age, and other tax exemptions and incentives.

Other insurance and public assistance measures such as railroad retirement (introduced in 1937), child nutrition (1946), disability insurance (1956), food stamps (1964), Medicare and Medicaid (1965), and Supplemental Security Insurance (1972), help many poor people, including elderly ones, to remain above the poverty level, which is now $11,611 for a family of four and $5,800 for one person (in 1987). Already three-fourths of the elderly are above the poverty-level income. There are some 32.5 million Americans (13.5 percent) living in poverty.

Medicare and Public Assistance

Human resources outlays by the federal government increased from $25 billion in 1960 to about $460 billion in 1986. The human resources share of the budget is estimated at about 50 percent, compared to 28 percent in 1960. The large increases in the welfare cost were the result of the Great Society's programs in the 1960s and beyond. Such programs, which were introduced to assist poor families, remain in place, although trimmed and tightened in the early 1980s.

Spending on health insurance programs for the elderly (Medicare) increased dramatically in recent years and is expected to continue rising. Thus, from $32 billion in 1980 it reached about $70 billion in 1986, and further increases are expected in future years as the number of retiring people grows.

The cutbacks for such social programs, about 8 percent overall, which were enacted in the early 1980s, especially affected low-income people. Some 50 percent of U.S. households, with incomes less than $20,000 a year, absorb 70 percent of the cuts; while 23 percent of all households, with incomes less than $10,000, absorb 40 percent of the cuts in federal spending. Great cutbacks were made in employment and training programs, child nutrition, welfare, and food stamps. Also, the number of students participating in the school meals program declined from 27 million to 24 million, and spending on guaranteed student loans for college students was cut by 27 percent.

Because Medicare absorbs large amounts of money, more than $70 billion annually, and is growing fast, strong criticism has been directed to this program. One of the reforms suggested requires that the government participates in the financing of the program, particularly of Part A Medicare, whose hospital benefits are not wage related. Other proposals require recipients to absorb more expenses, perhaps 10 percent of them.

In 1985 patients on Medicare paid an initial deductible of $400 against hospital charges for the first 60 days, $100 a day for the sixty-first through the ninetieth day in the hospital, and $200 for the daily cost after 90 days; coverage vanishes entirely after 150 days. Such cost-sharing curbs somewhat unnecessary care, and the cost to the government is less. However, some elderly people have no additional coverage or limited supplemental insurance and may skip or delay treatment. Some others, though, are so poor that their share is covered by Medicaid. It would seem that some kind of sliding payment based on income may be desirable by both the patients and the Medicare administration.

The rapidly rising cost of hospital care, especially room expenses, is part of the problem. Another financial problem is the aging of the population. The proportion of eligible people over the age of 65 increased from 9.6 percent in 1966 to 11.2 percent in 1988, while elderly over 80 increased from 1.6 to 2.4 percent during the same period. As medical advances keep people alive longer, health care costs are expected to grow.

A related problem exists with the Supplementary Medical Insurance (Medicare's Part B) that covers doctors' and outpatient services. Old people who want this additional insurance pay a small premium, but the Treasury contributes the rest, as it does for the catastrophic health insurance starting in January 1, 1989. Beneficiaries finance 20 percent of the Part B program and the Treasury the rest, 80 percent, after a $75 deductible. In 1983 the Treasury paid $18.2 billion for this insurance. The Treasury's contribution in 1988 was about $38 billion. To control these mounting Medicare expenses the government passed a law introducing preestablished rates for hospital reimbursement for a large number of categories, no matter how much more (or less) the hospital actually spends.

A similar set of ceilings on health spending and doctors' fees has been introduced by the Canadian government in ten provinces, where every citizen is guaranteed full medical and hospital coverage of a relatively high level of quality, although only 8 percent of the country's GNP goes for medical services as against 10 percent in the United States. However, there are conflicts over funding between the provinces and the central government, which pays about 40 percent of Medicare expenses. Also, a form of full medical coverage for every citizen has been introduced in the state of Massachusetts.

With the recently introduced predetermined rates for hospitals, treating elderly and disabled patients under the Medicare program, the government expects to slow down high hospital profits. With the previous retrospective system, which reimbursed hospitals based on actual cost, earnings of hospital management companies climbed to 30 and 35 pecent per year recently and their stock went up on the average from below $2 in 1975 to more than $55 in 1983. Even with the new standardized nationwide rates, earnings of hospital management companies such as Hospital Corporation of America, American Medical International, and Humana, Inc., are expected to range between 20 percent and 25 percent annually. However, such standard rates, which include emergency centers, ambulatory surgery centers, and home health care, are expected to slow down the burgeoning Medicare cost and provide incentives for cost-efficient health care.

Yet many state governors criticize the federal government for its restrictive rules on disability benefits. A 1980 law requires that beneficiaries be reexamined once every three years unless they are permanently disabled. As a result, some 374,000 people have been removed from the rolls in a period of two years. Social security administrators insist that strict rules and periodic examinations are needed to remove ineligible people from the rolls, amounting to 3.9 million beneficiaries and costing the government some $18 billion a year. However, state governors feel that these measures are hasty, harsh, and largely inhumane.

There are arguments that the swelling numbers of dependent elderly may lead to de jure or de facto impoverishment of the elderly in the future. Many elders suffer a social death because they are removed from the mainstream of life, being forced to retire and, for example, give up leadership positions in their communities, thus becoming virtual prisoners of their own homes.[10]

There is no doubt that the Medicare program, which covers more than 35 million Americans and costs large amounts of money annually, faces serious financial problems because of the growing elderly population, costly new medical technology, and, in many cases, inefficiency and inflation in hospital labor and supplies. Some 42 percent of hospital customers are Medicare patients, and this number is expected to rise. The new Medicare fixed fee, introduced by the government recently, should be coordinated with reimbursement rates for private insurers, mainly Blue Cross, to prevent hospitals from shifting overrun medical expenses. It seems that the only population group experiencing an increase in hospital admissions is that served by Medicare. Also, the cost of treating patients over 65 is twice as expensive as treating those under 65. To reduce hospital utilization and expenditures, copayments of up to 25 percent made by Medicare beneficiaries have been proposed. Moreover, increases in tobacco and alcohol taxes have been suggested as a perpetual financing of the program.

In order to reduce ever-growing Medicare costs, additional proposals aim at establishing in advance a flat, all-inclusive payment for medical services for each type of hospital case rather than for each individual service. Payment for the same illness and treatment would thus be the same, no matter how many services or how many doctors were involved. The same type of price constraints were introduced for hospitals in 1983 and proved to be successful in controlling costs. However, payments for treatment outside hospitals would not be affected by this proposal. Nonetheless, beneficiaries would save money because under current law they must pay 20 percent of all doctor's services.

To curb growing Medicare expenses, doctors' Medicare fees have been frozen since September 1984. Doctors, though, charge separately for services that they previously delivered as a package. Presently, each Medicare patient is classified in one of 468 diagnosis-related groups. But the number of physicians or services involved may be excessive, or length of hospital stays (averaging eight days now) may be excessive. For example, in a usual surgical case there may be a surgeon, an assistant surgeon, an anesthesiologist, a radiologist, a pathologist, a consulting specialist, and the patient's family doctor.

By controlling prices and the number of services through payment for a package of services for each patient, the government can save money and make doctors and hospitals share the financial risk. Such controls, which are supported by retirees, are opposed by some supply-siders. They argue that this policy is price fixing by government and that the deductible amounts should be raised to reduce the cost of Medicare, even though this might be politically undesirable.

Cost-of-Living Adjustment (COLA) and Other Changes

To avoid erosion of retirement benefits from inflation, in 1972 the U.S. government adopted a process of indexing benefits according to price-level changes.

In 1977, the indexing or automatic adjustment of pensions was related to changes in money wages, and not to changes in the Consumer Price Index (CPI), in order to include changes in productivity. This cost-of-living adjustment (COLA) occurred every first of July. Since 1983, such increases have taken place in early January of every year. However, indexing rates may be reduced or abolished altogether under the pressures of budget deficits.

A new law provides that if the trust funds drop to specified levels, any COLA increases will be based on the lower of the CPI increase or the increase in average wages. This may happen in periods of inflation, when benefit payments increase. When recession and unemployment as well as inflation occur at the same time, that is, when the economy is in stagflation, social security contributions may be reduced. However, when the economy upturns and a net cash inflow returns the trust funds to higher specified levels, benefit adjustments based on the CPI alone will be resumed and catch-up payments could be made.

With the social security amendments of 1983, the age of retirement during which full benefits begin was increased from 65 to 66 by the year 2009 and 67 by the year 2027. The new law gradually raises the retirement age by two months in each of a six-year period until it reaches 66 in the year 2009 and through another set of increases over subsequent six-year periods until it reaches 67 in 2027. For those who want to retire at the age of 62, the benefits will be reduced from the present maximum of 20 percent to 25 percent in the year 2009 and 30 percent in 2027. Presently, a worker's benefits are reduced for each month that income begins before the full-benefit age, with the maximum benefit reduction being 20 percent at age 62. Surviving widows or widowers can receive benefits after the age of 60.

For people who want to delay retirement beyond 65 but prior to 70, the delayed benefits are increased by 3 percent per year until 1989 and 8 percent per year for persons who reach age 65 after 1989 and until 2008.

Through 1989, recipients of social security aged 65–69 forfeit $1 of benefits for every $2 of earnings above $8,400. Beginning in 1990, however, the reduction will be $1 for every $3 earned. For recipients of benefits under age 65, the earning test is reduced to $6,120. Income earned by those above the age of 70 is not subject to any reduction.

The old formula for social security payment averages covered earnings over the number of years from 1956, or the year the employee becomes 26, if later, to the year of age 62. For persons eligible for benefits after 1985 with fewer than 30 years of participation, the benefits are somehow reduced.

Among the reforms concerning the financial viability of social security is the phasing out of benefits for college students 18 through 21. In addition, widows and widowers will lose benefits when their children turn 16 instead of 18.

To slow the rapid growth of the disability cost, which has shot up fivefold in a decade to more than $15 billion presently, recertification of the nearly five million Americans who get disability payments has been pursued from time to time.

Civil service retirement systems, based on length of service and pay, are more generous than social security and private pensions and allow employees to retire fairly early. The civil service plan of the United States covers about three million civilian employees and two million pensioners. Nearly half leave their jobs before the age of 60, and through moonlighting or working further in other jobs they can achieve additional pensions from social security. The U.S. government contributes 65 percent of the pension cost, 47 percent of which is not included in government agency budgets but is buried and picked up from general appropriations. Civil service benefits cost the government about 30 percent of payroll wages, compared to some 22 percent cost to employers for private and social security pensions combined. Although there are no serious problems at present, future pension liabilities are expected to exceed receipts and severe problems of financing civil service benefits may appear. Fringe benefits of government civilian employees are 76 percent higher than those in the private sector. The Veterans Administration alone pays out more than $15 billion a year in benefits.

All federal employees and legislative-branch employees hired after 1983, as well as employees of nonprofit organizations and state and local governments (including state and city colleges) are required to be under the social security system. Exception is made to institutions that have been withdrawn before April 29, 1983, and are remaining voluntarily out of the system. Presently, nine out of ten workers are earning protection under social security.

Statistically, women outlive men by five to eight years. One reason why could be that old women, especially widows, can take care of themselves better than men. Also, it may be that widows tend to be less lonely than widowers and do not care as much for late marriages. They experience friendships in their neighborhoods while men tend to make friends mostly around the workplace and lose them during retirement. Because women outlive men, there is the question of equal benefits for persons of both sexes with equal contributions, given that women are expected to collect more, on the average.

Men have greater trouble surviving alone than women perhaps because they lack the capability to adjust. Many who lost their wives during retirement tend to marry again; otherwise, they may die pretty soon. According to the Census Bureau, in 1930 the number of men and women above the age of 65 was roughly equal. But in 1988 there were about three women for every two men over 65, while above 85 the ratio of women to men was two to one. From 1950 to 1988 the number of Americans over 65 more than doubled.

Unemployment Insurance

Similar to other countries, the United States introduced unemployment insurance, together with the old-age and survivors' insurance, in 1935. It is a joint federal-state program in which employers of one or more workers pay 3.4 percent of the first $6,000 annual earnings to a trust fund of the federal government, which keeps a separate account for each state. By 1937 all states participated in the program. However, a few states impose taxes on employees also and some states use a higher tax rate. Although the tax was initially imposed on employers as being responsible for unemployment, it became more and more obvious that increase in unemployment in market economies is mainly the result of economic fluctuations and not much the result of the employers' policy.

To be entitled to unemployment benefits, a person must work for 52 weeks. The benefits, which amount to at least 50 percent of the weekly wage up to a certain maximum amount, are paid up to 26 weeks; but periodically, in recessions and other emergency cases, Congress extends benefits for more weeks.

In 1908 state governments introduced compensation for workers injured on the job. Such a compensation program, under which about three-fourths of industrial workers are covered, varies among states in regard to the amount and longevity of benefits.

PART II

TAXATION

5

Tax Revenue: Principles and Measures

A BRIEF HISTORICAL REVIEW

Taxation in the present-day sense probably did not exist in the Mediterranean world during biblical times. Tributes, tithes, tolls, and other levies were paid voluntarily to priests primarily on festal days. During Solomon's reign as king of the Hebrews (c. 973–933 B.C.), a corvée, or labor service, was extracted from the labor class, especially for the construction of roads and other public works.

Although there are different interpretations regarding income tax levying in ancient Greece, many sources suggest that tax payments were introduced by Solon's Laws (594 B.C.) or perhaps later (428 B.C.) for three classes (*pentacosiomedimni, knights, zeugites*). The lowest-income class (*thetes*) was exempted from taxation. Such taxes were proportional to income, estimated on the basis of landed property, the value of which was easy to assess.[1] Plato, it seems, supported this form of progressive taxation as simple and fair. When higher government expenditures were needed for wars or other reasons, more taxes were levied.[2] Along the same lines Demosthenes, a well-known politician and orator, advocated the distribution of the tax burden to larger numbers of people in the form of differentiated tax groups. Furthermore, he suggested that it is not proper to scare the rich. Such a tactic would result, not only in their refrain from paying taxes, but in their unwillingness to divulge the extent of their wealth.

During the Roman period, heavy taxation was imposed on plebeians and freemen to support an overgrown administrative apparatus. However, the establishment of the empire and the consequent consolidation of administration and finance made it possible to lighten the tax burden and to quiet potential discontent for a good part of the Roman period.

William Petty, a British economist, in his book *A Treatise of Taxes and Contributions* (1662) argued that taxation is inevitable for financing defense, justice, and other public services. He condemned expensive wars, however, as well as the extravagance of princes. He thought that the money collected should be spent primarily to stimulate the economy. Although taxes may be raised to create a reserve for emergencies, he argued, this is not to occur often because such money is withdrawn from productive circulation. Similarly to John Locke and Thomas Hobbes, Petty accepted the view that the state exists to protect the property of the individual who, in turn, should contribute toward the expenses of the state and recognize the utilitarian nature of taxation.

The French Physiocrats (1756–78) thought that labor applied to land was capable of producing goods whose value exceeded the factor cost; the difference, which they regarded as agricultural productivity or natural surplus, was called *produit net*. A single tax (*Impot unique*) upon this true net product could replace all other taxes, like property taxes (*taille*), sales taxes (*aides*), and salt taxes (*gabelle*), and solve many problems of misery and inequality. This concept was used later by the U.S. economist Henry George (1871), as will be explained later in this chapter.

Adam Smith thought that taxes to finance government expenditures must finally be paid from one of the different sorts of revenue, that is, rent, profit, or wages, or from all of them. With regard to taxes in general, he believed there are four maxims to be pursued. These maxims, or tax principles, are (1) equity, that is, tax payment in proportion to revenue; (2) certainty, in the sense that taxes ought not to be arbitrary as to the amount, time, and manner of payment; (3) convenience, that is, payment when the contributor is most likely to have the wherewithal to pay; and (4) avoidance of such related conditions as disincentives of production, evasions, and vexation or oppression by tax gatherers.[3]

Smith realized that there are difficulties of taxing people in proportion to their revenue. Because of the difficulty or impossibility of taxing directly and proportionally the revenue of its subjects, the state "endeavours to tax it indirectly by taxing their expense, which, it is supposed, will in most cases be nearly in proportion to their revenue."[4] This can take place by taxing the consumable commodities, primarily luxuries, upon which expenses are laid out. Smith argued that even direct taxes upon the wages of manufacturing labor, ceteris paribus, would be advanced by the employers and paid by the consumers.

Ricardo, on the other hand, thought that taxes are a portion of the produce of the land and labor of a country placed at the disposal of the government. They are ultimately paid either from the capital or the revenue of the country. They can be met either by an increased production or by a diminished consumption. But if there is no increased production or diminished, unproductive consumption, the taxes will fall on capital. As the capital of a country is diminished, its production will necessarily be diminished.[5] We can infer, then, that Ricardo was against taxes that would reduce capital formation and in favor of taxes on revenue or, more specifically, on unproductive consumption.

Henry George (1839–97), a neglected U.S. economist, proposed a single tax on land rent for the purpose of luring rich investors away from speculation in land and into productive enterprises. The speculative price of land stands in the way of productive ventures, and a single tax on land values would discourage such speculation in favor of capital formation and high productivity. To shift the burden of taxation from production and exchange to the value or rent of land would give new stimulus to production of wealth and promote equality in distribution.[6] Following the rationale of the Physiocrats and particularly François Quesnay and Mirabeau the Elder, Henry George thought that the numerous direct and indirect taxes kill the geese that lay the golden eggs by oppressing industry and hampering exchanges. By making hard-working people pay more for their energy and industry than others who are not working as hard (absentee owners, for instance) and by penalizing through taxation those who save more than the ones who consume and waste resources, we stifle opportunities and reduce wealth.

Although Henry George's proposals for reducing or eliminating taxes on industry and capital are today valuable and well accepted for purposes of stimulating production and employment, his suggestion of eliminating all forms of taxation except a single tax on the value or rent of land seems to be an impractical way of collecting huge amounts of public revenue in modern economies with high proportions of incomes from services and industry.

The socialists, particularly Karl Marx, viewed taxation and debt accumulation, primarily, as instruments of exploitation. However, it is said that "in capitalism man exploits man, in communism it is the other way around." According to Marx, banks place themselves by the side of governments and advance money to the state for privileges they receive. As a result, national debt increases, as do yearly payments for interest. The national loans enable governments to meet extraordinary expenses without the tax payers feeling the burden immediately, but eventually they necessitate increased taxes. The raising of taxation—caused by accumulation of debt—is not sufficient to meet increasing expenses, and this compels governments to resort to new loans. Therefore, public debt and the fiscal system corresponding to it play a great part in the capitalization of wealth and the exploitation of the masses. However, Marx in his book *Das Kapital* (1867) recommended heavy progressive income taxes and accumulated public debt as a means of overcoming the capitalist order.[7]

In contrast, the neoclassical economists, mainly Alfred Marshall (1890), placed emphasis on income and consumption taxes to finance public sector expenditures.

TAX PRINCIPLES

This section deals with the main principles of taxation and the problems of the subterranean economy. Included are the traditional principles of tax equity, tax shifting and incidence, and tax neutrality, as well as the income and substitution effects taxes exert on the economy. The next sections deal with tax revenue trends as proportions of national income for general, central, and state and local governments.

In addition to taxation, the methods of financing government expenditures are through printing and borrowing money. Governments in general have the authority for coining money. However, to print new money to cover government expenditures is highly inflationary. This has frequently been proved in many countries in which central banks are directly controlled by governments, particularly in developing countries.

In the United States, the power to coin money rests with Congress. With the establishment of the Federal Reserve Bank (Fed) in 1913, the amount of money supply is determined by the Fed, which is an independent institution. The seven members of the board of governors of the Fed are appointed for 14 years by the U.S. president with the consent of the Senate. All these seven members, plus the director of the New York Fed and four other directors from the 12 regional Feds in rotation, form the powerful Federal Reserve Open Market Committee (FOMC). The FOMC is responsible for buying and selling U.S. government securities and setting money supply targets, thereby affecting prices, employment, growth, and other economic goals of the country. When the Fed buys a government security, it pays with Federal Reserve notes or draws checks upon itself, thus creating money and directly monetizing the debt. However, the U.S. Treasury may borrow, primarily from the public at large, and thereby avoid such monetization.

Out of the three main ways of financing government expenditures (taxation, borrowing, and money creation), this chapter concentrates on taxation as a means of transferring resources from private to public use and promoting a more equal distribution. Later chapters examine the issues of borrowing to finance budget deficits and the problems arising from debt accumulation. Money creation itself is primarily an issue of monetary theory and policy and not much one of public finance; therefore it is not a central concern of this volume.

For a better understanding of the tax system, the meanings of the tax base and the tax rate structure should be clarified. Tax base is an item or an activity upon which a tax is imposed. There are three major tax bases: earnings or income, consumption, and wealth. They may be considered as economic tax bases, and as such they are related to each other. In addition, there are noneconomic tax bases such as individuals. The taxes upon them are known as head or poll taxes and are levied as lump-sum payments. Taxes on economic bases can be distinguished in general taxes, levied upon the whole base, and the more frequently used specific taxes, levied on a portion or an aspect of the tax base. In the case of specific taxes, exemptions and deductions are usually allowed, but not in the case of general taxes.

Tax structure refers to the types of taxes used by the government. Tax rate structure on the other hand, refers to the percentages of taxation on the tax base. A study of the tax structure and the tax rates is important for comparisons between different periods and among countries with different tax systems. There are three main tax rate schedules: proportional or flat (the same percentage regardless of the size of the tax base), progressive (increasing percentages with the size of the base), and regressive (decreasing percentages as the size of the base increases). The most important tax schedule in the United States is the progressive income tax, with rates rising as income increases.

Tax Equity

One of the main principles of taxation, supported by many economists including Adam Smith and Arthur Pigou, is equity, which refers to the fair distribution of the tax burdens among individuals or groups of people. It can be interpreted by the ability to pay and the equality of benefits to tax standards. The equity principle can be distinguished in horizontal and vertical equity. Horizontal equity requires that people in the same economic position pay the same amount of taxes. Vertical equity requires that the tax system consider differences in distribution and take higher portions of income from rich people, who have greater ability to pay than poor people.

For the implementation of the equity principle, the benefits theory and the ability-to-pay theory can be used. According to the benefits, or user-charge, theory, a linkage of tax payment to the benefits received should be established. Thus, public or quasi-public goods and services offered should be related to user charges or taxes levied. Such services may include postal, water, sewer, sidewalk, gas, hospital services, and state university education. The main problem in these cases is the measurement of cost and the related benefit, especially when there are substantial positive or negative externalities. However, when income elasticity of demand for public services is higher than one, there is an indication of support for financing such services. In general, the social optimum in taxation will be achieved when the marginal social cost of the tax burden is equal to the marginal social benefit from a public good or service used.

The principle of the ability to pay requires that taxes be paid according to the fiscal capacity of each person, which is best measured by income. High-income people should pay more taxes than low-income people, at a progressive rate, so that the welfare sacrifice would be the same or the marginal disutility in paying taxes would be the same. Thus, people with low income enjoy higher utility or satisfaction from a small amount of income that provides necessities of life than rich people who are using the same amount for luxuries. This is so because the marginal utility of income, or the welfare associated with each extra dollar, declines. To pay a dollar tax out of $10 income is more painful than to pay the one dollar tax out of $1,000 income.

Equity or fairness in tax treatment is satisfied when taxes paid by individuals are based on the benefits they receive from government expenditures. In competitive markets, the price of an incremental or marginal unit of a commodity is determined according to the marginal benefit or satisfaction of the buyer. In

Figure 5.1
Marginal Benefit Taxation

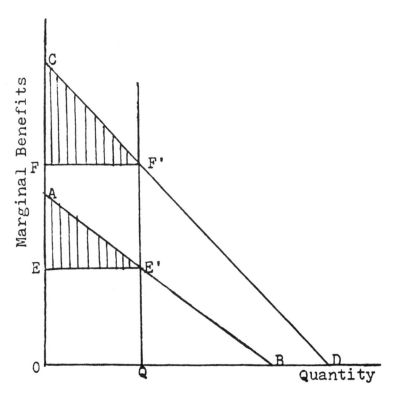

a similar way, the price (the tax) of an extra unit of a public good should be based on the marginal or extra benefit received. In that way, consumers in competitive markets enjoy a surplus, that is, the difference between what they were willing to pay and what they actually pay, which is not priced away. Likewise, taxpayers enjoy a similar surplus that is not taxed away.

Figure 5.1 shows that the marginal benefits of an individual consuming OQ units of a public good are OE, while those of another individual consuming the same units of that good, supplied in a fixed quantity (OQ) by the government, are OF. The marginal benefit taxation for the first individual with the marginal benefits curve AB, should be OE; and for the second individual, with the marginal benefit curve CD, it should be OF. Thus, the consumers' (taxpayers') surplus would be AEE' for the first and CFF' for the second individual.

Although it is difficult to match marginal benefits with taxes in public goods and services, an approximation can be made along these lines with user charges to finance the construction of bridges, tunnels, docks, airports, highways, and similar projects. On these grounds, the users should pay for such projects and services in the form of automobile and gasoline taxes, air fair taxes, bridge tolls, postal service charges, and the like. From a practical point of view, the concept of average-cost pricing is used, instead of marginalism. However, the difficulty of identifying beneficiaries and measuring related benefits remains.

Tax Shifting and Incidence

Tax shifting refers to the transfer of the tax burden away from its initial point to an ultimate point of impact. It has distributional effects as to the share of the final tax burden among individual households, sectors, and different regions of the economy. As such, it influences prices and output in product and factor markets and is affected by work-leisure choices and factor combinations in the production process. In the case of a tax replacing another of equal yield with budget expenditures remaining at the same level, there exists a differential incidence or placement. In the case of an equal increase in taxes and expenditures, there exists a balanced-budget incidence.

Through the market mechanism of supply and demand, all things being equal, a new tax or an increase in a tax is normally transferred or shifted, totally or partially, forward to consumers. On the other hand, a reduction or an elimination of a tax may allow part or all of the tax burden to be shifted backward through a price decline. A property tax can also be shifted through tax capitalization, which would mean a change in the expected returns and therefore in the price of the related capital good.

There may, of course, be cases in which a new tax does not lead to the change in price but to the reduction in the quality or size of the taxable good. This can be called a concealed or disguised tax shifting. However, as a result of higher prices from a new or a higher tax, some consumers may forgo buying the taxable good or may buy a cheaper one. In both cases, the consumer is less satisfied, and thus the total burden exceeds the revenue collected by the loss of satisfaction or efficiency (excess burden).

Depending on the market structure in which buyers and sellers operate, as well as on the elasticities of demand and supply, the tax burden may be shifted forward or backward. Under conditions of pure or perfect competition, where there are many sellers with a homogeneous product, the individual firm is pricetaker (horizontal demand, or average revenue, curve) and partial tax shifting would take place forward through industry forces. In the long run, some firms would be forced to exit the industry because of higher prices forced by an excise tax per unit product. This is so because the industry's demand curve is not horizontal but downsloping.

As Figure 5.2 shows, as a result of a tax, the quantity sold (Q) remained the same, as determined by the equilibrium point (marginal cost equals marginal revenue) where the firm maximizes profits or minimizes losses. However, the price increased from P to P' because of tax shifting. This can be so if other firms in the industry, under pure competition, are forced out and the remaining firms raise prices to cover the new cost due to taxation.

Figure 5.2
Tax Shifting in Pure Competition

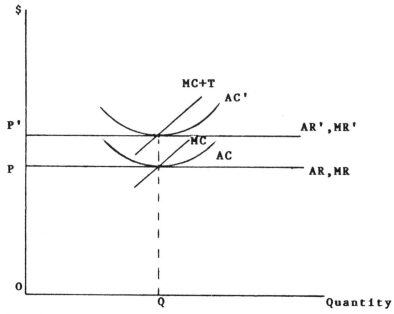

Figure 5.3
Tax Shifting under Monopolistic Conditions

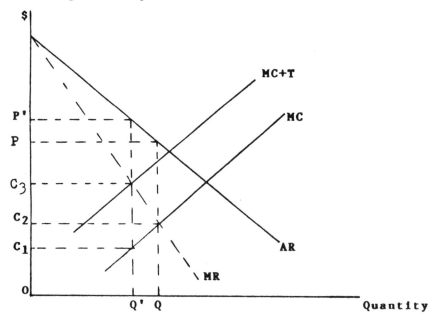

Under monopolistic conditions, where the demand curve of the firm is down-sloping, consumers and producers share the burden of taxation. As Figure 5.3 indicates, a tax per unit product would shift the marginal cost curve to the left, thus establishing a new marginal-cost–marginal-revenue equilibrium with a decline in quantity from Q to Q′ and an increase in price from P to P′. Consumers pay part of the tax (PP′) and producers absorb the rest. With lower quantity (Q′), producers have lower cost per unit (C_1) and can absorb part of the unit tax.

In competitive markets, demand and supply elasticities affect the partial equilibrium incidence of a tax on a single good, such as gasoline, beer, liquor, or tobacco. As a result of a tax on a particular item, the price and the quantity sold will change by an amount determined by the elasticities of demand and supply. If both demand and supply schedules or curves are elastic, price will rise less than the tax. The more elastic are both curves, the larger the decrease in quantity. The more elastic the supply and the less elastic the demand, the larger the increase in price.

In the previous analysis, the principle of partial equilibrium, that other things remain the same, was extensively used to determine the effects of a tax change on the price and quantity of a product. However, the partial equilibrium analysis is insufficient, since it ignores related changes in other prices and other markets. Instead, changes in prices and quantities of all goods and factors should be considered in a general equilibrium framework. In the interdependent system of the economy, therefore, the behavior of consumers toward a taxed product will affect prices and quantities of other products, as well as the return to capital and labor.

Long-run general equilibrium tax incidence analysis involves such elements as work-leisure behavior, capital-labor ratios, budgetary choices, and other multiple interacting variables requiring complex econometric models for the statistical measurement of the related coefficients. In real life, many taxes affect many industries and many sectors of the economy. Thus, a tax on income from interest discourages saving and may reduce investment financing. This may reduce demand for labor and lower productivity and wages. Likewise, a corporate income tax may affect not only business investment but also returns to capital and in the long run returns to labor. In turn, foreign trade, capital flow, and the equilibrium of the entire economy will be affected—a process that requires a general equilibrium analysis.

Assuming other things to be the same, the less the elasticity of demand, the higher the tax shifting to consumers; and the less the elasticity of supply, the higher the tax shifting to producers. If price elasticity of demand is zero, quantity demanded would be the same and the whole amount of tax would be shifted forward to consumers. If demand is perfectly elastic, the supply curve would shift to the left, equilibrium would be established at lower quantity, and the final incidence of total tax per unit would fall on producers. If supply is perfectly inelastic (vertical supply curve) the whole amount of tax per unit would be shifted backward to producers. In contrast, if supply is perfectly elastic, a sales tax would be shifted entirely forward to consumers (shift of the supply curve upward) and, depending on the elasticity of demand, the quantity sold would be reduced.

Tax Neutrality: Income and Substitution Effects

Tax neutrality exists when market choices of people are not distorted by the tax. A neutral tax, although having an income effect, does not cause substitution effect, and so consumers' preference schedules remain unaffected. In general, taxes do affect economic variables such as output, employment, and inflation, for which discussion takes place in later chapters.

Because of the price distortion caused by an excise or other tax, an excess burden falls on the consumer as he or she is forced to shift from a desirable or optimal choice. If everyone pays the same amount, as in the case of lump-sum tax (a head tax), then excess burden or deadweight loss can be avoided. But this may be in conflict with the equity principle, which is based on the ability to pay, and so policymakers should attempt some kind of trade-off between excess burden or efficiency cost and equity.

Figure 5.4 shows the pretax equilibrium at point A and at price OP and quantity OQ. With a sales tax the supply curve (S) rises to S + T and the new after-tax equilibrium is at point B. The new price increases to OP', quantity declines to OQ', and tax revenue is equal to P"P'BD. Before the tax, consumers paid OPAQ but were willing to pay OFAQ. The difference, PFA, is known as the consumers' surplus. After the tax, the consumers' surplus declined to P'FB; that is a decrease equal to P'PAB. From this, government collects revenue PP'BC and the rest, ABC, is a deadweight or loss to the consumers. Likewise, the producers' surplus (PAQ) is, after tax, reduced to P"DQ'. The government collects revenue PCDP" from the producers and the rest ACD is the loss to the producers. The consumers' and the producers' loss together, ABD, is the excess burden or deadweight loss to the economy.

However, arguments on excess burden, which had some importance in the past, have gradually lost significance in theory and in practice because of recent advances and efficient policies tending to minimize such burdensome distortions in the trade-off between equity and efficiency.

Because of the increase in population and the growth of consumption, commodity demand increases. Assuming that the supply curve (S) of a commodity has the shape of that in Figure 5.5, an upward shift of the demand curve from D_1 to D_2 would lead to a higher price from P_1 to P_2 and an increase in supply from Q_1 to Q_2. If at quantity Q_2 supply becomes fixed or monopolistic, a new shift of demand to D_3 would mean a new higher price P_3, but the same quantity Q_2. If the price is fixed at P_2 by the government, in spite of higher demand D_3 then a shortage $Q_2 Q_3$ would appear—which might necessitate rationing.

If a tax is imposed per commodity unit, equal to price increase P_2P_3, the tax

Figure 5.4
Excess Burden of a Sales Tax

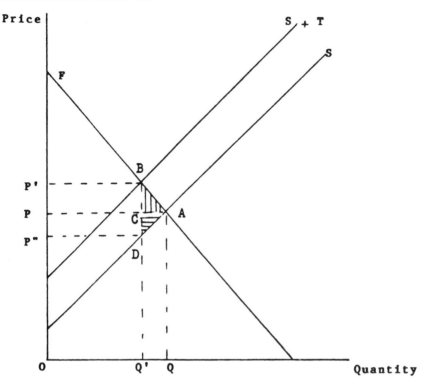

would be absorbed by the producer with fixed supply Q_2. The consumer with demand curve D_3 would pay a price P_3 and enjoy the same quantity Q_2. The tax would have no effect on price and quantity. It would not distort people's market choices and as such is a neutral tax. At the same time, the government collects taxes $P_2 P_3$ per unit of a commodity or a resource fixed in supply, such as land, without generating unwanted side effects.

As shown in Figure 5.6, in the presence of an income tax the budget line is AB, whose slope is the income earned by giving up additional units of leisure and vice versa. An income tax reduction would increase the taxpayer's money income, shifting budget line AB to a final position AB" and the utility or indifference curve I to II, which is parallel to and higher than I. The movement from point a, where curve I is tangent to the budget line AB, to point b, where the same curve I is tangent to A'B' (parallel to AB"), shows the substitution of leisure for more work and income because of less taxes (non-neutral effect). The movement from point b to point c shows the income effect of tax reduction. At point c, the taxpayer enjoys not only more income, but also more leisure than at b. Macroeconomically, however, such a government policy of tax reduction

Figure 5.5
Equilibrium Price and Quantity of a Commodity after Tax

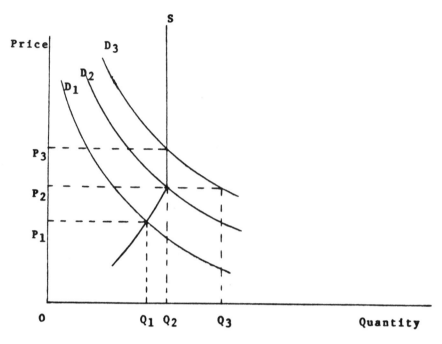

may lead to the replacement of work by leisure (less labor supply), particularly by groups such as part-time workers, married women, and early retirees.

A tax on interest income may have a substitution effect and an income effect. It may induce people to substitute consumption for saving (non-neutrality), or it may make them save more in order to maintain consumption in future periods (income effect). It is expected, though, that the substitution effect would be stronger than the income effect and saving would be discouraged in favor of present consumption. Such a substitution effect would cause an excess burden or a deadweight loss to the economy.

Figure 5.7 shows that an excise tax is less efficient than an income tax. Assuming other things to be the same, an imposition of income tax on the consumer would shift the budget line from AB, where there is no tax, to A′B′ and the equilibrium point from a to b. The resource transfer in terms of commodity X would be BB′ and the loss in utility from indifference curve I to II would be equal to the resource transfer. Therefore, no excess loss or deadweight is imposed on the economy. However, an excise tax on X, which will lead to the same amount of tax revenue (BB′ or AA′), would bring about a parallel shift of the utility or indifference curve II to III. The equilibrium point c is the tangent point of III to the new budget line AB‴, along line A′B′, resulting from the increase in the relative price of X because of the tax. It yields the same

Figure 5.6
Substitution and Income Effects of a Tax Reduction

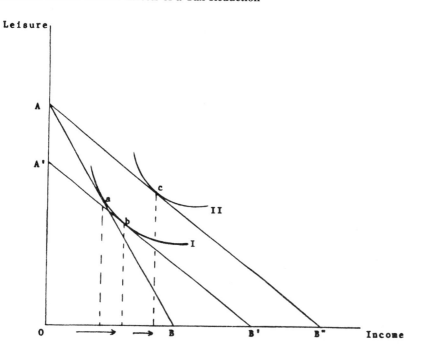

amount of tax revenue (BB') but an excess burden B'B", equal to the distance
from II to III. The same analysis holds for an entire economy if the budget lines
are used as production possibility lines and the utility curves as social indifference
curves.[8]

Proportional, Progressive, and Regressive Taxes

In the case of proportional or flat tax rates, the marginal tax rate (MTR) is
equal to the average tax rate (ATR) and the tax line is horizontal to the tax base
axis, as Figure 5.8 shows. In progressive taxation, the marginal tax line is positive
(moving upward) as the tax base expands, and the average tax line is also positive
but growing at a lower rate, so that at each point MTR > ATR. In contrast, in
regressive taxes the marginal tax line is declining as the tax base grows larger,
and the average tax line is also declining but to a lesser extent (MTR < ATR).

Proportional or flat tax rates remain constant regardless of the size of the
income or any other tax base. General retail sales taxes, collected by many states
and localities, belong to this category. Progressive or graduated tax rates are the
ones that increase as the size of the tax base increases. Personal income and
corporation income taxes are examples of such tax bases on which progressive

Figure 5.7
Excess Burden from an Excise Tax Compared to an Income Tax

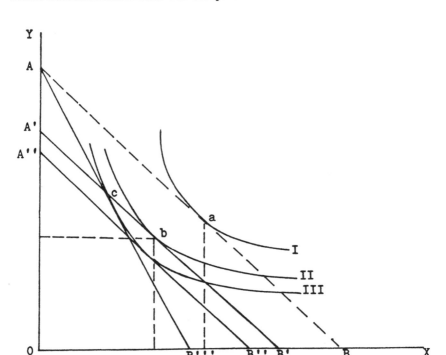

rates are levied. Regressive tax rates, which decline as the tax base rises, include capital stock taxes imposed on business incorporated within some states.

As the tax base expands, a statutorily progressive tax yields increasingly larger amounts of revenue to the government. The opposite occurs with a regressive tax, while a proportional tax yields intermediate results. A progressive income tax can be considered as an automatic stabilizer in the same sense that it automatically withdraws proportionally more revenue than the increase in income in a cyclical upswing of the economy and proportionally less revenue in its downswing. Note here that when ad hoc decisions are used for tax or other budgetary changes, we refer to discretionary fiscal stabilizers.

Progressive personal income taxes encourage leisure and discourage work incentives. In such allocational non-neutrality, tax payers try to substitute leisure for work (this is the substitution effect or work-leisure trade-off) depending on the progressiveness of the rates of taxation. It may be argued, though, that because taxation reduces disposable income, taxpayers are expected to maintain after-tax purchasing power by additional work (this is the income effect). However, it seems that the substitution effect is more powerful than the income effect,

Figure 5.8
Progressive, Proportional or Flat, and Regressive Tax Rates

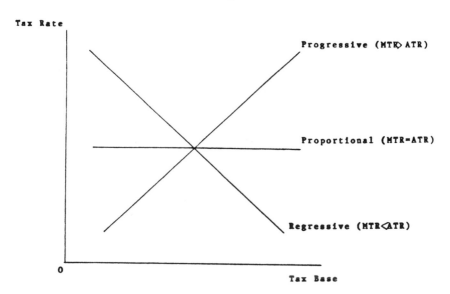

particularly in highly taxed personal income groups, except when noneconomic motives of work, such as social prestige or personal power, are present.

Figure 5.9 shows that in a 100 percent marginal income tax no work will occur and the whole area OB will be leisure. If there is no personal income tax (line AB), the work-leisure indifference curve (W_1) dictates how much time will be devoted for work (L_1B) and how much time will be available for leisure (OL_1). The same thing can be observed with proportional income tax. In such a case the line AB will be at a lower level, somewhere between AC, and the area of work will be smaller than L_1B but larger than L_2B.

The more usual case is with a progressive personal income tax at less than 100 percent marginal rate (curve BC). Assuming an indifference curve W_2 parallel to W_1 (preserving the preference pattern of the taxpayers), the time available for work, which is determined by the point of tangency of W_2 on curve CB, becomes smaller (L_2B) and that of leisure larger (OL_2). This progressiveness distorts further the neutral work-leisure trade-off. Thus, the higher the marginal rates of personal income tax, the less the work incentives and the more the leisure induced. When the individual does not work (that is, when he or she buys leisure), the after-tax income lost is the opportunity cost. Increase in leisure can take place mainly through longer vacations, early retirement, greater absenteeism, and less overtime work.

Similar results are expected in total tax revenue. As Figure 5.10 exhibits, total tax revenues at first grows with growing tax rates, but after a certain point higher tax rates are associated with lower amounts of tax revenues. Thus, when tax

Figure 5.9
Work-Leisure Trade-off as a Result of Income Tax Changes

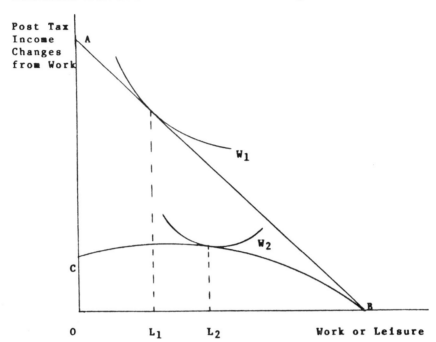

rates (t) in the vertical axis increase from t_1 to t_{opt} (optimum tax rate), tax revenues along the horizontal axis increase from R_1 to R_{opt} (optimum tax revenue). However, when tax rates increase further than t_{opt} say at t_2, tax revenues decline to R_2. This is known as the famous (or, as some say, infamous) Laffer curve, named after Professor Arthur Laffer who popularized it.

There is not much empirical research to verify this relationship of tax rates and tax revenues, supported primarily by supply-side economists. It seems, though, that the so-called secondary workers, such as teenagers and women, are most responsive to changes in after-tax income. Although in the very short run a decrease in tax rates may not result in an increase in tax revenue, in the long run efforts not to reduce tax liabilities, stimulation in work effort, and increase in investment and productivity are expected to create a higher rate of economic growth and enhance overall tax revenue.

Special interest constituencies press for higher levels of spending that need higher taxes. Since millions of taxpayers do not represent an effectively organized interest group, the result is ever-growing taxes. Thus, the taxes paid by the median-income family of the United States increased from $9 in 1948 to $2,218 in 1983, that is, by 246 times. More than 90 percent of taxable income flows from brackets of $35,000 per year or less.

Figure 5.10
The Relationship of Tax Rates and Tax Revenue

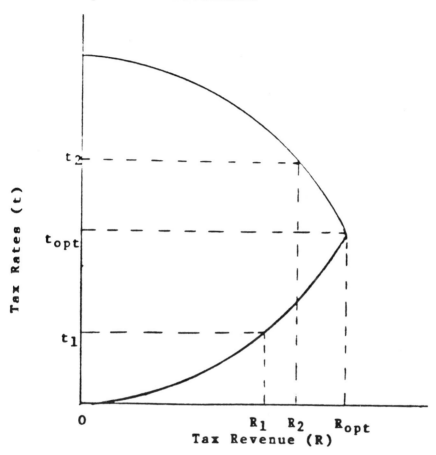

For purposes of providing budgetary revenue and restricting personal consumption and wealth accumulation, progressive income taxes and consumption taxes are used in all economies, including the socialist ones. However, maximum tax limits are introduced to minimize disincentive effects on labor allocation, performance, and improvement of skills. For recent reforms reducing tax rates see Chapter 7.

TAX EVASION: THE SUBTERRANEAN ECONOMY

The subterranean economy, that is, that portion of national output which involves tax evasion, is described in many ways: underground, black, unrecorded, concealed, dual, twilight, parallel, cash, hidden, moonlight, and clandestine. Reasons for participation in the subterranean, or underground, economy may be to evade taxes, to avoid losing government benefits, to circumvent regulations, to bypass trade union vigilance, and to have flexibility in employment and remuneration of labor. In the last case, primary or secondary jobs may not be reported. This could result in inappropriate policies.

The main method used to estimate the size of the subterranean economy is that based on the discrepancies between income and expenditures. Here, it is assumed that income estimates and reporting are biased but expenditures are not. An approximation of tax evasion can be made by comparing income tax revenues, as proportions of national income, of different countries with similar tax rates. Thus, if income taxes in a country with a progressive tax system similar to that of the United States absorb 10 percent of total national income, compared with 16 percent in the United States, tax evasion in the first country is about 6 percent of the national income.

There are estimates that the U.S. subterranean economy is about 14 percent of the measured national income.[9] More than $3 billion is the annual loss from sales taxes in New York State and localities alone. About half of the subterranean income lies in classical illegal activities, while the rest lies only in tax evasion activities. Tax avoidance, which is legal, and tax evasion, which is illegal, may be merged into a new term *avoision*.

Recent studies indicate that the underground, or unofficial, economy is not only sizable but also growing faster than the official, or recorded, economy. Among the most important causes of subterranean economic activities, particularly in the United States, Britain, and the Scandinavian countries, is tax evasion. If people perceive that public expenditure is wasteful or the tax burden is heavy and inequitably distributed, they may tend not to participate in the official, or above-ground, economic activities. Also, when tax administrations are poor and ineffective, underground economic activities are likely to flourish.

High income taxes and social security contributions bring about a black market for labor. In a labor black market both employers and employees gain from no tax and no social security payments. Moreover, regulations that relate to labor markets may be circumvented or ignored, and this leads to low tax or no tax payment. Such regulations may cover minimum wages, alien workers, minors, retirees, overtime, and working women. Other black market economic activities involve goods because of price controls, rationing, import quotas, export bans, and forced sales of commodities to government agencies or to marketing boards. In all these cases a hidden market is developed and the end result is a loss of tax revenue from unreported transactions and income. Black markets for goods reached epidemic proportions in the United States during World War II, and since then have become widespread in some highly regulated countries. In addition to black markets for labor and goods is the black market for money. Constraints on interest rates and credit controls result in such money black markets, as well as loan sharking operations and nonreporting of interest income.

There are also some activities, such as illegal drugs, prostitution, illegal gambling, and other criminal actions that affect tax levying. Such illegal activities in the United States range between one-third and one-half of the underground economy. Being forbidden by law, these prohibited services are not reported and income earned escapes measurement and tax payment.

Under-the-counter contributions to public employees who can issue specific licenses as waivers from particular regulations and avoid delays for special permissions for government services are parts of bureaucratic corruption that generate incomes and do not pay taxes. It is argued, however, that such under-the-counter payments oil the bureaucratic mechanism, making it more efficient and compensating the public employees for low wages.

Because of underground activities, income and employment expand. However, from the point of view of public finance, government expenditures increase and tax revenues decrease, and income distribution is distorted. Those who earn underground incomes continue to enjoy public services in the form of protection, schooling, roads, health services, and the like, although they pay less taxes or no taxes compared with other taxpayers. Moreover, official employment records are distorted, the rate of economic growth is underestimated, the rate of inflation is also distorted, and fiscal and monetary policies become less effective. It is estimated that if the underground employment is considered, the actual unemployment rate may be more than 2 percent lower than the official rate. Monetary policy is also likely to be distorted as money expansion, related only to the official economy, ignores a good part of income transactions.

In spite of governmental measures to minimize tax disincentives, tax evasion remains. The primary culprits are middlemen, scientists, artists, and enterprises. To eliminate or reduce tax evasion and loopholes, governments from time to time try to dig deep in high incomes but are "carried out with a sieve."

Because the number of individuals not paying or underpaying taxes has gradually been increasing, the Internal Revenue Service (IRS) is in the process of using computerized information regarding the lifestyles of individuals who fail to pay their income taxes. Such information includes the neighborhoods and the number of years families live there, as well as the model and year of cars owned. Census Bureau statistics, telephone books, automobile registration files, and similar publicly available records are expected to provide related data. But the procedure is very troublesome, and there may be the question of the violation of privacy. In addition, the cost involved for the collection of data may be high.

More detailed historical research has revealed that the underground economy in the United States has increased from $0.55 billion or 0.6 percent of GNP in 1930 to $14.4 billion or 5.07 percent of GNP in 1950, to $45 billion or 4.6 percent of GNP in 1970, and $154.3 billion or 6.07 percent of GNP in 1980.[10] These figures do not include criminal activities. The trend seems to have accelerated in recent years, especially since the mid–1970s, mainly because of the substantial increase in marginal tax rates due to inflation. However, the tax cuts enacted in 1981 and 1986 are expected to reverse this trend.

By working off-the-books, craftsmen and craftswomen, moonlighting professionals, and other workers (mostly immigrants, minorities, or women) manage to escape taxes. But they lose social security benefits, minimum wages, health insurance, and other safety measures, and thus they return toward the "tyranny of the free market." Finally, corporate America sometimes exploits the underground economy by entering into subcontracts with small entrepreneurs.

GENERAL GOVERNMENT REVENUE

Average and Marginal Taxes

To see the relationship of tax revenue (T) to income (Y) and to trace changes in these two variables, the average propensity to tax (APT), the marginal propensity to tax (MPT), and the income elasticity of taxation (E_t) can be used as follows:

$$APT = \frac{T}{Y}$$
$$MPT = \frac{\Delta T}{\Delta Y}$$
$$E_t = \frac{\Delta T/T}{\Delta Y/Y}$$

The average tax rate is the percentage of income absorbed by taxes, whereas the marginal tax rate is the ratio of change in tax revenue over change in income.

The income elasticity of taxation (E_t) relates the percentage change in tax revenue to the percentage change in income over a period of time. If the elasticity is more than one ($E_t > 1$), this relationship is elastic. If it is equal to one ($E_t = 1$), there is unitary elasticity and the proportion of tax change is equal to that of income change. If it is less than one ($E_t < 1$), the relationship is inelastic.

The governmental revenue raised through taxation may be given by

$$Ti = \sum_{i=1}^{n} t_i B_i \qquad i = 1, 2, 3, \ldots, n \text{ years}$$

where T stands for tax revenue, t for the tax rate, and B the tax base. That is, the tax yield to the government in a particular time period equals the summation of tax rates times the tax base per year for the period considered. Tax base, such as income, is the object of taxation, and tax rate is the amount of tax per unit of tax base.[11]

The built-in flexibility of taxes, which may be defined as the change in tax yield related to a change in income, is the marginal tax rate or bracket rate. Thus, the U.S. marginal taxes of total government, related to national income, were 32.5 percent in 1940–50, 39.6 percent in 1950–60, 41.3 percent in 1960–70, 1970–80, and 36.2 percent in 1980–85. These empirical results indicate that the U.S. marginal tax rates were higher than zero ($t > 0$) in these years, indicating that the tax structure of the United States has built-in flexibility. Further, the income elasticity of taxation, which is applicable to long-run revenue productivity of the tax system—or the ratio of the percentage change in taxes over the percentage change in income—was higher than one in these years (1.4 in 1950–60, 1.2 in 1960–70, 1970–80, and 1.1 in 1980–85).

It seems that the United States and many other countries are slowly moving away from what Thomas Jefferson suggested when he said that "government governs best which governs least." Indeed, the powers of governments to "police" the economy and to "secure the public interest" are growing. As noted earlier, defense and internal security, unemployment insurance and old-age pensions, welfare programs, minimum-wage determination and compulsory collective bargaining, controls on banking operations and financial markets, and a host of regulations dealing with such issues as restricting monopolistic practices, improving working conditions and, in many instances, ownership of some utilities and even productive enterprises are under governmental or public domain. Governments, in turn, finance all those operations primarily by taxation, by borrowing (through selling bonds or other securities to the public), and by issuing new money. All things being equal, the last method of financing government expenditures, that is, issuing new money, is inflationary when the growth of money supply exceeds the growth of real production. To make public operations less bureaucratic and more efficient, efforts are made to increase the quality of civil servants and the civil service through training and mechanization as well as to abolish graft and waste by "cutting out fat without cutting muscle."

General Government Revenue Trends

Total taxes or general government receipts, as a percentage of national income, increased from 13.3 percent in 1929 to 22.2 percent in 1940 and 29.0 percent in 1950. As Figure 5.11 shows, this trend has continued in the years since 1960, and general government receipts have increased from 33.6 percent in 1960 to 35.2 percent of national income in 1985.[12] A higher increase can be observed in the tax-income ratios of the EEC countries as well as in those of Japan. Such increases in tax revenue that are larger than national income indicate that the public sector is growing more than the private one.

The upward trend in total taxes as proportions of national income has been due to the gradual growth of direct (or income) taxes since the 1950s. On the other hand, indirect taxes, as percentages of national income, have remained constant or even declined slightly during the years.

Social security taxes, which increased steadily from 3 percent of national income in 1950 to around 8 percent in the 1980s, have contributed largely to growing proportions of total taxation. If social security contributions were excluded, general government taxes would be fairly constant during the entire period (around 25 percent of national income). Actually, central or federal government taxes declined from 19.6 percent of national income in the 1950s to

Figure 5.11
Total Receipts of General, Federal, and State-Local Governments as Percentages of National Income (current prices)

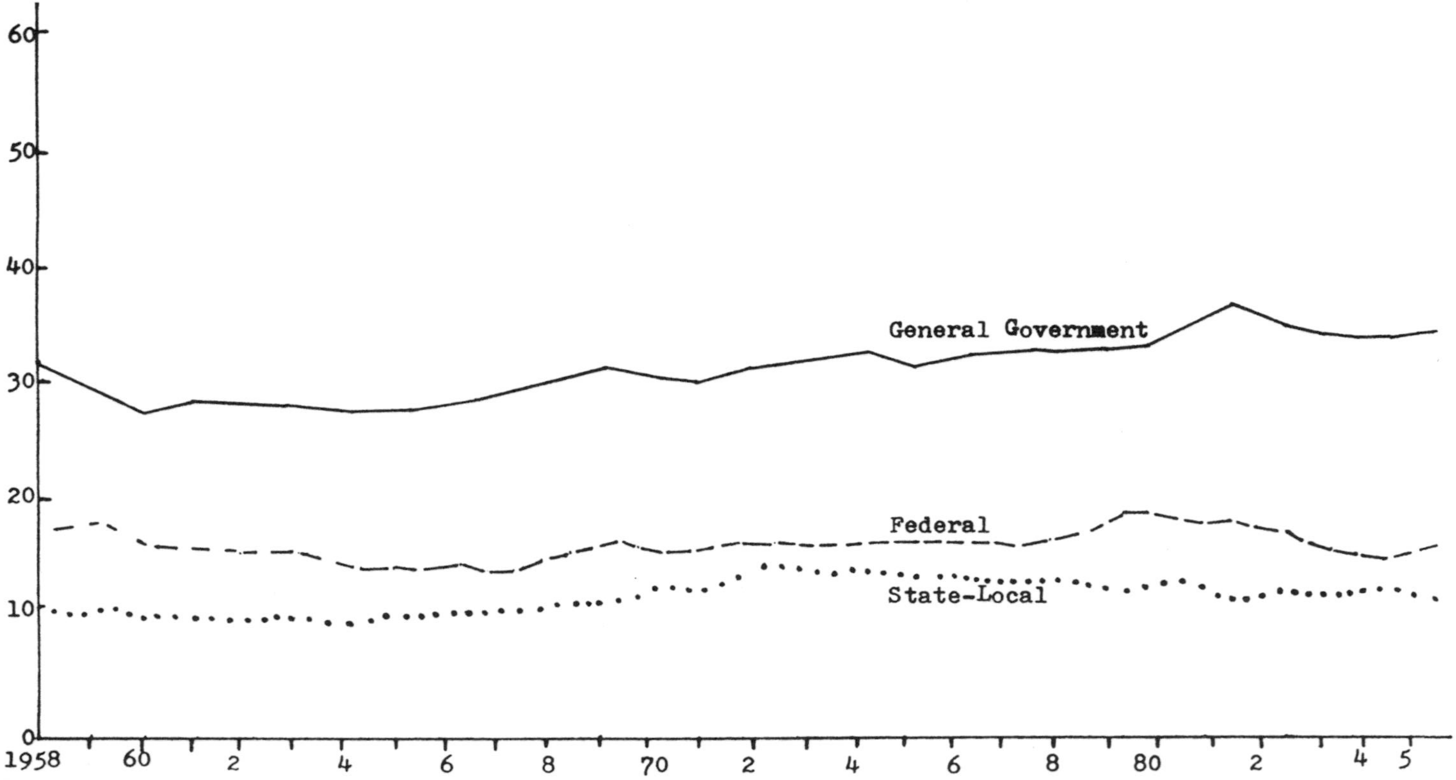

Source: Organization for Economic Cooperation and Development, *National Accounts*, various issues.

16.7 in the 1960s, 15.4 percent in the 1970s, and about 15.4 percent in the 1980s. This decline occurred in the direct taxes, but overall indirect taxes remained constant (around 10 percent of national income) and state and local taxes increased in the entire period. Therefore, the frequently heard cries about the ever-bigger federal tax bite and the related screams of distress are simply not justified. In fact, the rate of national taxation is considerably lower in the United States than in other market economies.

For the EEC, average taxes were higher than those in the United States and close to those in Canada. Comparing the main EEC countries with the United States as well as Japan, we can see that France has the highest percentage of income absorbed by taxation, followed by West Germany, the United Kingdom and Italy, the United States, and Japan. Moreover, in all these countries there was an upward trend of taxes to income ratios, during the years since 1950.

FEDERAL GOVERNMENT RECEIPTS

The tax structure and the particular taxes of the federal government play a major role in the question: Who bears the tax burden and what are the tax effects on the economy? Up to 1913 U.S. government revenue was based on indirect taxes, mainly on tariffs and excises. After being introduced through the Sixteenth Amendment, income taxes gradually became more important than the other previous types of taxes.

As shown in Table 5.1, federal government receipts increased 8-fold from 1960 to 1986 and about 20-fold from 1950. Presently, the main sources of federal budget receipts are individual income taxes, social insurance, corporate income taxes, and excises. Lesser amounts of revenue are provided by deposits of earnings by Federal Reserve System (FRS), customs duties, and estate and gift taxes. Remaining budget expenditures, that is, deficits, are financed through borrowing, which accounts for about 20 percent of total taxes collected per year. The largest increases took place in contributions for social insurance and personal income taxes. Corporate profit taxes, excises, customs duties and estate and gift taxes have not increased much in the years since World War II. As a percentage of GNP the federal tax revenue, omitting wartime peaks, changed from around 2 percent in 1900–20 to 4–6 percent in 1920–40, 14 percent in 1950, 18 percent in 1960, 20 percent in 1970, again 20 percent in 1980, and 19.2 percent (estimated) in 1989.

Figure 5.12 exhibits federal government revenue by major financial sector and source. Since 1950, significant changes occurred in the main sources of budget revenue. Social security revenue increased from 13 percent of the total federal revenue to almost 30 percent, followed by personal taxes, which increased from 39 percent in 1950 to 41 percent in 1984–85. Corporation income taxes declined (from 28.3 percent to 7.6 percent of total tax revenue), as did indirect business taxes. These figures indicate the sizable increase in individual taxes, in the form of income and social security taxes, and the large decreases in corporation taxes

Table 5.1
Federal Budget Receipts in Selected Fiscal Years
(billions of dollars)

Source	1950	1960	1970	1980	1987	1989*
Individual Income Taxes	15.7	40.7	90.4	244.1	392.6	412.4
Corporation Income Taxes	10.4	21.5	32.4	64.6	83.9	117.7
Social Insurance Taxes and Contributions	4.4	14.7	45.3	157.8	303.3	354.6
Excise Taxes	7.5	11.7	15.7	24.3	32.5	35.1
Estate and Gift Taxes	0.7	1.6	3.6	6.4	7.5	7.8
Customs Duties	0.4	1.1	2.4	7.1	15.1	17.2
Miscellaneous Receipts Deposit of Earnings by Federal Reserve System	0.2		3.3	11.8	16.8	16.4
All Other	1.5	1.2	0.2	1.0	2.5	3.4
Total	40.9	92.5	193.7	517.1	854.1	964.7

*Estimated

Source: *Economic Report of the President*, various issues; and U.S. Department of Commerce, Bureau of the Census, *Historical Statistics of the United States, Colonial Times to 1970*, 1975, p. 1105.

and indirect business taxes. With the 1986 and 1987 tax reforms, however, these last two forms of taxation are expected to rise, while personal income taxes are expected to decline somewhat. Social security contributions, on the other hand, are expected to be relatively constant or slightly increased.

STATE AND LOCAL GOVERNMENT REVENUE

Sources of Revenue

The U.S. fiscal structure is characterized by a multilevel system with federal, state, and local government units. While the federal government provides primarily for defense, foreign affairs, justice and other national-level services, state governments provide mainly for education, social welfare, highways, and health. Local governments provide for local services such as police and fire protection, water supply, garbage disposal, and sewage. These public services have the characteristics of joint consumption and largely nonexcludability and as such cannot be effectively provided by private markets. The federal or central government may consider intervention in lower-level jurisdiction as needed to correct

Figure 5.12
Federal Government Revenue by Major Financial Sector and Source: 1984–85

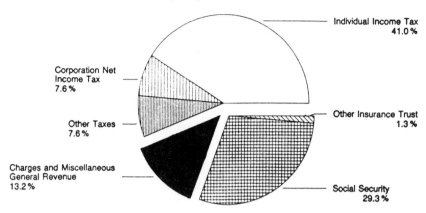

Source: U.S. Department of Commerce, Bureau of the Census, *Governmental Finances in 1984–85*, GF, no. 5, p. xviii.

inefficiencies in allocation or to subsidize services for a higher degree of equalization among states and localities.

Intergovernmental subsidies or grants may be conditional or unconditional and matching or nonmatching. They may take place through revenue distribution to local units or directly to needy residents. A personal welfare scheme or a negative income tax may improve horizontal equity in the U.S. multiunit government, for it comforts states and localities with strong fiscal pressures due to public welfare programs and other urban burdens. But expectations are that federal revenue-sharing funds to state, and especially to local, governments would be reduced or eliminated under the pressures of federal deficits, so that cities and other localities will have to find new financial sources or else cut their services.

State and local revenues have been and continue to be based primarily on sales and property taxes and to a lesser extent on income taxes. Although income taxes on the state and local levels have increased in recent decades, they are still proportionally small. Table 5.2 presents the dramatic increase of state and local government revenue since 1948; Figure 5.13 shows the percentage distribution by major financial sector. State taxes increased from 3.4 percent of GNP in 1950 to 4.5 percent in 1960, 6.0 in 1970, around 7 percent in 1980, and 9.4 percent in 1986. On the other hand, local government taxes remained constant at around 3 percent to 4 percent of GNP during those same periods, as they were from the beginning of the present century.

As mentioned previously, the U.S. federation is characterized by substantial state and local government economic activities. To finance the activities of some 82,600 local government units, large amounts of revenues are provided by federal government revenue sharing, mainly in the form of conditional grants for public

Table 5.2
State and Local Government Receipts
(billions of dollars)

Year	Total	Personal tax and nontax receipts	Corpo- rate profits tax accruals	Indirect business tax and nontax accruals	Contribu- tions for social insurance	Federal grants-in- aid
1948	13.0	1.5	0.5	9.3	0.6	1.1
1950	21.3	2.5	0.8	14.6	1.1	2.3
1960	50.0	6.8	1.2	32.0	3.4	6.5
1970	135.8	23.6	3.7	74.8	9.2	24.4
1971	153.5	27.0	4.3	83.1	10.2	29.0
1972	179.3	33.8	5.3	91.2	11.5	37.5
1973	196.4	37.3	6.0	99.6	13.0	40.6
1974	213.1	40.5	6.7	107.4	14.6	43.9
1975	230.6	44.7	7.3	116.2	16.8	54.6
1976	270.1	51.5	9.6	128.4	19.5	61.1
1977	300.1	58.3	11.4	140.7	22.1	67.5
1978	330.3	66.2	12.1	150.0	24.7	77.3
1979	355.3	73.7	13.6	160.1	27.4	80.5
1980	390.0	82.6	14.5	174.5	29.7	88.7
1981	425.6	94.5	15.4	195.3	32.5	87.9
1982	449.4	104.9	14.0	210.8	35.8	83.9
1983	487.7	116.1	15.9	231.0	38.5	86.2
1984	540.8	130.3	19.5	256.3	41.1	93.6
1985	577.5	140.9	18.2	275.4	44.2	99.0
1986	618.8	149.3	21.3	296.8	44.5	106.9
1987*	652.3	160.9	27.2	313.6	46.1	104.7

*Estimated

Source: U.S. Department of Commerce, Bureau of Economic Analysis.

welfare, education, employment, highways, housing, and health functions. Total revenue sharing, or federal aid to state and local government units, increased from $1.1 billion in 1946 to $6.5 billion in 1960, $24.4 in 1970, $88.7 in 1980, and $105 billion in 1987. Likewise, state governments provide revenue, or tax sharing, to city and other local governments, coming primarily from excise taxes, gasoline, and general retail taxes. To coordinate intergovernmental externalities and have fair results, states and localities with higher per capita income match grants with higher percentage taxes of their own.

State and local government revenue by states are not much different than expenditures (which have been presented in the previous chapter) because of the balanced budget requirement. A sizable amount of such revenue ($104 billion out of a total $619 billion in 1986) comes from the federal government in the form of grants or aid. California receives the largest amount of aid ($13 billion in 1986), followed by New York ($11 billion), Pennsylvania ($5 billion), Illinois

Figure 5.13
**State and Local Government Revenue by Major Financial Sector and Source:
1984–85**

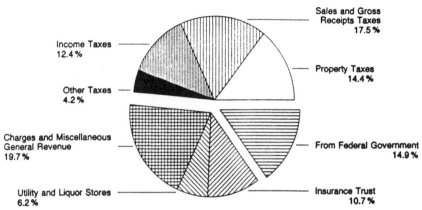

Source: U.S. Department of Commerce, Bureau of the Census, *Governmental Finances in 1984–
85*, GF, no. 5, p. xviii.

and Texas (close to $5 billion), and Michigan and Ohio (about $4 billion each).
Delaware, Nebraska, and Vermont receive the lowest amounts of federal aid
(around $300 million annually). Income support, housing, and transportation are
among the state and local programs strongly financed by the federal government.

However, the sharing of federal revenues with state and local governments
presents complex interaction problems, regarding not only the administration of
funds but also restrictions and regulations on matters of racial, sexual, and
religious discrimination, environmental protection, and other activities provided
by federal laws. Such federal funds may be used for any purpose (block grants)
or for specific purposes (categorical grants), and they may match state expenditures (matching funds).

More specifically, for states the main sources of revenue are sales taxes (about
30 percent of the total state taxes), federal grants-in-aid (24 percent), individual
income taxes (around 17 percent), corporation income taxes (5 percent), motor
vehicle and operator's licenses (4 percent), and property taxes (2 percent). Property taxes, which were once the main source of state revenue, are now the most
important local taxes (around 80 percent of total local revenue). Many local
governments also levy sales taxes (about 10 percent of total revenue), personal
income taxes (5 percent), and payroll taxes (4 percent). Alaska has the highest
state and local taxes; Arkansas, the lowest. Texas and Georgia also have low
state taxes per capita.

About 40 U.S. states and the District of Columbia levy personal income taxes,
including Alabama, Delaware, Indiana, Kentucky, Maryland, Michigan, Missouri, New York, Ohio, and Pennsylvania. Many states allow personal income
taxes for local governments in major cities, including Birmingham, Wilmington,

Lexington, Baltimore, Detroit, Kansas City, New York, Akron, Cincinnati, Dayton, Philadelphia, and Washington, D.C. However, such local income taxes are small, varying mostly between 1 percent and 2 percent, except in New York, Philadelphia and Washington, D.C., which have higher rates.

Marginal income tax rates for New York State and New York City are relatively high. For the state, they vary from 2 percent for taxable income up to $1,100 and 8.75 percent for income over $50,000. For the city of New York, they vary from 1.5 percent for taxable income up to $2,600 to 4.1 percent for income over $60,000 for single taxpayers. Before 1987, New York City single dwellers used to pay 43.3 percent taxes for taxable income $25,000 (25 percent federal, 14 percent state and 4.3 percent city taxes); for income above $81,000, they used to pay 68.3 percent taxes (50 percent federal, 14 percent state, and 4.3 percent city taxes) plus 5 percent of the total city tax as resident tax. After the tax reforms of 1981, these rates prevailed for income from wages as well as other forms of income (rent, interest, dividend, capital gains, and profit, for example). Before these reforms the marginal federal tax rates for nonwage income was up to 70 percent. Therefore, before 1981, New Yorkers with income above the highest bracket used to pay tax rates up to 88.3 percent; that is, less than 12 percent of the income they made remained at their disposal.

As a result of the social security amendments of 1983, more than 20 states collect taxes on social security benefits. Some states, though, including New York and New Jersey, passed legislation exempting social security benefits from taxation. Such a taxation is considered equitable because the tax falls on middle-income and upper-income retirees (with above $25,000 annual adjusted gross income, plus half the amount of social security benefits for single taxpayers and $32,000 for couples). The portion of the benefits subject to tax is the lesser of 50 percent of the excess over the base amount or 50 percent of the benefits. Federal taxes on social security benefits, which affect some 10 percent of the 36 million recipient Americans, are security funds and cover growing expenses. However, state and local taxes on such benefits are mostly used to help cover shortfalls in general operating budgets.

Some 45 states and a number of cities in the United States levy corporation income taxes, which vary from 1 percent in Arkansas to 5 percent in Alabama, Colorado, Florida, Maine, Missouri, New Mexico, and Vermont; 10 percent in Connecticut and New York; and 12 percent in Minnesota. Local governments also impose corporation income taxes varying from 1 percent to 2 percent, except for New York, which levies 10 percent. Such differentiation in corporation income taxes affects investment and other business decisions among different states and cities and has serious employment and income effects.

California levies 9.6 percent taxes on the profits of multinational companies. For assessment, it uses a worldwide unitary method of taxation based on a percentage of a company's global payroll, property, and sales to prevent corporations from shielding their profits by shifting them from California to low-tax areas. A number of companies, including IBM, Coca Cola, Sony Corporation, and Royal Dutch/Shell Group, have assailed the method as double taxation and are fighting it in court. A new proposal would base the tax only on a percentage of the profits multinationals make in the United States or charge them a fee of 2/100 of 1 percent of their assets within the state (this is the water's edge approach). However, because of threats of retaliation by other countries, notably Britain, there are expectations that the U.S. government will limit such unitary taxation altogether.

To encourage greater literacy, many individuals and businesses, particularly the publishing firms, want states and cities to exempt books from sales taxes. As the argument goes, state and city sales taxes, totaling 8.25 percent in New York City alone, impede the free flow of information. They are taxes on knowledge and as such should be eliminated, as they have been on other essential products.

The fact that the federal government picks up part of the state tax increases had in the past induced some states, including New York, to introduce high state tax rises. Reforms suggested to eliminate federal tax deductions for state and local taxes are expected to put all the states on an equal footing. But highly taxed states like New York and Massachusetts would pay higher taxes after the implementation of such reforms.

Inflation bracket creep and high property taxes ignited tax revolts in certain localities and states, notably in California (the result was Proposition 13). Such tax rebellions took place, mainly in the 1970s, because voters judged government programs not to be worth the taxes extracted from them and they forced politicians to act on their belief. As a result, taxes were cut to stimulate demand, in a Keynesian tradition, and increase production, as well as to please voters.

Federal funds to state and local governments, which increased substantially after 1972, permit local officials to implement programs without the pain of raising new taxes to finance them. States and localities use such funds to support police and fire protection, sanitation, education, health care, libraries, and parks and other social and recreational facilities. Such grants may be conditional or unconditional, depending on whether restrictions are placed on their use. Usually, conditional grants are provided by the grantor with the requirement that they are matched by certain proportions of local funds of the recipient or the grantee, so that some control of the related intergovernmental externalities or spillovers is exercised. But there are also tax credits and tax deductions, which are intergovernmental devices that allow taxpayers to meet their tax liabilities to one unit of government by paying taxes to another unit and subtracting taxes paid before or after the application of the tax rate to the tax base. However, large deficits in federal budgets are forcing arguments for reduction or complete elimination of such grants in the future.

Differences in State Taxes: Revenue Incentives

As noted earlier, state and local revenue come mostly from sales and property taxes and to a lesser extent from federal grants and income taxes. Alaska,

Figure 5.14
General Revenue of State Governments by Source: 1986

Total: $393.1 Billion

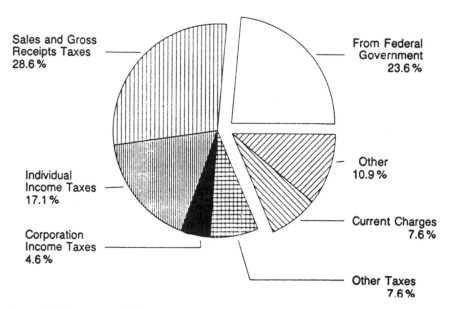

Sales and Gross Receipts Taxes 28.6%

From Federal Government 23.6%

Other 10.9%

Individual Income Taxes 17.1%

Current Charges 7.6%

Corporation Income Taxes 4.6%

Other Taxes 7.6%

Source: U.S. Department of Commerce, Bureau of the Census, *Governmental Finances, 1986*, GF 86, no. 5, p. xix.

Wyoming, New York, Hawaii, and California have high state taxes, while Arkansas, Mississippi, Alabama, and Texas have low state taxes.[13] Figure 5.14 shows general revenue of state governments by source. The largest proportion of revenue comes from sales taxes, followed by grants from the federal government and individual income taxes.

Many local governments have been experiencing a drastic fall in revenues due partly to the loss of economic activity and of resident population and partly to central government cutbacks. Such fiscal stress and nasty trade-offs tend to affect primarily minority and poor groups. A number of cities offer incentives for industrial and commercial development, either through discretionary policy of special incentive boards or through predetermined guidelines. Such incentives are based primarily on the number of jobs and the size of enterprises created mainly in poor or less-developed sections of the cities and their suburbs. Although from time to time there is criticism that there may be bias in the process of incentives allocation, such incentives may prove to be effective tools for stimulating the development of neglected areas in large cities.

To revive regional development, cities and states may provide realty tax and other incentives for projects that may create jobs and revitalize commercial activities. In New York, for example, housebuilders and renovators of offices and stores do not pay full taxes on improvements until seven years after their operation starts, while the nontax period may be extended to 22 years for industrial and commercial buildings in depressed areas. A better system would be to reduce tax rates on all improvements and raise the taxes on the land where they are located. If buildings were taxed at lower rates than land, cheap land in depressed sections of the cities would become attractive for factories and commercial sites, whereas land with high value and higher tax rates would become less attractive for industrial construction.

A serious financial problem of local and state governments is that services are reduced and taxes are raised in periods of economic downswings and recessions, yet services are restored and probably taxes are cut in periods of recoveries. This problem is associated with the constitutional prohibition of all states, except Vermont, to run a deficit. Presently, states producing energy, minerals, lumber, and farm products are experiencing declines in severance taxes and other revenue. On the other hand, manufacturing states in the Great Lakes and the Middle Atlantic are doing well, as are states with high growth in technology, such as California, Massachusetts, and New York.

In its effort to reduce budget deficits, the federal government is contemplating reforms to increase tax payments, especially by states that have or are expected to have surpluses. Such state budget surpluses would continue, if present tax and spending trends continue to be the same in the future. To avoid high tax payments, primarily because of the proposed no deductions for state and local taxes from federal taxes, surplus states such as New York and New Jersey are moving toward reducing their own taxes.

Tax proposals to eliminate deductions for state and local income taxes, and property and other taxes, would affect state fiscal positions in different ways. Taxpayers in states with high state taxes would bear a heavier burden if these proposals are implemented. Thus, New York, with relatively high deductible state and local taxes per capita, would owe more in federal income taxes compared to Alabama, with low deductible taxes per capita. Next in line are Massachusetts, California, Iowa, Arizona, Pennsylvania, and Texas. The main argument of this proposal is that citizens in low-tax states get smaller deductions and exemptions and pay proportionally more taxes to the federal or central government compared to high-tax states. Therefore, taxpayers in low-tax states subsidize those in high-tax states. In order to correct this unequal burden, high-tax states should reduce their taxes. However, counterproposals suggest that high-tax states such as New York and California face higher expenses to pay for local police, courts and jails, and other disbursements for enforcing laws on drug traffic, immigration, and other regulations of national interest.

Pollution Controls

Different degrees of industrialization are associated with higher or lower degrees of pollution and toxic waste in different states and they demand different degrees of cleaning expenses. From that point of view, a waste-end tax on companies according to the toxicity of the waste disposed, and not on the raw material used, as largely prevails now, would be more effective as an economic incentive to encourage recycling and other alternatives to disposal. This waste-end measure has already been introduced by New York and some other states.

Private firms consider their own internal production cost in planning and implementing their policy of profit maximization. This cost, however, is usually less than the cost to society. The differential cost is absorbed by the public or the consumers affected by pollution and other disamenities generated by the producers. Pollution is a serious problem, especially for urban societies, and state and local governments and in many cases the federal government try to reduce air, water, land, and noise pollution by subsidies, direct regulations, and effluent charges.[14]

In Figure 5.15 optimum pollution control is at the point where marginal cost (MC) is equal to marginal benefit (MB). The net benefit is A. The area under the MB curve shows the polluter's total liability for damages. However, it pays the polluter to reduce pollution up to point L because MC is less than MB. The damages to pay C for the pollution he or she does not remove plus B for the additional cost will be the lowest possible total cost of pollution abatement. Ideally, an effluent charge or a tax must be equal to OP per unit of pollution (the toxicity or the discharged wastes). It will then pay the polluter to reduce pollution to the level of cleanliness L because MC is less than the tax liability. Therefore, industrial units or projects with high costs (including pollution costs) to benefits ratios (C/B) should be discouraged. This would be so when

$$\left(\sum_{t=0}^{n} \frac{C_t}{(1+i)^t} \bigg/ \sum_{t=0}^{n} \frac{B_t}{(1+i)^t} \right) > 1$$

where i is the social discount rate.

Tax-Exempt Bonds

Under the U.S. Constitution, state and local governments can issue tax-exempt bonds, sometimes called municipals or "munis." Also, public institutions such as highway authorities and hospitals, can issue tax-exempt bonds to finance their investment projects and other operations. Justification for this special status of such bonds is to bar government authorities from taxing each other's securities. The bonds represent loans repaid on specific dates with prorated interest payments, usually twice a year. Defaults are rare in such bonds, but the buyers bear the risk of selling them at a depressed price when interest rates rise, or the state and local governments can call them before they mature. When people buy bonds issued by their own states and cities, they are usually exempted from the taxes of these jurisdictions.

Figure 5.15
Optimal Pollution Control (MC = MB)

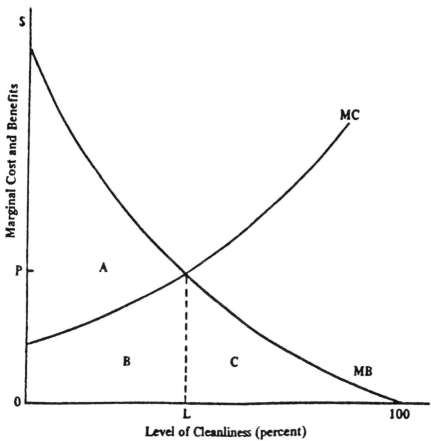

Level of Cleanliness (percent)

Tax-exempt bonds may also be used to raise funds to be relent to businesses in the cities or for mortgages for low-income families. The tax exclusion of interest on state and local securities gives a great advantage to high-income taxpayers with capital income, who accept a lower before-tax yield.

Depending on the degree of liquidity and some other risk elements, the bonds are rated (AAA, AA, A, BB, B, and so on) and their yields vary. On the other hand, dividends of common stocks of electric and gas distribution and some other utilities may enjoy favorable tax treatment, in addition to secured income and the benefits of long-run capital gains they may enjoy when the stocks are sold after a period of time, usually six months.

The exemption of interest earned from state and local bonds, as well as that of the salaries of government employees, was originated from Supreme Court decisions of the early 1800s. About 100 years later (1918), the Supreme Court decided that salaries of state and local government employees and interest from bonds can be taxed by the federal government. However, because of pressures from state and local governments, as well as high-income investors, such interest is still exempted, although there are strong arguments to narrow such exemptions to certain state and local government bonds.

Borrowing to finance capital projects has the advantage of spreading cost throughout the years of the lifetime of the projects and among the people using them. In that way, the users of the projects' services are responsible for paying the taxes required for servicing and amortizing the related debt. Moreover, in the process of debt management, state and local governments do not have to bother much with economic stabilization policies. Such complicated policies concern primarily the federal government and the monetary authorities. In some states and localities, the authorization of qualified voters may be required for certain projects or bond issues. For servicing and retiring the debt, serial bonds may replace sinking funds; that is, capital may be financed by bonds spread over the life of a project, instead of using funds accumulated through taxes.

Of the two main kinds of state and local government bonds, that is, the general obligation bonds and revenue bonds, the first are guaranteed by the borrowing government for the payments of interest and the principal, while for the second the users are responsible. The revenue bonds are used mainly by governments and public agencies or enterprises not only to finance roads, waterworks, electric utilities, and other facilities but also development projects in certain regions. Debt payments for such bonds are made by collected tolls, fees, rents, and other charges paid by the users. Because of legal limitations in issuing general obligation bonds, the issue of state and local government revenue bonds to finance debt is growing in recent years. However, since 1969 Congress has limited the tax exemption privilege of industrial development bonds to $5 million, and further limitations are expected in the near future. Also, according to the 1983 social security amendments, tax-free interest income from bonds is included in the adjusted gross income, which is taxed if it exceeds a certain amount.

Some 44 states and the District of Columbia levy small taxes on owners of municipal bonds, with limited advantages to in-state municipals over out-of-state bonds. Although the nominal state-maximum tax rates on income vary, the actual or effective rate is much lower due to tax savings by deducting these taxes from income on federal returns.

As a result of tax-exempt bonds, if bond buyers belong to a 28 percent tax bracket, for example, and the yield is 10 percent, the after-tax return would be 13.89 percent. If state and city taxes are considered (for example, 10 percent for New York State and 4 percent for New York City, for income above $50,000), then the after-tax return for triple tax-exempt bonds (federal, state, and city) would be 17.41 percent. In some states, excluding New York, there is a personal property tax varying from $1 to $5 for each $1,000 of par or market value of the municipals. Moreover, in most states there is a capital gains tax on municipals that is collected when the bonds are sold or mature.

Also, U.S. Treasury securities may be exempted from state and local taxes. They are mainly bonds issued at $1,000 units with more than ten years' maturity, notes at $5,000 with less than ten years' maturity, and three-month and six-month Treasury bills at more than $10,000 denominations. Tax-exempt bonds may include perpetual bonds. In such bonds, the government promises to pay a fixed amount to the holder of the bond every year, forever. Britain and other countries have already introduced such bonds, called Consols. The price of a Consol is equal to the coupon divided by the yield or the return.

Another form of borrowing, not only by Uncle Sam but also by municipalities and corporations, is by offering zero-coupon bonds. They can be bought at a fraction of their face value. The initial investment and the accumulated interest are collected when the bonds mature. Brokerage firms such as Merrill Lynch have their own versions of zero-coupon bonds called tigers. They buy a huge chunk of U.S. Treasury, municipal, and corporate bonds, put them in an escrow account, and offer pieces of them to investors, especially to those planning for the education of their children and retirement.

A zero-coupon bond is issued at a very large discount from face value and pays no current interest, as do conventional bonds. At maturity, the accumulated compounded interest is paid in a lump sum. Such bonds, however, are less liquid and more vulnerable to interest rate changes than other bonds. When inflation rises, interest rates normally rise and the loss of purchasing power is great for zero-coupon bonds with long-term fixed rates. For these bonds, future cash interest payments cannot be reinvested at higher rates, as can be done with conventional bonds. Moreover, income taxes must be paid on the imputed or phantom interest of these bonds every year, except if they are tax-exempt or are held in a tax-deferred account such as an individual retirement or Keogh account.

According to Moody's bond surveys, interest rates on long-term municipals are less (around 70 percent), on the average, compared to long-term corporate bonds. The reason for that difference is that municipal bonds are exempt from federal income taxes and in most cases from state and city taxes. This is known as the doctrine of reciprocal immunity, according to which individual states are immune from federal interference in their affairs as, likewise, the federal government is immune from state interference (Supreme Court case of *McCulloch v. Maryland* in 1819, and *Pollock* v. *Farmers' Loan and Trust Company* in 1895).

Among the different kinds of municipal bonds, the revenue bonds, which are issued to finance particular revenue-producing projects and are usually secured solely by the revenue from those projects, have particular importance because their number has grown rapidly in recent years to about 70 percent of all annual new issues, that is, double that of a decade ago. Such bonds are issued primarily for highways, turnpikes, and public utilities, but recently also to finance hospitals, housing, pollution control equipment, public power projects, convention centers, and sports stadiums.

Commercial banks are the largest investors in municipal bonds, followed by fire, casualty, and trust companies and individuals. Municipal securities brokers and dealers are under the rules of the Securities and Exchange Commission (SEC) and the Municipal Securities Rulemaking Board (MSRB), which was established by Congress in 1975. Trades in municipals are made over the counter (or over the phone).

However, the tax exemption status of the municipals has recently been subject to repeated assaults at the federal level, especially against certain types of municipals for purposes of revenue collection. But the arguments in favor of tax exemption invoke the constitutional protection of separation of federal and state jurisdictions on these matters. The fear that tax reform measures would impose restrictions on the sales of tax-exempt securities increases the offer of new issues, especially when interest rates are expected to increase. As a result, a large number of long-term and short-term tax-exempt bonds have been issued, recently.

The new measures that have lowered the federal government's top individual income tax will reduce demand for tax-exempt municipal and state bonds and increase interest rates paid for such bonds. Also, the Treasury wants to eliminate tax exemptions for municipal borrowing for private-purpose projects such as industrial development and pollution control. It is proposed that even tax exemption for general obligation bonds should end if such bonds finance projects that are more than 1 percent privately owned. In addition to the suggested elimination of the deduction of state and local taxes from federal income taxes, severe cuts are proposed in housing, public transit, and economic development programs, as well as sewage treatment and other federal subsidies to states and municipalities. As a result of these measures, the cost of borrowing by state and local governments will increase substantially and vital facilities and services can be expected to be curtailed.

6

Tax Structure

DIRECT AND INDIRECT TAXES

Following the survey of tax principles and trends for general, federal, and local government revenue in the previous chapter, this chapter concentrates on the distinction between direct (or income) and indirect (or consumption) taxes. Direct taxes are those that are imposed primarily on individuals; they are personal income taxes and the less important lump-sum (or head) taxes. Indirect taxes are those that are imposed initially on objects (in rem taxes) such as sales and property taxes.

Direct Taxes

Considering allocative and incentive effects, one must seriously question whether direct, or income, taxation is better than indirect, or commodity, taxation, or whether there is an appropriate balance or combination of these two types of taxation. Switching from income taxes to commodity taxes increases incentives to work and enhances productivity at first. But an increase in prices from commodity taxes would most probably nullify the increase in earnings from a reduction in income taxes and leave incentives unchanged.[1]

For income taxation to be fair, it should be linked to the principle of the ability to pay. As mentioned earlier, Adam Smith thought that subjects should contribute toward the support of the government in proportion to their respective abilities. John Stuart Mill also stated that whatever the required sacrifice by the government, it should be made to bear as nearly as possible with the same pressure upon all; that is, an equal proportion of utility should be sacrificed from income taxes.[2] This is what Edgeworth called "equal marginal sacrifice," or equal marginal utility, which implies equal post-tax income satisfaction. From the standpoint of incentives and skills, tax rates should not be very high; otherwise we may end up in cutting down the tree to get the fruit, to use the example that Montesquieu brings from among the savages.

Empirically, direct tax flexibility in relation to income (marginal direct tax) first declined slightly from 0.18 in the 1950s to 0.15 in the 1960s and then increased to 0.18 in the 1970s and 0.20 in the 1980s. Similarly, income elasticities of direct taxation were higher than one, primarily in the 1970s. Ongoing high rates of inflation, which raised the rates of progressive income taxes, seemed to be responsible for this upturn for the marginal rate of direct taxes.

The elasticities of direct taxes with respect to inflation (measured as the ratio of current to constant dollars GDP) were higher than the elasticities of indirect taxes to inflation. This indicates that, beyond their mutual influence, inflation transfers purchasing power from the private to the public sector because of the progressive nature of direct taxes. Moreover, that the elasticities of direct taxes in relation to inflation were higher than those of indirect taxes may suggest a substitution of direct with indirect taxes.

Direct taxes as percentages of total revenue of general government (state and local governments included) changed from 65 percent in 1960, to 66 percent in 1970, 67 percent in 1980, and 66 percent in 1985. In contrast, indirect taxes declined, accordingly, and gave a 207 ratio of direct to indirect taxes in 1970 and 243 in 1985. As percentages of national income, direct taxes increased from 18 percent in 1958 to 22 percent in 1970 and 23 percent in 1985. Almost the same trends prevail in the United Kingdom, as well as in West Germany, France, and Italy, but with higher percentages. This sizable growth of direct taxes, including social security contributions, is primarily responsible for the increase in taxation in the United States and other market economies.

As percentages of total government revenue, direct taxes are far higher (about double) in developed countries than in developing countries, while indirect taxes are comparatively higher in developing countries. More or less, what prevails in developing countries can be observed in centrally planned economies. However, as per capita income increases, direct taxes also increase in proportion to income for almost all countries regardless of their system.

Indirect Taxes

Indirect taxes, which are levied against goods and services and have no immediate effect on people, include excises (mainly on tobacco, beverages, fuel, cosmetics, travel), sales taxes, turnover taxes, and stamps and tariffs. They are largely regressive, taking a large fraction of their revenue from the low-income groups; their proportions decline with increases in income. In the United States and Canada, they are levied principally by individual states and localities. Figure 6.1 shows that indirect taxes were constant and around 10 percent of national income for the United States and 15 percent for the EEC from the 1950s onward.

Figure 6.1
Indirect Taxes as Percentages of National Income: United States and the EEC (average of France, Germany, Italy, and the United Kingdom)

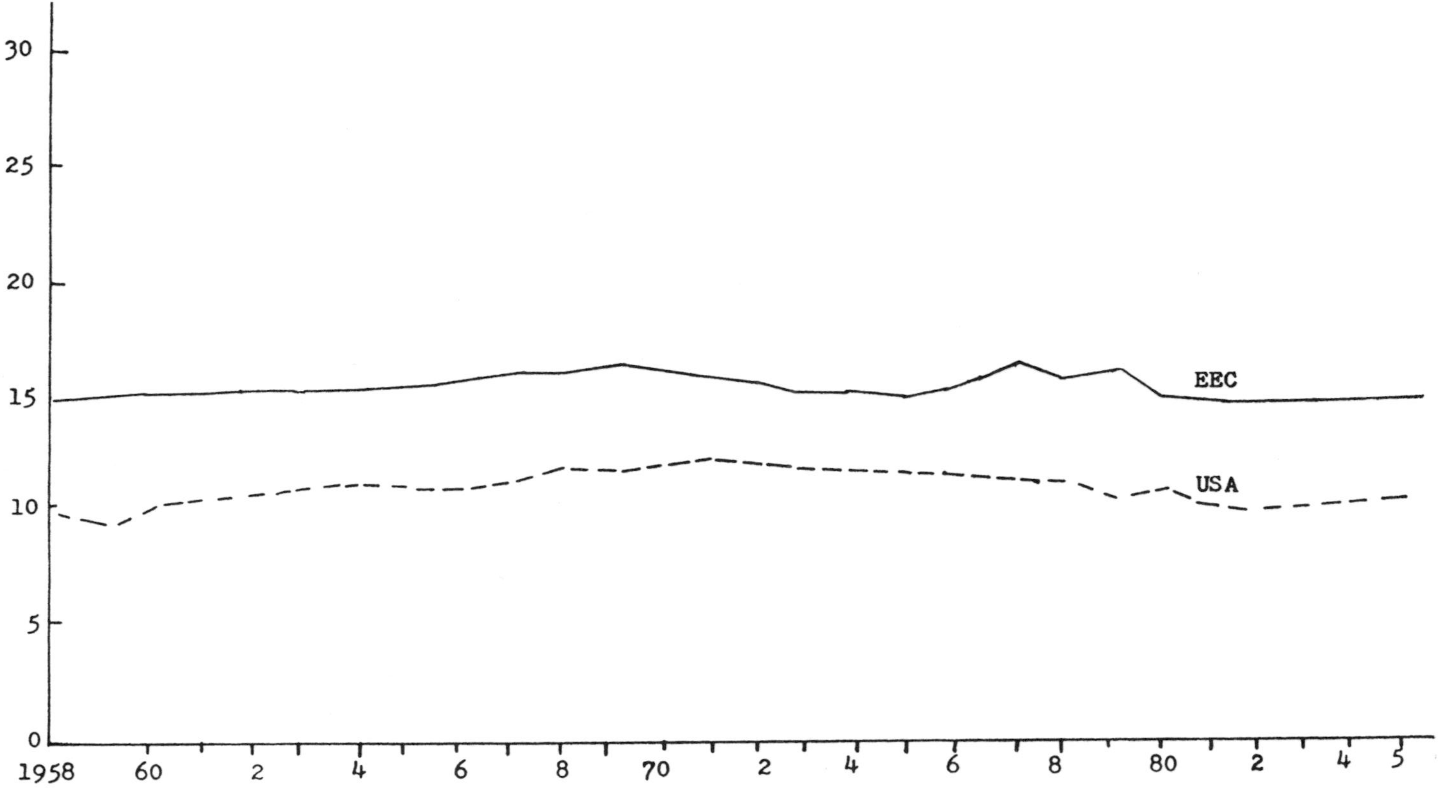

Source: OECD, *National Accounts*, various issues.

137

There is discussion on introducing consumption taxes even in the place of income taxes. The consumption tax form requires all the receipts of the taxpayer to be listed. Then savings (in the form of deposits in savings banks, pension plans, and purchase of stocks, bonds, or houses) and expenses for basic needs would be subtracted and the difference taxed. After special treatment for medical expenses, purchase of certain consumer durables, and other borderline activities, progressive consumption tax rates may be used to raise revenue. This type of tax, it is argued, would contribute to more capital formation and the acceptance of more responsibility and risk because it would provide sufficient financial incentives. Such a consumption tax would, the argument continues, raise enough revenue to eliminate the need for corporate taxes, which sometimes may be swollen because of mismeasurement of depreciation and false profits on inventories because of inflation. Also, it would tax a good portion of tax-free income in subterranean economic activities, which escape measurement and tax levying.

The elasticities of indirect taxes, with respect to private consumption, imports, and GDP for the periods 1950–60 and 1960–70 were greater than one. In the 1970s, however, the elasticities were less than one and lower in the United States than in the EEC. These results indicate that during the 1970s the relative growth of indirect taxes in the United States was lower than the growth in the other variables (private consumption, GDP, and particularly imports).[3] The dramatic increases in the value of oil imports without a similar increase in tariffs on imported oil and contrary to what is customary in the EEC and other countries (where oil prices are more than double those prevailing in the United States) seemed to be responsible for the differences. In the 1980s, the elasticities of indirect taxes, with respect to private consumption, imports, and GDP, were all close to one.

Indirect taxes as percentages of general government taxes are, on the average, lower in developed market economies than in developing countries. Large amounts of indirect taxes in developing countries come from customs duties or tariffs. On the other hand, centrally planned economies have high indirect taxes, primarily turnover taxes, and low direct taxes compared to developed market economies, or even to developing or low-income countries. Therefore, the ratio of direct (primarily income taxes and social security contributions) to indirect taxes is relatively low. It is mostly less than 40 percent, compared to more than 150 percent for most of the Western market economies and around 30–60 percent for most of the developing countries. Moreover, in most of the countries considered indirect taxes are constant or are declining in proportion to total taxes.

PERSONAL INCOME TAXES

Income taxes are levied by the federal government, and also by most states and some cities, which follow, by and large, the federal tax pattern. The Sixteenth Amendment of the Constitution gave Congress the power to lay and collect taxes. In 1913, the first revenue act was passed and many other tax acts and laws have been enacted since then. Although there had been some short-lived periods of federal personal income taxes since 1861, the official establishment of such taxes, together with corporation income taxes, started in 1913 with the ratification of the Sixteenth Amendment of the Constitution.

The main source of U.S. budgetary revenue is personal income taxes. Gross or total income, which includes wages and salaries, rent, interest, dividends, royalties, and profits from unincorporated business activities, adjusted for certain related costs (as form 1040 shows), is reduced by deductions and exemptions to determine taxable income. An important personal exemption is the $2,000 ($1,900 in 1987) per taxpayer, spouse, and each dependent. If what remains is less than $2,540 for single and $3,760 (in 1987) for joint returns, no income tax is paid. If the standard deduction is used, no allowances for dependents is permitted. Before 1985, personal exemptions were $1,000 per dependent, while the deductions were $2,300 and $3,400, respectively.

In case taxpayers prefer to itemize deductions instead of using the above standard deduction, they can deduct from income such expenses as state and local taxes, interest paid on mortgages and other consumer loans, medical expenses above a certain amount, charitable contributions, casualty losses, and some other expense related to the earned income. Usually, long-term capital gains (over six months) pay less taxes than other forms of income do.

Around 70 percent of Americans choose the standard deduction. Over 90 percent of taxes are collected from the employers through withholding. This effective method, which was introduced during World War II, has the advantage of collecting tax revenue gradually as income is earned, instead of waiting for the period of a year. However, for certain kinds of income such as dividends and interest, there is no withholding and the taxpayer must file the related papers and pay the taxes.

As it is known, every taxpayer is responsible to file his or her tax returns. However, about one-fourth of the taxpayers underpay and three-fourths overpay taxes. The first group pays the difference, and the second group receives refunds from the Treasury. Because it is difficult for the Internal Revenue Service to audit over 80 million American returns, spot checks are made, especially in particular professional groups such as doctors and business people.

The Tax Reform Act of 1969 limited the maximum tax rate on earned income (wages, salaries, and professional activities, for example) to 50 percent. The purpose of this limitation was to avoid stifling work incentives and reducing labor productivity. For other forms of income, such as income from capital, the rates were reduced in 1981 from 70 to 50 percent. With progressive taxation, as long as marginal tax rates grow, average tax rates too are growing, although at smaller percentages.

For married individuals filing a joint return with exemptions, the present tax rates are 15 percent for taxable income up to $29,750 and 28 percent for higher taxable income, with an extra charge of 5 percent for certain income ranges ($71,900 to $171,900).[4] Before 1987, such tax rates used to start at 11 percent

Form 1040

Department of the Treasury—Internal Revenue Service

U.S. Individual Income Tax Return 1988

OMB No. 1545-0074

For the year Jan.–Dec. 31, 1988, or other tax year beginning , 1988, ending , 19

Label

Use IRS label. Otherwise, please print or type.

Your first name and initial (if joint return, also give spouse's name and initial) | Last name

Your social security number

Present home address (number, street, and apt. no. or rural route) (If a P.O. Box, see page 6 of Instructions.)

Spouse's social security number

City, town or post office, state, and ZIP code

For Privacy Act and Paperwork Reduction Act Notice, see Instructions.

Presidential Election Campaign

Do you want $1 to go to this fund? . . . . Yes ▢ No ▢

If joint return, does your spouse want $1 to go to this fund? . . Yes ▢ No ▢

Note: Checking "Yes" will not change your tax or reduce your refund.

Filing Status

Check only one box.

1 ▢ Single

2 ▢ Married filing joint return (even if only one had income)

3 ▢ Married filing separate return. Enter spouse's social security no. above and full name here. _____

4 ▢ Head of household (with qualifying person). (See page 7 of Instructions.) If the qualifying person is your child but not your dependent, enter child's name here. _____

5 ▢ Qualifying widow(er) with dependent child (year spouse died ▶ 19). (See page 7 of Instructions.)

Exemptions

(See Instructions on page 8.)

6a ▢ Yourself If someone (such as your parent) can claim you as a dependent, do not check box 6a. But be sure to check the box on line 33b on page 2. . . . .

b ▢ Spouse . . . .

No. of boxes checked on 6a and 6b

c Dependents:

(1) Name (first, initial, and last name)	(2) Check if under age 5	(3) If age 5 or older, dependent's social security number	(4) Relationship	(5) No. of months lived in your home in 1988

No. of your children on 6c who:
● lived with you
● didn't live with you due to divorce or separation

No. of other dependents listed on 6c

If more than 6 dependents, see Instructions on page 8.

d If your child didn't live with you but is claimed as your dependent under a pre-1985 agreement, check here ▶ ▢

e Total number of exemptions claimed . . . .

Add numbers entered on lines above ▶

Income

Please attach Copy B of your Forms W-2, W-2G, and W-2P here.

If you do not have a W-2, see page 6 of Instructions.

7 Wages, salaries, tips, etc. (attach Form(s) W-2) . . . . | 7

8a Taxable interest income (also attach Schedule B if over $400) . . . . | 8a

b Tax-exempt interest income (see page 11). DON'T include on line 8a | 8b

9 Dividend income (also attach Schedule B if over $400) . . . . | 9

10 Taxable refunds of state and local income taxes, if any, from worksheet on page 11 of Instructions . | 10

11 Alimony received . . . . | 11

12 Business income or (loss) (attach Schedule C) . . . . | 12

13 Capital gain or (loss) (attach Schedule D) . . . . | 13

14 Capital gain distributions not reported on line 13 (see page 11) . . . . | 14

15 Other gains or (losses) (attach Form 4797) . . . . | 15

16a Total IRA distributions . . | 16a | | 16b Taxable amount (see page 11) | 16b

17a Total pensions and annuities | 17a | | 17b Taxable amount (see page 12) | 17b

18 Rents, royalties, partnerships, estates, trusts, etc. (attach Schedule E) . | 18

19 Farm income or (loss) (attach Schedule F) . . . . | 19

20 Unemployment compensation (insurance) (see page 13) . . . . | 20

Please attach check or money order here

21a Social security benefits (see page 13) . . | 21a |

b Taxable amount, if any, from the worksheet on page 13 . . . . | 21b

22 Other income (list type and amount—see page 13) _____ | 22

23 Add the amounts shown in the far right column for lines 7 through 22. This is your total income ▶ | 23

Adjustments to Income

(See Instructions on page 13.)

24 Reimbursed employee business expenses from Form 2106, line 13 . | 24

25a Your IRA deduction, from applicable worksheet on page 14 or 15 | 25a

b Spouse's IRA deduction, from applicable worksheet on page 14 or 15 | 25b

26 Self-employed health insurance deduction, from worksheet on page 15 | 26

27 Keogh retirement plan and self-employed SEP deduction . | 27

28 Penalty on early withdrawal of savings . . . . . | 28

29 Alimony paid (recipient's last name _____ and social security no. _____) | 29

30 Add lines 24 through 29. These are your total adjustments . . . . ▶ | 30

Adjusted Gross Income

31 Subtract line 30 from line 23. This is your adjusted gross income. If this line is less than $18,576 and a child lived with you, see "Earned Income Credit" (line 56) on page 19 of the Instructions. If you want IRS to figure your tax, see page 16 of the Instructions ▶ | 31

140

Tax Compu-tation	**32**	Amount from line 31 (adjusted gross income)	**32**	
	33a	Check if: ☐ You were 65 or older ☐ Blind; ☐ Spouse was 65 or older ☐ Blind.		
		Add the number of boxes checked and enter the total here . . . . ▶ **33a** ☐		
	b	If someone (such as your parent) can claim you as a dependent, check here . . ▶ **33b** ☐		
	c	If you are married filing a separate return and your spouse itemizes deductions, or you are a dual-status alien, see page 16 and check here . . . . ▶ **33c** ☐		
	34	Enter the larger of: { ● Your **standard deduction** (from page 17 of the Instructions), OR ● Your **itemized deductions** (from Schedule A, line 26). If you itemize, attach Schedule A and check here ▶ ☐ }	**34**	
	35	Subtract line 34 from line 32. Enter the result here	**35**	
	36	Multiply $1,950 by the total number of exemptions claimed on line 6e	**36** ·	
	37	**Taxable income.** Subtract line 36 from line 35. Enter the result (if less than zero, enter zero) . .	**37**	
		Caution: If under age 14 and you have more than $1,000 of investment income, check here ▶ ☐ and see page 17 to see if you have to use Form 8615 to figure your tax.		
	38	Enter tax. Check if from: ☐ Tax Table, ☐ Tax Rate Schedules, or ☐ Form 8615 . . .	**38**	
	39	Additional taxes (see page 17). Check if from: ☐ Form 4970 ☐ Form 4972	**39**	
	40	Add lines 38 and 39. Enter the total . . . . ▶	**40**	
Credits (See Instructions on page 18.)	**41**	Credit for child and dependent care expenses (attach Form 2441)	**41**	
	42	Credit for the elderly or the disabled (attach Schedule R) . . .	**42**	
	43	Foreign tax credit (attach Form 1116)	**43**	
	44	General business credit. Check if from: ☐ Form 3800 or ☐ Form (specify) _____ . . .	**44**	
	45	Credit for prior year minimum tax (attach Form 8801)	**45**	
	46	Add lines 41 through 45. Enter the total	**46**	
	47	Subtract line 46 from line 40. Enter the result (if less than zero, enter zero) . . . . . . ▶	**47**	
Other Taxes (Including Advance EIC Payments)	**48**	Self-employment tax (attach Schedule SE)	**48**	
	49	Alternative minimum tax (attach Form 6251)	**49**	
	50	Recapture taxes (see page 18). Check if from: ☐ Form 4255 ☐ Form 8611 . .	**50**	
	51	Social security tax on tip income not reported to employer (attach Form 4137) . . .	**51**	
	52	Tax on an IRA or a qualified retirement plan (attach Form 5329)	**52**	
	53	Add lines 47 through 52. This is your total tax . . . . ▶	**53**	
Payments Attach Forms W-2, W-2G, and W-2P to front.	**54**	Federal income tax withheld (If any is from Form(s) 1099, check ▶ ☐)	**54**	
	55	1988 estimated tax payments and amount applied from 1987 return	**55**	
	56	Earned income credit (see page 19)	**56**	
	57	Amount paid with Form 4868 (extension request).	**57**	
	58	Excess social security tax and RRTA tax withheld (see page 20)	**58**	
	59	Credit for Federal tax on fuels (attach Form 4136). . . .	**59**	
	60	Regulated investment company credit (attach Form 2439) . . .	**60**	
	61	Add lines 54 through 60. These are your total payments . . . . ▶	**61**	
Refund or Amount You Owe	**62**	If line 61 is larger than line 53, enter amount **OVERPAID** . . . . ▶	**62**	
	63	Amount of line 62 to be **REFUNDED TO YOU** . . . . ▶	**63**	
	64	Amount of line 62 to be applied to your 1989 estimated tax . . ▶ **64**		
	65	If line 53 is larger than line 61, enter **AMOUNT YOU OWE**. Attach check or money order for full amount payable to "Internal Revenue Service." Write your social security number, daytime phone number, and "1988 Form 1040" on it	**65**	
		Check ▶ ☐ if Form 2210 (2210F) is attached. See page 21. Penalty: $		

Please Sign Here

Under penalties of perjury, I declare that I have examined this return and accompanying schedules and statements, and to the best of my knowledge and belief, they are true, correct, and complete. Declaration of preparer (other than taxpayer) is based on all information of which preparer has any knowledge.

▶ Your signature	Date	Your occupation
▶ Spouse's signature (if joint return. BOTH must sign)	Date	Spouse's occupation

Paid Preparer's Use Only

Preparer's signature ▶	Date	Check if self-employed ☐	Preparer's social security no
Firm's name (or yours if self employed) and address ▶		E I No.	
		ZIP code	

141

for income in excess of the standard deduction and would progressively grow to higher percentages, through 15 income brackets, up to 50 percent.

Presently, the tax rates for single individuals with no dependents are the following:

Taxable income	Tax rates (percent)
Not over $17,850	15
Over $17,850 up to $43,150	28
Over $43,150 up to $100,480	33
Over $100,480	28

For married individuals filing a joint return with two exemptions the tax rates are the following:

Taxable income	Tax rates (percent)
Not over $29,750	15
Over $29,750 up to $71,900	28
Over $71,900 up to $171,090	33
Over $171,090	28

For married individuals filing separate returns with one exemption the tax rates are the following:

Taxable income	Tax rates (percent)
Not over $14,875	15
Over $14,875 up to $35,950	28
Over $35,950 up to $124,220	33
Over $124,220	28

Progressive personal income taxes have automatic countercyclical effects on the economy. However, they discourage work effort and alter the work-leisure trade-off. Such a substitution of leisure for work effort tends to reduce labor productivity and economic growth.

The 23 percent income tax cut of 1981, across the board, resulted in a proportionately larger reduction of taxes for high-income people. Thus, a couple with taxable income of $15,000 a year received $474, or a 5 percent tax cut annually, while a $50,000 couple received $3,410, as compared to the $25,632 cut, or 18 percentage points, for a $200,000 couple; that is, the last couple received a cut three and a half times larger than the percentage of the first couple.

As a result of the 1981 and 1986 tax rate cuts and the increase in defense spending, annually there occur huge budget deficits that threaten to paralyze fiscal policy. In such cases, fears of recession may prevent fiscal actions to cut budget deficits through decreasing spending or tax increases. Moreover, large budget deficits may aggravate the problems of debt-ridden developing countries, increase the danger of insolvency of banks and thrift institutions, and cause a national and international crisis. (Later chapters of the book deal with this topic in more detail.)

If stimulative actions are taken to avoid recessions and eventual depressions, there is the risk of exacerbating inflation. It is true that the cost-push double-digit inflation of the 1970s has been reduced to about 4 percent annually in the 1980s, but mainly because of the decline in oil prices.[5] However, increases in spending or reduction in taxes may increase both demand-pull inflation and budget deficits. To adjust taxes to inflation, a tax cut equal to the inflation rate was implemented in 1985 and thereafter. This rate of tax cut or indexing was 3.7 percent for the year 1986.

Negative Taxation

Among the various schemes that have been suggested to mitigate the problem of income inequalities and to improve social welfare is the program of negative income tax (NIT). In such a program the government or the city will guarantee an income to every family according to its size. Any person unable to work, either because of sickness and age or because no job is available, will receive a basic income sufficient to maintain his family at a determined standard of living.

An administratively efficient welfare scheme may be that in which each individual reporting an annual income below a fixed income floor will receive a supplementary payment up to this amount in monthly checks. The dilemma in such a welfare policy is how to guarantee an individual's income without destroying the incentive to work and creating a Solomonic bureaucracy.

To avoid severe disincentives to work, such a welfare scheme can permit individuals to earn up to a certain amount without facing reduction in the guarantee level. For higher earnings the guarantee can be reduced, say, to half of every additional dollar earned again up to a certain amount. An alternative scheme could be to establish a progressive NIT on earnings per hour. The higher the hourly earnings, the lower the supplementary income by the government, until it becomes zero.

The Tax Reduction Act of 1975 introduced special relief for low-income earners with dependents. It allowed a 10 percent credit against tax of earned income up to $5,000. The credit was reduced by 10 percent of income in excess of $5,000 and up to $10,000, or what was considered as the poverty level, in which amount it became zero. If the credit applied was higher than the tax liability, then a refund was given. This form of NIT is used to a larger degree in other countries such as Sweden.

However, the earned-income credit is a weak form of negative taxation or government transfer, for it excludes income received from other sources, such as capital income and pensions, and applies only to taxpayers or dependents. From the standpoint of welfare, a stronger or fuller negative taxation or a progressive taxation with a downward extension would provide a better and more efficient system of alleviating poverty and replacing the present system of cash and in-kind benefits or transfers.

An appropriate NIT program should not discourage work and should be combined with proper on-the-job training and skills attainment. A lower than 100 percent rate would provide income up the poverty level, but it will preserve incentives to work. This can be done to some extent by introducing negative income tax below the 100 percent rate, say at 50 percent, and raising the poverty level, say to $14,000. Thus, with income of $14,000 NIT payment would reach zero; with $8,000 income, NIT payment would be $3,000, or ($14,000 − $8,000) × .50; with $4,000, it would be $5,000; and with zero income, $7,000.

In conclusion, as long as the socioeconomic system of a country is unable to provide jobs for people able and willing to work, some form of negative taxation or other federal or state assistance, such as the Supplemental Security Income (SSI), seems to be socially and economically needed.

PAYROLL TAXES AND PENSION PLANS

Social Security Financing

The social security program, which was established in 1935 by President F. D. Roosevelt, was and still is financed by equal contributions of employees and employers. Since 1943 employers have been required to withhold taxes on wages and salaries. Because of the program's political popularity, benefits have been greatly increased, as have been tax rates for its financing, especially after the 1977 amendments. Thus, from a 2 percent (1 percent payable by employees and 1 by employers) tax levied on the first $3,000 of earned income in 1935, the tax rate gradually increased to 4.8 percent on the first $7,800 in 1970 and 15.02 percent on $45,000 in 1988. It will rise to 15.3 percent in 1990 on a maximum income from wages and will increase automatically in the future to keep pace with rises in average wage levels. Self-employed persons pay three-fourths the total employer-employee taxes of other workers (13.02 percent in 1988), which taxes will increase up to 15.3 percent in 1990.[6] Some civil service, state, local, and railroad employees have their own special retirement plans.

There are today in the 1980s six wage earners supporting one retiree, compared to the 30 to 1 ratio some 30 years ago. By the time baby boomers retire in 2015, two taxpayers will be supporting one recipient of benefits. With higher payments than receipts in the social security system, we seem be mortgaging our children's future. Up to 1958, collected payroll taxes had exceeded benefit payments; but after that year, the reverse occurred. The introduction of disability coverage in 1956 and hospital insurance (Medicare) played a major role in this reversal.

Relying on a pay-as-you-go process or on intergenerational transfer, the system may provide more benefits than the revenues collected to pay for them. To be self-supporting and financially sound, the system must collect sufficient employment taxes or contributions to equal the discounted value of the benefits expected, as is the case with private insurance funds. The present system has managed to pay its bills easily for the last four decades only because the ratio of wages to benefits remained satisfactory.

Although payroll taxes (a form of forced savings) replace private savings for retirement, the social security program seems to discourage saving for investment and high productivity because it provides old-age security and the possibility of earlier retirement. Thus, if one retires between the ages of 65 and 70, for every additional dollar earned above $8,400 income (or $4,920 below the age of 65), there would be a one-half dollar reduction in benefits. However, if the government is investing pension funds, public investment may offset private investment as long as receipts exceed payments in the pay-as-you-go process of financing, in which this year's contributions are used to pay this year's benefits. Also, there is a trend on the part of the employers to substitute capital for labor to avoid paying high payroll taxes, which are largely shifted forward. Such a practice of replacing labor with machinery reduces demand for labor and tends to increase unemployment and decrease payroll tax revenue.

Income in excess of the annual amount subject to payroll taxation is not included in such tax levying. Also, the five years of lowest earnings are not included in the calculations for the determination of benefits. By 1990, the combined social security payroll tax is scheduled to be 7.65 percent of earnings for employer and employee each; 5.1 percent of which would be Old-Age and Survivors Insurance (OASI), 1.1 percent Disability Insurance (DI), and 1.45 percent Health Insurance (HI). Of the total money collected, about 70 percent goes to OASI, 10 percent to DI, and 20 percent to Medicare.

An additional payroll tax paid by the employer is collected by the federal government for unemployment insurance. Such insurance is provided by state law, and the tax goes in the unemployment trust fund of the U.S. Treasury. Because payments are higher than revenue in these insurance programs, payroll taxes may be raised and, if expanded medical protection is included, they may be more than 25 percent of earnings, as they are in some European countries. Therefore, a value-added tax or other budget revenue may be used to finance partially or totally such social insurance programs.

From the administrative point of view, the payroll tax does not present problems because it is collected by the employer, and self-employed persons file returns and pay their taxes themselves. Overwithholding above the set ceiling may be credited against personal income taxes. The tax, then, is proportional up to the upper limit and regressive thereafter. Since labor supply is fairly inelastic, the tax burden falls largely on labor. In the short run, however, and depending on the bargaining power of unions, additional payroll taxes may be partially absorbed by the employer, thus reducing profits; or they may, more frequently, be passed on to consumers through price raising. The fact that capital income is excluded makes the payroll tax less equitable compared to other taxes and supports the argument to substitute it with an overall income tax.

Moreover, greater payroll taxes lead to growing pressures for wage increases, which in turn contribute to inflation and depress employment, since employers are discouraged by higher labor costs to hire more workers. Probably, no increases or even cuts in payroll taxes in less-developed areas of a country may encourage job creation in regions with pockets of unemployment.

Current tax exemptions for health insurance payments encourage excessive insurance purchase and even overuse of medical care. This is the main reason of proposed plans to reduce tax subsidies that contribute to high health care cost and inflation. Such plans suggest that employer contributions to health insurance above $75 a month for a person or $175 a month for a family be included in the employee's gross income. This proposal would affect some 30 percent of all civilian workers and employees, but it would not affect low-income working people.

Contributions Related to Benefits

To compare social security payments or taxes (t) on income (Y) with expected benefits (B), the variables should be converted to present values with an appropriate rate of discount (r). For a fair treatment, they should be equal; that is,

$$\frac{t_1 Y_1}{(1+r)^1} + \frac{t_2 Y_2}{(1+r)^2} + \ldots + \frac{t_k Y_k}{(1+r)^k} = \frac{B_{k+1}}{(1+r)^{k+1}} + \frac{B_{k+2}}{(1+r)^{k+2}} + \ldots + \frac{B_n}{(1+r)^n}$$

If the present value of benefits is higher than the present value of payments, then individual net social security wealth will be positive. If it is less, then the resulted wealth will be negative.

Given the recent measures on social security, the Congressional Budget Office predicts that after 1985, and for some 75 years, contributions will be higher than payments for retirement and a surplus will be realized. Therefore, when social security is separated from the regular or consolidated budget under new legislation that becomes effective in 1992, the system will be sound, standing on its own merit. By that time social security contributions will, it is estimated, be $69 billion higher than outlays. The 1988 social security surplus is expected to be $40.8 billion ($333.2 billion revenue and $292.4 outlays). These calculations include indexation of benefits for inflation as it prevails now. However, with ever-growing expenditures for Medicare hospital insurance (Part A) and nonhospital Medicare services (Part B), the system is headed for trouble unless such accelerated costs are reduced.

The maximum yearly social security taxes increased from $30 in 1940 to $45 in 1950, $144 in 1960, $374 in 1970, $1,588 in 1980, and $3,379 in 1988 (estimated). By 1990, a tax rate of 7.65 percent against a maximum earnings base of $51,600 is scheduled to bring a yearly tax of $3,947. The Social Security Amendment of April 20, 1983, introduced many changes in the system in order to stave off expected large deficits. An important change concerns the tax rates, as well as the maximum earnings to be taxed, which were increased gradually.

Swelling government deficits, high interest rates, and low economic growth have in the past led to severe criticism of the growing entitlement programs and resulted in quests for reforms in social security contributions and benefits. Demands for equity and fairness call for a deep analysis of these programs from the viewpoint of intergenerational bias and inequity, so that discrimination between today's and tomorrow's retirees be reduced or eliminated.

The intergenerational inequity ratio can be determined by comparing social security contributions with benefits. It is estimated that this ratio is about three to one in favor of today's retirees and against those who retire after the year 2010 (the baby boomers). If the economy performs poorly in the meantime, this ratio is expected to increase, and vice versa. As a result, one can expect reforms dealing with higher contributions, raising the retirement age, or reducing related benefits.

Presently a worker retiring at the age of 65 will receive all his or her contributions and accrued interest, in current dollars, in about 3 or 4 years; but for a baby-boomer retiring after 2010, it will take some 15 years to recover contributions if he or she is still around. Thus, there seems to be an inherent subsidization of the old by the young. However, because more than 30 million Americans are senior citizens, it is politically difficult to push for such reforms as deindexation and reductions in social security benefits. At the same time, the interests of young working persons should not be increasingly jeopardized, regarding future benefits and present low-interest loans for homes, as well as availability of jobs. Otherwise, the already precarious support for the system by younger workers could be undermined.

The proportions of retirees to working people is increasing, not only because of the declining rate of population growth, but also because life expectancy at age 65 increases. This graying of America, as mentioned earlier, has, in the long-run, forced many reforms in the system in recent years, including the gradual increase in payroll tax rates as well as the raising of payroll tax ceilings and the age of retirement.

To prevent the national retirement system from falling into disarray, new revenues and cost reductions are needed. However, it should be understood that social security is only a supplement designed to ensure that old folks are somehow comfortable at home and no one suffers from extreme poverty. It is not a pool of revenue collected from payroll taxes to be invested for returns until benefits begin. The social security program is designed primarily for a partial replacement of wages lost as a result of a worker's retirement, disability, or death.

Beginning January 1, 1984, part of social security benefits became subject to taxation. Thus, retirees with income of more than $25,000, or $32,000 for married taxpayers filing jointly, are subject to federal taxes upon half of their social security benefits. The taxable income is 50 percent of the income exceeding the above specified amounts, in which half of social security benefits are included. But it cannot exceed half of the benefits. For example, if a single taxpayer had an adjusted gross income of $29,000, in which interest is included, and social security of $6,000, he or she ought to report $3,000 of social security benefits as taxable income. Thus,

Income	$29,000
Half Benefits	3,000
	32,000
Base Amount	25,000
Difference	7,000
50% of the Difference	3,500
Taxable Social Security Benefit (cannot exceed half the benefit)	3,000

The proceeds of this tax go to the social security trust fund from which the benefits are paid. Hence, in order to relieve the social security system from financial pressures, work disincentives should be removed, work opportunities for the retirees extended, and earnings ceilings dropped.

The elimination of work disincentives from people receiving retirement benefits would help increase revenue from social security and income taxes, as well as improve national productivity. Older persons able and willing to work could continue working in order to supplement inadequate incomes, especially in the coming years in which more and more retirees and fewer and fewer workers are expected. However, such measures should be considered hand in hand with policies of employment for young people. In addition, civil service personnel and other groups with separate insurance programs should also be included under an overall system. To this end, the reform law of 1983 introduced a requirement that new federal employees and all employees of nonprofit organizations join social security starting January 1, 1984.

On the other hand, social security revenues are expected to increase because of the growing production and therefore higher wages expected in the future. If one assumes an average productivity rate of 3 percent per year (as in 1947–65) up to 2020, real production would be 120 percent more than present production.

If average annual productivity remains about 1 percent, as it was in the last decade, total production would nonetheless increase by 50 percent. Therefore, revitalizing production could help solve many problems, including retirement financing. To insure the long-term financial integrity of the politically delicate system of social security and to enhance the confidence of the contributors, economic policies toward high productivity are to be expected.

IRA and Keogh Plans

Individual retirement accounts (IRA) and Keogh plans are tax-sheltered retirement accounts. To boost their retirement income, individuals can deposit interest-earning savings in thrift institutions and defer tax payments for such deposits. Already, billions of dollars have been deposited to banks and other thrift institutions for that purpose.

Individuals can put 100 percent of their earned income into an IRA, with a limit of $2,000 per year, as long as they are not covered by a retirement plan at work (unless their income is under $50,000 on joint returns or below $35,000 on single returns). If there is a nonworking spouse, the working spouse can set up an additional account, but the two accounts together may total no more than $2,250, with at least $250 of that amount in the account of the nonworking spouse. Until recently a self-employed person could also put up to $30,000 or 25 percent of earnings, whichever was less, into a special retirement program known as a Keogh plan, deducting all these dollars from taxable income. In 1986, this amount was reduced to $7,000. However, there is a 10 percent penalty for early withdrawals (before the age of 59 1/2) from all qualified retirement plans, not just IRAs. In addition, income taxes must be paid for the money taken out (Section 401k of the tax code introduced in 1978).

The Employee Retirement Income Security Act (ERISA) of 1974 sets certain limits in case employers decided to establish a pension plan. Thus, employees must be included in the plan after one year's employment or when they become 25 years old, whichever event comes later. However, it is suggested that the maximum amount of tax-deferred income that a professional corporation (PC) can lay aside in a pension plan be reduced.

Under the spirit of deregulation in the banking system, the $2,500 minimum investment in Super NOW (negotiated order of withdrawal) accounts and money market accounts has been removed. As a result, Keogh and IRA accounts and any other accounts permitting deposits lower than the $2,500 amount can be shifted to Super NOW and money market accounts to enjoy higher interest rates. Also, the interest rate on ordinary passbook accounts in commercial banks was recently increased from 5.25 percent to 5.5 percent to be equal to that given by savings and loan institutions for decades.

Growing proportions of fringe benefits have been used during the years since 1950 to avoid taxes. Such untaxed benefits, which increased from 2 percent of the wages in 1950 to more than 10 percent presently, include employer contributions to pension funds, health insurance premiums, employer-paid child care, dental care, legal fees, and commuting costs. It is estimated that from such optional, untaxed benefits the government is losing more than $100 billion in revenue per year.

Other deferred-tax contributions to pension funds have been established by professional organizations such as those of teachers, doctors, and engineers.

Cross-Sectional Review

Comparatively speaking, the share of social security contributions to government revenue is far higher in advanced Western countries than in the developing countries. It varies from 40 percent for France to 34 percent for Italy, 26 percent for Japan, and 25 percent for the United States. Contributions to social security in developing nations, as statistical data show, are very low, at around 10 percent or less. They vary from 4 percent for Venezuela to 8 percent for Peru and the Philippines, 11 percent for Colombia, and 13 percent for Turkey.

From 1950 to the present almost all countries have shown a trend of growing social security contributions. For the United States, such contributions increased from 10 percent of general government revenue in 1950 to 15 percent in 1960, 20 percent in 1970, and 23 percent in 1985. Such trends indicate that social insurance improves as the countries achieve higher levels of development. For in contrast, in low-income countries such as Brazil, Sri Lanka, and Zimbabwe, these contributions are very low, even below 1 percent.

A similar review of social security contributions as percentages of employees' compensations indicates that rich countries withhold far higher proportions of workers' incomes for retirement and other social benefits than poor countries. Moreover, such contributions have gradually increased for all countries considered. Thus, for the United States, they were raised from 4.4 percent in 1950 to 7 percent in 1960, 9.5 percent in 1970, 13 percent in 1980, and 15.02 percent in 1988. Japan and the United Kingdom have about the same social security taxes on employees compensations as the United States, while France, Germany, Italy, and Sweden have far higher payroll taxes, varying from 22 percent to 33 percent of the employee's income.

CORPORATE INCOME TAXES

As indicated earlier, the Sixteenth Amendment to the Constitution of the United States of 1913 opened the way for government income taxes for individuals as well as corporations. The federal corporation income tax rates before 1987 varied from 15 percent on income up to $25,000 to 46 percent on income above $100,000. From $25,000 to $50,000 the tax rate was 18 percent; from $50,000 to $75,000 it was 30 percent; from $75,000 to $100,000 the rate was 40 percent; and above that income it was 46 percent. Although most corporations are taxed at lower than the maximum rate, the bulk of the tax base (90 percent) is offered by large corporations. States absorb about 10 percent of the total corporation income taxes, and the federal government absorbs the rest.

Although the income tax rates for corporations were reduced by the Tax Reform Act of 1986, the graduated structure was retained in order to encourage growth of small businesses. The number of corporate income tax brackets was reduced from five to three, and the maximum tax rate dropped from 46 to 34 percent as follows:[7]

Taxable income	Tax rates (percent)
Not over $50,000	15
Over $50,000 but not over $75,000	25
Over $75,000	34

Corporations invest in plant and equipment and create jobs. They therefore deserve and get a number of incentive provisions such as investment tax credit, accelerated depreciation, and employment credit. Moreover, many provisions for personal income apply *pari passu* to business income from proprietorship, partnership, or corporations. However, there are questions of double taxation of corporation income (profits) and dividends (distributed profits). As the argument against corporate taxes goes, only individuals, not legal business entities, can bear the disutility of tax burdens.

The corporation income tax has been criticized on the grounds that it taxes corporations as independent entities without considering the tax brackets of individual shareholders and that it leads to a low level of business investment. Consequently, reforms have been suggested to integrate corporate and individual income taxes, thus making the corporation a withholding unit for individual income taxes.

Tax rates for corporations were reduced from 52 percent to 48 percent in 1964, raised temporarily by 10 percent during the Vietnam War, then reduced again in 1978 to 46 percent and in 1986 to the current level of 34 percent.

Corporate Tax Revenue and Loopholes

The corporation income tax now raises revenue only 2.4 percent of GNP (1988 estimate), compared with 3.3 percent in 1970, 4.4 percent in 1960, and 5.4 percent in 1953. As a percentage of federal revenue, it now accounts for only 12.8 percent as compared to 16.9 percent in 1970, 23.5 percent in 1960, and 28.4 percent in 1953.[8] This sizable decline in the proportional revenue from corporation income taxes is due to such reforms as investment tax credit and accelerated depreciation allowances. Some people, including President Ronald Reagan, have called for the abolition of the corporate tax altogether, while many profitable companies, especially growing ones, cannot use all of their tax benefits.

Effective corporate tax rates vary from industry to industry. For instance, in 1984 tax rates as a percentage of profits were 35 percent for finance, insurance, and real estate corporations; 31 percent for petroleum and coal products industries; 28 percent for crude petroleum and natural gas corporations; 23 percent for retail trade; 13 percent for communications; and 6 percent for construction. Because of tax loopholes, such as investment tax credit or oil depletion and allowances and intangible drilling expenses, some corporations are paying small amounts of taxes or nothing while others are paying high proportions of their profits.

The present complex tax system, with all its loopholes and differentiations, distorts the allocation of capital and labor and harms productivity, employment, and growth in the economy. It tends to shift business capital spending away from modern long-term plants toward short-lived equipment and office furniture. As a result of tax exemptions and tax subsidies, corporate tax payments have fallen from 25 percent of federal revenue in the years 1950 through 1969 to about 10 percent in the 1980s. During the early years of the 1980s some 250 major companies paid an average of 14 percent income taxes, varying from 46 percent for Whirlpool Corporation to 28 percent for IBM and Digital Equipment; 25 percent for the makers of computers, technical instruments, and textiles; 4 percent for Sears; close to zero for chemical companies; and virtually nothing for General Electric, Sperry Corporation, Control Data, Wang Laboratories, and for other industries such as airlines, timber companies, and railroads.

As a result of the accelerated depreciation provisions of the 1981 tax act and other investment credits, corporate cash flows improved markedly. This triggered an investment boom, which in turn led to the upswing of the economy in subsequent years.

Corporate profit taxes increased from $22.3 billion in 1960 to $32.2 billion in the fiscal year 1970 and $69.9 billion in 1980. Later on, they started declining. In 1983 they dropped to $54.3 billion; that is a decrease of 22.3 percent over 1980. This resulted from the severe recession of 1981–82 and the corporate tax cuts of 1981.

To control abuses in tax privileges and cafeteria-style fringe benefits, the Deficit Reduction Act of 1984 was enacted. It provides that employer educational assistance is not tax deductible unless the training is specifically related to the employee's present job. Moreover, employee discounts cannot be larger than 20 percent and workers' salaries cannot be reduced for contributions to health plans and health care expenses, known as zero-balance reimbursement accounts, or Zebras. Other fringe benefits such as free airline tickets to employees, free parking at corporate headquarters, group legal services, extra vacation days, paintings and decorations for the office, and subscriptions to business periodicals are also affected. As a result, corporate benefit packages and flexible health and other plans remain uncertain.

Macroeconomically, a certain proportion of national income or product is paid in total taxes per year by individuals and corporations. Corporate taxes are passed on to individuals in the form of higher prices. Even if they pay taxes from profits, consumers bear the final burden because profits themselves are the result of prices that are higher than the cost of production. Given this system, a fairer approach would be a simple tax directed at the final taxpayer, that is, the individual. A value-added tax or some other form of consumption tax could be used to replace partially or totally corporation income taxes. A tax on the value added (gross receipts minus purchases from other firms) by each firm would reduce the burden of capital-intensive industries and help the balance of payments by keeping more capital at home and attracting capital from abroad.

In recent years major defense contractors have paid no taxes or even negative taxes (that is, they have received a refund). Thus, Grumman and Lockheed paid no taxes at all in 1981–83, while General Electric paid -$283 million, Boeing -$142, Weyerhauser -$139, Dupont -$139, General Dynamics -$71, and Northrop Corporation -$42 million. Similar corporations—Martin Marietta, Rockwell International, Union Carbide, RCA, Texaco, Xerox, and TRW, for example—paid relatively small amounts of taxes or collected sizable rebates.

Because corporate income taxes fall ultimately on people, elimination of such taxes would simplify the tax system and certainly make it fairer. Progressivity of personal and corporate income taxes does not seem to preserve social equity and does not provide an efficient means of raising needed amounts of tax revenue. It does not contribute much to the well-being of the poor, the sick, and the old; yet it demoralizes the rich. Along these lines, one may argue that government spending for social security, Medicare, education, and other social services contributes more to the reduction of inequality than progressive taxation. A consumption tax system or, more specifically, a value-added tax system with some progressivity depending on the degree of necessity could replace partially or totally the present personal and corporate income tax system, which is riddled with inefficiencies and fraud.[9]

ESTATE AND GIFT TAXES

Death taxes and gift taxes complement income taxes so that tax avoidance from unrealized capital gains and other sources can be limited. Death taxes can be distinguished in estate taxes, which concern the entire property at death, and the inheritance taxes, which concern the bequest going to each heir or legatee. They are both wealth-transfer taxes with some progressivity and are used to implement the ability-to-pay principle for equity in tax distribution. Gift taxes are paid by the donor, not the donee, and are also progressive.

A Brief History

Death taxes were first introduced by the U.S. federal government in 1798 and became permanent in 1916. To prevent interstate competition for aged rich residents, the Revenue Act of 1926 permitted the states to levy up to 80 percent of the federal estate tax liability, which otherwise would be collected by the federal government. On the other hand, federal gift taxes were not introduced until 1924 and reformed in 1932. In 1976, both estate and gift taxes were integrated into one federal tax code, replacing the $60,000 estate tax exemption and the $30,000 lifetime gift tax exemption with a uniform set of tax rates for both bequests and gifts.

The Economic Recovery Tax Act (ERTA) of 1981 reduced the top estate tax rate from 70 percent to 50 percent for estates over $2.5 million. Rates start at 18 percent on the first $10,000 taxable estate. Also the tax exemption for estates of up to $175,000 was increased gradually after 1981 to $600,000 after 1987. Thus, there will be no estate or gift tax on taxable transfers aggregating $600,000 or less after 1987. Mainly because of inflation, ERTA expanded the gift tax exclusion from $3,000, which had prevailed since 1942, to $10,000 per donee annually. However, gifts made within three years of death may be subject to estate taxation. Unlimited exclusion is available for gifts made for paying education expenses (tuition) or medical expenses.

All states in the United States except Nevada now have death taxes either in the form of a pickup tax (collecting the full amount of the federal tax credit), an estate tax, or an inheritance tax (concentrating attention on the person who receives the bequest). Some states have two and some others all three types of death taxes. Pennsylvania was the first to introduce a state death tax in 1825, while other states followed up to the Civil War, after which a laxity prevailed. New York revived a 5 percent transfer-of-property tax in 1885, and other states followed with different rates and exemptions (varying from $5,000 to $100,000). Gift taxes, which are mostly unified with estate taxes, exist in many states.

Some Negative Effects

Although the final burden of the estate tax seems to rest with the recipient, the testator, prevented from the free disposition of his or her wealth, bears a portion of the final tax incidence. As a result the testator will try to use various devices, such as the formation of trust funds to bequeath the estate to charitable or educational institutions, and make before-death gifts to escape taxation. Other effects of estate taxes may be early retirement, longer vacations, less work for income earning, and less saving and capital formation. Retirement decisions may not be affected much by death taxes, however, since a person may choose to work longer to supplement taxes and leave the same value of property to his or her survivors. Therefore, the work-leisure substitution effect and the post-tax income effect may not be as powerful in this case. The effects of death taxes on consumption-saving incentives may be significant, though, since they distort saving and investment decisions. Thus, death and gift taxes affect growth negatively by breaking up ownership, but they are not important tools as automatic or discretionary fiscal stabilizers. Presently, federal revenues from estate and gift taxes are only about $6 billion per year ($5.8 billion in 1988, estimated), or less than 1 percent of the total budget revenue, compared to $1.6 billion in 1960, $3.6 billion in 1970, and $6.4 billion in 1980. It is estimated that about two-thirds of capital accumulation is due to inheritances.

Distributional Effects

Progressive death and gift taxes perform an important function in market economies. They are used for a greater equality in the distribution of wealth. This is in accordance with the arguments of Aristotle and John Stuart Mill, who supported a limit on the accumulation of wealth by individuals. As noted before, although Aristotle supported private property, suggesting that "common ownership means common neglect," he favored a limit to acquisition of wealth itself justified by the anxiety about livelihood. According to Aristotle, the pursuit of wealth in excess of this limit can be considered a corruption or an unnatural form of acquisition. Limiting wealth acquisition—and thus limiting corruption—is a major purpose of progressive taxations in capitalist societies, although death and gift taxes are modestly progressive in the United States. The taxation of transfers of wealth contributes also to the closing of some tax loopholes, such as tax-exempt interest on state and local government securities that is mostly accumulated and transferred in the form of gifts or inheritance. Such a taxation provides one means toward a greater equality of opportunity without causing major disincentives in savings and investment.

However, there are some negative distributional effects of death and gift taxes. Persons with legal skills can implement estate and property transfers to avoid horizontal and vertical equity taxes. Thus, gifts to charitable institutions and nonprofit organizations, which number more than 800,000 in the United States, are tax exempt. Also, trusts, that is legal arrangements dealing with the administration of funds for an individual or organization, are used to avoid paying taxes for property transfers to a later generation (grandchildren or remaindermen, for example). The law permits the establishment of a trust by wealthy persons, naming other persons (spouses and children, for example) as life tenants entitled to income from the trust and then transfer the property to remaindermen without paying estate taxes again. Therefore, estate taxes are paid initially when the originator of a trust fund dies and not again when the property is transferred to the remaindermen. This is a widely used technique to skip paying taxes for a generation. Also, the Tax Reform Act of 1984 lets parents place cash or other assets in trust for a child for a minimum of 10 years during which all the income produced is taxed at the child's tax rate. Such large tax credits, interspousal transfer exemptions, and other sizable deductions mitigate the redistributive impact of the estate taxes.

PROPERTY TAXES

Property or capital values can be converted into income while income streams can be converted into capital values through a discount or interest rate. Likewise, capital taxes can be converted into income taxes and vice versa. In practice, however, property or capital taxes are imposed directly on the value of assets (in rem) and tend to be proportional, and not progressive or regressive as are personal taxes. Property or capital taxes tend to discriminate against income from assets, while income taxes tend to discriminate against income from labor offered by people, who cannot be depreciated, as can capital assets. Thus, investment in real assets is allowed to depreciate but not investment in human capital (education).

As mentioned earlier, the Physiocrats in France and Henry George in the United States considered agriculture as the only productive sector. Therefore, taxation should be imposed upon the surplus, or net product, of land received by the landlords (this should be a single tax). Adam Smith and David Ricardo in England thought that the relative value of products depends on the amount of labor involved, as later Karl Marx believed also. However, Ricardo explained that the value of land products is determined by the cost (labor) involved in the production of marginal (poor or nonrent) land. Then tax should be imposed on the rent of the rich lands, which rent is considered a surplus for the landlords. As population increases, poorer lands are cultivated and higher rents are collected by the owners of lands, which Ricardo called "the original and indestructible powers of the soil." Rent, then, is not a real cost but the result of price.[10]

Modern theories consider rent as the return on any resource, not only on land. This is known as economic rent, which can be defined as the return on a resource above opportunity costs, or what the resource would earn elsewhere in an alternative use. For example, an actor or a TV news-caster can earn $200,000, but in alternative jobs may earn $40,000. The difference ($160,000) is economic rent, or surplus, which should be subject to taxation.

An increase in demand for land, which is fixed in supply, leads to higher return or economic rent. A tax upon it is rather neutral in its effect on resource allocation and can hardly be shifted. In the long run, however, land and capital are considered complementary assets for individual owners, and some tax burden on land may be shifted to capital. Immobile property cannot easily escape taxation and constitutes the main source of income for municipalities, townships, and counties. Less important sources for local revenues are user fees for local services, automobile licensing, and consumption (sales) taxes. Tax rates tend to average from 1 percent to 4 percent of the true value of the property, although there is some degree of arbitrary evaluation in assessing market values.

The assessment—that is, the discovery and evaluation, of realty (land and buildings)—is not as difficult as is that of personal property. The property tax burden may be concentrated on the owner of property (tax capitalization) or on the consumer (renter). The effect of a general property tax would be the reduction of the capital value of the assets involved, since their values would be determined by discounting the expected net income stream.

Taxes on land are mainly borne by landowners who, on the average, have high income. Taxes on structures, which have relatively higher property value than land, reduce consumption of housing services and are regressive. In proportion to income, they decline as income rises, as does housing consumption. Property taxes, particularly real estate taxes, differ in the numerous municipalities and localities. With different tax rates gross rates of return will differ among localities. Thus, if locality A imposed a 4 percent annual capital income tax and locality B 6 percent and the rate of return before tax was 8 percent in both, the cost of capital in A would be 12 percent and in B 14 percent. Prices of goods produced in high-tax B locality would be relatively higher until the difference would be dissipated through capital flows into locality A, with a higher net rate of return.

In the case of housing, where there is inelastic demand, property taxes may be shifted forward to consumers and turn out to be regressive or backward to labor. Policymakers may use such taxes on residential, commercial, and industrial structures to discourage urban centralization and encourage investment decentralization in suburbs and specified rural areas. Special industrial locations may be used also for purposes of environmental protection.

Property taxes are based on the value of assets or capital stock at a particular time. Investment, made out of income, during a period, increase capital stock. Income, on the other hand, depends on the accumulated capital over the years or is equal to capital times the inverse of capital-output ratio. It seems, then, that property taxes are taxes on previous incomes, while taxable income includes part of property income, and so on. This leads to a multifold taxation of income invested into assets and discourages capital formation and economic growth.

Site value tax, or tax on economic rent of land, especially in urban centers or seashore resorts, is justified because of the unearned value created from rising demand of land fixed in supply. Thus, a shift in demand from D to D' in Figure 6.2 leads to a higher price from P to P', commanding a higher rent and justifying a site value tax. However, increments of land and other capital gains are seldom marketed, and so site value is difficult to assess. Moreover, buildings and improvements are produced, but land or sites are not. Thus, a differentiation of assessment values, and therefore of taxation, should be made on land and property improvements. One will recall that, and according to David Ricardo, a tax on the nonreproducible properties of land falls on economic rent and cannot be shifted forward. This economic rent, constituting unearned income, should, according to Henry George, be the basis for introducing a single tax while abolishing other forms of taxation.

Property taxes, which were known in ancient times, during the feudal period in Europe, and colonial times in the United States, constitute the main source of local government revenue; indeed, more than 80 percent of local tax revenue in the United States comes from property taxes. They are levied on the assessed value of a property. Such assessed value varies from less than 15 percent to 50 percent of the real value, with a national average of about 30 percent. The tax base of such taxes can be classified as real assets and financial assets. Real, or tangible, assets include land (farm and nonfarm), structures (residential and

Figure 6.2
Site Value Taxation

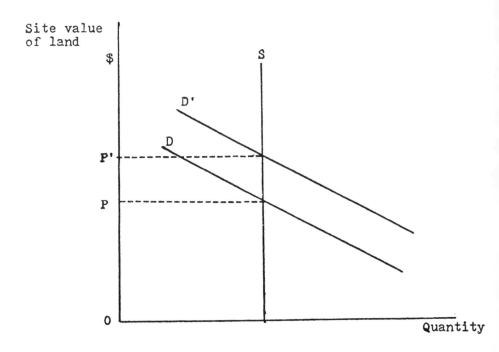

nonresidential; buildings, fences, and other improvements), and equipment (machinery, consumer durables, and inventories). Financial, or intangible, assets include stocks, bank deposits, and bonds and other debt instruments.

The total value of real assets, that is, the total value of national wealth, is estimated to be about three times the total production, or GNP. This can be inferred from the relative constancy of the capital output ratio, which prevails for all countries over time, as statistical measures indicate.[11]

There exist different levels of property tax rates among countries and even among various political jurisdictions in the same country. In assessment, real estate tax differentials and exemptions may be used by local governments to discourage establishment of industries in urban areas with high pollution and to attract them in less-developed regions. Such exemptions may include the sale of free tax bonds for the construction and development of state and local government industries; they may also include property owned by certain charitable organizations and by elderly and poor people. In many cases, all debt obligations on assets are deductible. In addition, a net worth tax is used in a number of European, Asian, and Latin American countries in which corporations are mostly exempted.

CONSUMPTION TAXES

In view of large budget deficits and the consequent high interest rates, inflationary pressures, and crippled competitiveness in world markets, there have been thoughts about changing the tax system toward penalizing consumption and encouraging saving and investment. Previous policies provided strong incentives to borrow and consume mainly to increase overall demand. Such policies led to low rates of saving, insufficient investment, and slow rates of productivity growth. Low rates of investment in plant, equipment, and innovation, in turn, reduced the rates of real economic growth and allowed inflationary spirals.

A consumption-based tax can replace partially the present system through a national sales tax or value-added tax. In a less radical change, it can limit tax deduction of consumer interest payments or defer taxes on income that is saved. A nonregressive consumption tax would attract money under productive investment shelters and encourage capital accumulation and innovations. Measures that tend to stimulate saving and growth in productivity, in addition to consumption taxes, are those that reduce tax rates on capital gains, establish individual retirement accounts, and limit restriction on the interest rates institutions can pay to small savers.

Financing expanding governmental services in a noninflationary manner is one of the main problems of public policy for all governments. In recent years, there has been a growing interest in proposals for taxing consumption expenditures as an alternative to taxing income, that is, to switch gradually from taxes on income earned to those on income spent. Indirect taxes, which include turnover taxes, value-added taxes, tariffs, and sales taxes, are primarily expenditure taxes and as such are affected by changes in consumption, imports, and inflation.

The main problem of consumption taxes is to raise a given revenue from a consumer by taxing the commodities he or she consumes in such a way that the vestultant loss in utility is minimized. To achieve that the tax, as a proportion of the consumer price of each good, should be inversely related to elasticity of demand for such commodities.

It is generally accepted that higher rates of growth in productivity require higher rates of capital investment, which, in turn, can be financed by higher rates of saving. To discourage consumption in favor of saving, heavier taxation on consumption expenditures is proposed by a number of economists.[12] They argue that the use of consumption taxes as substitutes for income taxes would encourage saving and stimulate incentives for work and high productivity. Therefore, such taxes on present consumption may be considered as subsidies to saving; whereas taxes on savings or interests, which prevail in the United States, are equivalent to subsidies to present consumption. Thus, it may be that this form of taxation may be partially responsible for ongoing inflation.

Another form of consumption tax is that on gasoline, especially on the oil imported from the members of the Organization of Petroleum Exporting Countries (OPEC). With oil prices tumbling in the mid–1980s, a tax on imported oil would provide large amounts of revenue, indirectly coming from the pockets of OPEC, which increased prices drastically and unilaterally in the 1970s. Such a tax would keep demand at low levels and help conservation and environmental protection.

From the standpoint of economic growth, consumption seems to be a better tax indicator than actual income. A person who consumes uses resources for his or her own satisfaction, but a person who saves contributes more to the betterment of society by financing capital formation and stimulating employment and growth. It would be better for a person to be taxed on what he or she takes out of society's production rather than what he or she contributes to it. Taxation, then, is to restrain private use of resources and make way for government expenditure. These arguments were promulgated years ago by Thomas Hobbes and indirectly by Adam Smith in his support of investment for increasing the wealth of nations. Presently this line of reasoning is supported by Nicholas Kaldor and William Andrews, as well as by other economists.

Sales Taxes

Consumption or transactions taxes include general sales taxes, excise taxes, severance taxes, turnover taxes, and value-added taxes. Sales taxes produce about 50 percent of state and 10 percent of federal consumption or expenditure taxes imposed on sellers' gross receipts of product transactions and paid by households or consumers. They are impersonal (in rem) taxes and can be placed at one or more than one stage. They may be based on GNP, that is, on both consumer and capital goods or, more usually, on consumption expenditures.

Excise taxes are selective taxes on specific products, such as liquor, gasoline, tires, tobacco, telephone services, air transportation, customs duties, and pollution costs. When they are used to penalize extravagant or harmful consumption, regarding especially alcoholic beverages and tobacco, they are called sumptuary taxes. They are levied primarily by the federal government on a unit-of-product basis (unit tax) or as a percentage of price (*ad valorem* tax).

In place of excise taxes, user charges can be levied. In this case fees are collected to finance particular public services such as urban mass transit or highway and road construction, for which a special trust fund can be established. Although it is difficult to match benefits and user charges, even an approximation of cost-benefit analysis can be beneficial, especially from a political point of view. Another related tax is the severance tax, used by some 33 states usually on gross receipts from natural resources such as minerals, fish, and timber. It may be used to replace a property tax and has the advantage of helping resource conservation.

Value-Added Taxes

The value-added tax (VAT) is primarily a consumption tax and as such is included in indirect taxes. The VAT, which has been introduced by the EEC member states, is a proportional tax on the value of all goods and services included in a firm's invoices, reduced by the amount of previous VAT liability. As the supporters of VAT argue, this tax is simple: It reduces consumption expenditures, decreases tax evasion, improves the flexibility of the tax structure, and stimulates investment and economic growth. As a tax upon the difference between the total value of output minus the value of purchased material inputs, it helps policymakers determine whether demand for consumer goods is growing in an inflationary way. Thus, VAT can be used to regulate demand. However, additional value-added taxes, when first introduced, would more than likely be passed on to the consumers in the form of rising prices.

Policymakers and economists in the United States and other countries have started contemplating the introduction of VAT as a substitute for personal income taxes. By shifting the nation's tax burden away from taxes on income and profits and toward sales or value-added taxes, supporters believe, would stimulate production incentives and discourage consumption expenditures. However, they argue, care should be taken to avoid overburdening low-income and middle-income consumers upon whom such taxes primarily fall. This can be achieved by providing tax exemptions for the necessities of life, such as food, modest rental payments, or a small home. Also, a VAT can be coupled with a rebate on low incomes and exports.

When a VAT permits firms to subtract purchases of capital goods from the tax base, it takes the form of a general consumption tax. When capital goods are not subtracted (except depreciation allowances), the VAT is equivalent to a tax on national income, that is, on the total value added from wages, rents, interest, and profits. The VAT can be calculated by subtracting from sales all purchases from other firms and applying a tax upon the difference. It can also be applied to all sales, and then the tax paid on goods purchased can be deducted. The latter, the so-called tax credit method, is easiest to apply. Also, it facilitates export remissions and thereby encourages competition of domestic firms in foreign markets.

With the introduction of the value-added taxes, there would be less confusion over tax legislation, which the mass production of laws and regulations has created in the already saturated legal profession. They, like sales taxes, are simple and fair and catch both the tax evaders and the tax avoiders.

Such modifications and simplifications of the tax system would help small and medium enterprises, since the disadvantages of turnover taxes, which favor vertical integration, would also be eliminated. Instead, the horizon would be clearer for them to adjust their size in such a way that they can enjoy the best results in economy of scale and factor productivity, preserving at the same time their independence.

The value-added tax, a form of which was adopted by the state of Michigan in 1953, repealed in 1967, and reenacted in the mid–1970s, is levied on the increments of the value of goods and services at each stage of production and distribution. It extends to the retail stages of virtually all sectors, including services. It covers more taxpayers than other forms of taxation; and because it usually increases revenue and reduces evasion, many countries have introduced it. But it often increases the burden of the tax authorities, and so policymakers hesitate to adopt it.

Although it is argued that the introduction of the VAT leads to inflation, empirical research has shown that in the majority of the countries that introduced the VAT, it had minor or no impact on inflation.[13] This was particularly so in countries such as Austria, France, Korea, the Netherlands, and Norway, in which the authorities imposed temporary price controls to offset expected once-and-for-all increase in prices due to the introduction of the VAT or in which the VAT replaced other forms of taxation. In a few countries the anticipation of the introduction of a VAT acted as a trigger for wage increases and credit expansion, which led to inflationary pressures. The uncertainty induced by the tax change might have a major effect on the vicious circle of wage-price increases, although the direct effect of the VAT might probably be trivial. Furthermore, when the VAT is introduced at times of economic slowdown or recessions, traders are expected not to pass the tax on to consumers in the form of higher prices, as happened in West Germany.

Multiple rates of a VAT can be used to eliminate the regressivity likely to be associated with a single rate of such a tax. However, this increases administrative complexities, compliance costs, and distortions in consumption to the extent that such progressivity is probably unjustified.

In the United States most states levy sales taxes at widely different rates. However, in other countries circumstances are different because VATs have either replaced inefficient turnover or cascade taxes (for example, in France, Germany, and the Netherlands) or been required for EEC membership (as in the case of the United Kingdom, Greece, Spain, and Portugal). In France, the VAT was introduced in 1954, where presently it raises about 50 percent of tax revenue. In West Germany, the VAT was proposed in 1918 and introduced in 1967. There it provides 13 percent of government revenue. In Britain, it provides 15 percent and in the EEC 10 percent of the overall tax revenue.

One of the major criticisms against consumption taxes and particularly VATs is that they are hidden sales taxes and absorb higher proportions of income from the poor and lower from the rich; whereas, income taxes are open, so that people can see them better than the VAT. However, the unequal results of consumption taxes come from the higher inequality in the distribution of income and wealth. A better distribution of income makes the difference between consumption and income taxes less important and the value-added taxes more attractive. As long as there is high income inequality, income taxes of some progressive form or a combination of consumption and income taxes is required. Moreover, some form of progressivity can be introduced in consumption or indirect taxes.

It is argued that federal or central government value-added taxes would interfere with state and local sales taxes in decentralized federations like the United States. However, this can be arranged through the proper coordination of the different forms of consumption taxes (VAT, sales, excises, customs duties, and so on).

Although no tax is the best tax, the introduction of some form of value-added tax may provide sufficient revenue to shrink budget deficits and encourage saving for productive investment. With flexible exchange rates and rapidly growing international transactions, a simple and universally adjusted tax system is desirable. Even though a value-added tax would lead to an increase in administrative costs and a rise in prices when first introduced, in the long run it would replace many other tax regulations that are complicated and confusing. Sooner or later, therefore, it would infiltrate the U.S. tax system. The U.S. Treasury estimates that a broad-based value-added tax of 10 percent would raise about $250 billion, covering a substantial part of total consumption expenditures. However, critics argue that in the short run it would raise consumer prices by nearly 8 percent and would require 20,000 additional personnel, costing about $700 million to enforce it. Also, it is considered by many Congressional representatives as politically risky, for it may increase federal intrusion into the sales tax area of the states and cities.

To raise additional funds in order to clean up hazardous waste sites (Superfund Program), Congress passed a form of value-added tax, which could be the progenitor of an even broader national sales tax. This historic addition to the federal government's revenue source is a levy on the enhancement of a product's value at each stage of production. It is expected to apply only to some 30,000 companies and to exclude service industries, exports, and companies with annual sales of less than $5 million. This form of taxation may be the forerunner of a broad-based national value-added tax as a way to provide budgetary revenue or to reduce income taxes. It will also capture some of the underground revenue that now escapes taxation and help solve some problems of budget deficits and trade imbalances.

Cross-Sectional Survey

Comparatively speaking, other developed and developing market economies have the same tax structure as the United States, but with some deviations depending on the stage of their economic development. Thus, the countries of the EEC have a tax system based mainly on a progressive income tax on individuals, a proportional tax on corporations, and a value-added tax, replacing previous complex turnover taxes.[14] Mostly, statutory income tax rates are growing from 5 percent to 60 percent in the EEC countries. There is also a small property or real estate tax collected mainly by local governments. This last tax also exists in Japan, where national taxes are levied in equal proportion mainly on personal income, corporate income, and commodities and services (indirect taxes). In the EEC, however, corporate tax revenue is about 3 percent to 4 percent of the GNP.

The revenues of the EEC countries as a group come primarily from VAT (1 percent of the VAT collected by the member nations goes into the EEC common pot), customs duties, and special levies on agricultural imports (including sugar duties). Revenue from VAT is about 50 percent of the total revenue of the EEC, as a unit separate from that of the individual member countries. In 1983, that amount was 11 billion European Currency Units (ECUs), or about $10 billion. The EEC revenue from customs duties was close to 8 billion ECUs, and that from agricultural levies and sugar was about 3 billion ECUs. Most of the collected revenues are spent for the support of prices of agricultural products by a special EEC fund known as the Fond Europeen d' Orientation et de Garantie Agricole (FEOGA) (about two-thirds); around 10 percent for the regional development of backward areas; and the rest for social policies, research, energy, and aid to third world countries (about 6 percent). Greece, Italy, Portugal, Spain, and to some extent France are the main recipients of subsidies for agricultural products and regional development.

Serious financial problems have appeared with the budget of the EEC with about two-thirds of its approximately $20 billion annual receipts spent for farm subsidies. The countries of the north, primarily Britain and to some extent West Germany, object to farm subsidization and have asked for a revised farm policy to eliminate food surpluses which then are sold on world markets. Australia, the United States, and other countries, which export farm products, complain that the agricultural policy of the EEC leads to unfair competition against their own products.

The planned economies, following largely the Soviet economic model, rely heavily on turnover taxes to provide revenue and to balance supply and demand.[15] If the authorities establish a low price OP for a commodity whose market supply (S) and demand (D) curves meet at a higher point, as shown in Figure 6.3, the difference QQ' is shortage. In this case rationing would take place. When the planners want to avoid shortages and rationing, they impose a turnover tax, PP', thereby moving prices close to the equilibrium of supply and demand and collecting budgetary revenue equal to PP' per unit of the commodity considered. If there is a shift in demand to D' and planners prefer to have the same quantity, they simply further raise turnover taxes, P'P", thus determining a final price, OP", and collecting PP" unit taxes.

The turnover taxes therefore play an adjustment role of supply and demand similar to profits in capitalist economies and a distribution role by discriminating between necessary goods (housing, medical care, transportation, education, books) for which there is a small or no turnover tax and luxurious goods (cars, videos, vodka) with high taxes. Prices incorporating taxes, then, play a limited allocative role in socialist economies and are used for demand-and-supply manipulation, for income distribution, and partially for tax revenue.

Through input-output models, the planners manipulate relative prices and sectoral imbalances in demand and supply to stimulate investment and promote growth. Political leadership selects priority projects consistent with their targets

Figure 6.3
Turnover Tax in Planned Economies

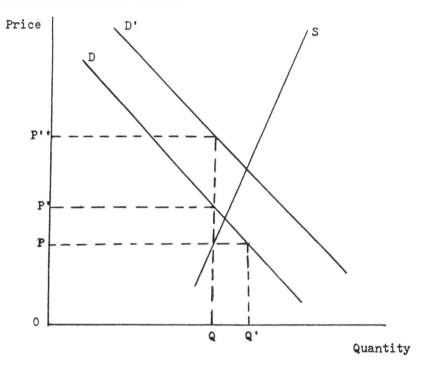

and deviates from the price mechanism for resource allocation. Usually manufacturing is favored over the traditional agricultural sector, as are other social
services (education, health, culture) through cheap credit, tax reductions, and
undervalued foreign currency. As a result, severe shortages of some goods are
accompanied by large stocks in others. To correct such sectoral imbalances,
rationing and tax-cum-subsidy measures are used. That is the way to avoid
extensive productivity losses due to misallocations of resources and effective
protection from imports. In 1988, the Soviet Union introduced a progressive tax
on private income varying from 27 percent for monthly income above $830 to
50 percent for monthly income above $1,160, 70 percent for monthly income
above $1,660, and 90 percent for monthly income above $2,480. For monthly
income up to $830 (500 rubles), taxes are 13 percent, as paid by government
workers (this had been the top tax rate since 1916, and even before, under Czarist
Russia, until the 1988 progressive tax was set in place).

7

Effects of Taxation on the Economy

IMPACTS ON SAVING AND CAPITAL FORMATION

There are three main institutional originating sectors for domestic savings: the household, business enterprise, and government. Governmental savings can be made through taxation, public borrowing, or inflation. Taxation, imposed by government, forces the public to reduce spending in order to save enough money to pay off taxes. In that case, government saving is the excess of tax revenue over expenditure. Other possible means of financing government expenditures are through expanding governmental debt, that is, by selling securities (bills, notes, bonds) on a voluntary basis to households and business, by creating debt in bank notes, or by issuing flat government currency. Inflation or increase in prices can be regarded as a form of quasi-forced saving if the government is financing its deficit in an inflationary fashion. As the government bids resources away from other sectors, prices tend to rise and consumption is reduced.

The share of government (central, state, and local) in total savings depends primarily on the degree of governmental intervention on the economic activities of the country. However, one should keep in mind that savings contributions, especially by governments, depend on economic fluctuations and related fiscal and monetary policies.

Fiscal policy, particularly tax policy, has a profound impact upon savings and investment. Capacity output and economic growth depend on capital formation and saving, which are influenced by governmental policies on taxation and expenditures. Such policies affect the average and primarily the marginal propensity to save and, therefore, the division of income or output between consumption and capital formation. Moreover, accepting the Keynesian macroeconomic theory that higher income leads to higher proportions of savings, a policy of more progressive taxation would impose a heavy burden on savings and investment financing.

Taxation on capital or on income from capital tends to reduce the net return on savings and investment and to encourage consumption rather than capital formation. Also, it tends to discourage thriftiness for supplementing social security benefits, aside from its distorting effects on resource allocation. Individuals consume less or save out of present income in order to enjoy more consumption in the future. The forgone current consumption is channeled into capital formation so that productive capacity is increased over and above the depreciation rate of the existing capital stock.

The market interest rate is the link between present consumption forgone and expected future consumption. High interest rates, assuming other things remain the same, generate lower preference for present consumption in favor of more saving or more future consumption and vice versa. A capital tax or an interest tax encourages present consumption and discourages investment, which is an important component of real economic growth. However, if the government uses tax revenue for investment, capital stock grows and reduction of private investment is replaced by a public sector investment, so that economic growth can continue.

Contrary to what David Ricardo argued, there seems to be a difference between financing government spending through additional taxes and through selling bonds to the public. Increase in taxes is expected to reduce productive incentives and to cut more on private spending. On the other hand, selling government bonds is expected to reduce more on saving, which would be directed mostly toward new capital formation. Although government bonds represent future tax obligations when amortization of debt takes place, the fact is that debts are usually growing instead of being paid back by almost all governments. Moreover, deficit financing is, on many occasions, used for countercyclical purposes, that is, to stimulate aggregate demand and reduce unemployment. But in many instances such policies have led to inflationary spirals, which proved to be difficult to control without drastic fiscal and monetary measures. In any case, accumulation of real debt represents a shifting of the tax burden onto the next generations, and it is rather discouraging capital formation and real growth.

The Economic Recovery Act (ERA) of 1981 and the Tax Reform Act of 1986 introduced the largest tax cuts in the history of the United States, thus reducing personal tax rates and tax liabilities by more than $100 billion dollars annually. This was done mainly to stimulate incentives for all taxpayers to work, save, and invest. Also, individuals were offered the chance to defer income taxes through special retirement accounts, and businesses were allowed to write off investment more rapidly and provided with other incentives for more capital formation.

In spite of all these incentives, rates of saving remained the same, and business investment increased only slightly in subsequent years. This was so because individuals spent more for consumption, while business people remained skeptical about future expansion in an economy with large budget deficits and high interest rates. In addition, much of the money (about $25 billion annually) that went to retirement accounts was shifted from taxable savings. Therefore, the tax reductions proved to be crude Keynesian tools unable to stimulate sizable savings and investment mainly because of the other unwise fiscal and monetary instruments that led to huge deficits. Thus, U.S. private savings remain only around 4 percent of GNP. If, however, the purchase of cars and other durables is considered as investment, and corporate retained earnings are included, then the saving rate would be between 10 percent and 12 percent.

Tax cuts and other fiscal incentives work well when there are ample savings to finance additional investment. With incentives, investors may earn more; but the lack of saving for investment engenders more competition for available capital and interest rates are driven up. It may therefore be unwise to use incentives to encourage investment when large budget deficits exist simply because sufficient funds are not available. The use of investment incentives, without reducing budget deficits, increases demand for capital, raises interest rates, and reduces growth.

Effects of Social Security on Saving

As to the economic effects of social security benefits, it would seem that not much change in saving takes place and only a slight decline in the labor force participation rate of older people occurs. Depending on the lifetime earnings stream of individuals, their marital status, and the employment conditions of their spouses, incentives to retire change and social security seems to subsidize extra work for early retirees. However, other policy tools may be more effective in modifying saving behavior and stimulating labor supply of the elderly.

It is estimated that the social security system reduces personal saving by about 50 percent—and this has serious ramifications for capital formation and output. This is so because the availability of benefits reduces the desire to accumulate assets for retirement (asset substitution effect). However, social security benefits induce earlier retirement, which requires higher rates of saving during the earning years to realize a desirable level of retirement income (this is called the retirement effect). The net effect depends on the relative strengths of these offsetting forces.[1]

Social security, which increases consumption, not saving, consequently places a drag on capital formation. Yet indexed benefits stimulate inflation and raise interest rates. However, the argument that social security benefits discourage private saving has certain flaws. Individuals may save to improve the economic and social position of their children and possibly their grandchildren. Also, in the pay-as-you-go system, working people, paying more than they expect to receive, may be relieved by the idea that among present beneficiary retirees are their parents or grandparents, whom they have at least a moral obligation to support in their old age. Moreover, some people prefer to go on and save, regardless of their expected retirement benefits, just to increase their wealth, particularly in their old age when they may not be able to continue accumulation of capital. Others want to leave property to their children or other heirs. This practice depends, among other things, on the inheritance taxes and the whole fabric of the socioeconomic system of the country. Some other people may need to save in order to offset reduced support from their children, the result of the availability of retirement benefits. On the other hand, social security payments may displace private dissaving by the old. Thus, it is difficult to accept that, on the average, net saving would increase without social security. One should also consider the unsocial side effects of eliminating social insurance or relying on profit-maximizing private organizations for health insurance.

Societies in the past used different measures to deal with the problems of old age and disability. In ancient Sparta, for example, the strict laws of Lycurgus provided for such persons to be exterminated by being thrown in a rough canyon. The American Indians, in contrast, respected their elders; those who were dying remained under the cover of sheltering trees awaiting their death. Extended families in developing nations today care for the old and disabled members of the clan because, in many cases, there exist no social security, medicare, nursing homes, and other protective programs.

The United States seems to follow the road taken by ancient Athens and Rome, however, as well as that of modern Sweden and Britain; to wit, it travels from affluence to altruism and perhaps to atrophy. To avoid the last stage, incentives for work and high productivity must be preserved, while bureaucracy and inefficiency must be discouraged. Presently, the major defects of the U.S. social security system are due to its attempt to serve both the insurance and the welfare objectives of the country. However, it is difficult to achieve these two objectives. It seems that splitting social security into its welfare and insurance components and funding the welfare segment out of general taxation would stabilize the system and eliminate the shadow of its bankruptcy.

Effects of Tax Changes on Economic Growth

Supply-side economists argue that tax cuts are self-financing through incentive effects on work, saving, investment, or tax nonavoidance. However, all three major taxcuts during this century (in the 1920s, 1960s, and 1980s) had small effects on raising tax revenue in the short run. The tax cut by the Kennedy administration in 1962, which can be considered as a Keynesian prescription with a supply-side flavor, had limited effects on tax revenues and significant stimulating effects on consumption. The 1981 tax cut had similar effects. In both cases tax revenues increased in the top brackets but not in the other income groups. It was estimated that only from the top 1.4 percent of tax returns, representing incomes of more than $75,000, tax revenue rose 4.3 percent; whereas for the rest of the income groups, tax revenues fell.[2] Even this small increase in tax revenue could be attributed to an increase in incomes from inflation, stimulated mainly from deficit spending, and to a rise in capital gains taxes. Moreover, when the Kennedy-Johnson tax cuts were enacted, inflation was only 1.2 percent and the budget deficit was virtually zero; whereas when the Reagan tax cuts were enacted inflation was 8 percent and the budget deficit close to $200 billion. The fact that inflation was kept low in the following few years despite the large deficit spendings and large tax cuts could be attributed to tight monetary policy, lower oil prices, foreign capital inflow, more competition in deregulated industries, and restraint in labor cost due to the deep recession of 1981–82. The effects of the tax rates reduction of 1986 on economic growth remain to be seen.

As argued earlier, tax policies play an important role in investment and growth rates. Countries with a relatively low average tax burden achieve higher real rates of economic growth than do countries with high tax burdens. Low taxes increase incentives to save and invest, to work hard, and to innovate toward higher levels of production. With high rates of economic growth, in turn, the tax base is expanded, total tax revenue increases, and government services are enhanced.

Empirically, tax increases had negative effects upon economic growth in the post–1950s period. Thus, an increase of 1 percent in the tax–GNP ratio was associated with a decrease in the rate of economic growth of 0.57 percent. When investment and labor force growth were introduced as additional independent variables, the GNP growth reduction, as a result of a 1 percent increase in the tax–GNP ratio, was 0.30 percent. Likewise, an increase in the total tax ratio of 1 percentage point was associated with a reduction in the rate of growth of investment by 0.66 percent.[3]

In low-tax countries employment rises more rapidly, as do investment and productivity. The reverse seems to be true for high-tax countries. Moreover, highly taxed affluent societies prefer leisure to hard work and high performance, and the result is low production incentives, a reduced competitive stimulus, relaxation in the introduction of modern technology, and retarded productivity growth.

Fiscal policies dealing with economic growth projections and sectoral investment allocation, explicitly or implicitly, use the incremental capital output ratio (ICOR), which is assumed to be constant. The higher the rate of economic growth projected, the higher the rate of investment (public and private) needed.[4] In turn, investment can be financed by savings that are derived from the public or the private sector or from abroad through net capital inflow. The primary concern of fiscal policy, then, is how to insure sufficient saving to finance projected investment without leading to an overall deficient demand and unemployment.

Thus assuming a rate of economic growth (g) of 4 percent, an ICOR (v) equal to 3, a government consumption rate (c) of 20 percent, a marginal private saving rate (s) of 6 percent, a net foreign capital outflow (f) of 10 percent, and an income velocity (k) of 4, it follows from the equation that a tax rate (t) (the tax to national income ratio) of 16 percent (0.1596) would be required:

$$t = \frac{c - s + g(v - 1/k) - f}{1 - s}$$

$$t = \frac{0.20 - 0.06 + 0.04(3 - 1/4) - 0.10}{1 - 0.06}$$

$$= \frac{0.14 + 0.12 - 0.01 - 0.10}{0.94}$$

$$= \frac{0.26 - 0.11}{0.94} = \frac{0.15}{0.94} = 0.1596$$

However, the capital output ratio, average or incremental, which is used to project saving or taxation to finance investment, is not a guide to the profitability or desirability of investment projects because it does not measure the average or marginal rate of return on capital. In order to determine in which sector or industry capital formation is more productive, the relative contribution of the services of capital or the property income share must be considered along with the capital output ratio.

From the viewpoint of society as a whole, social marginal productivity (SMP), namely, the additional national income or product and the improvement in the balance of payments of a country resulting from an additional unit of investment, private or public, is an effective tool in the hands of the government to weigh investment priorities or the improvement in social welfare. The social return on capital can be measured by dividing the value of output (V) minus the cost (C) of materials, depreciation, and labor over investment (I); that is (V - C)/I.

TAX INCENTIVES AND PRODUCTIVITY

Economic behavior in recent years focuses too much attention on consumption and not enough on investment to increase the capacity of productivity. To induce the private sector to consume less and save more, tax reforms, the cutting down of regulations, and the introduction of policies intended to increase investment are suggested to spur production incentives and expand supply. With such policies, total demand in the economy would not be diminished, but the mix would be different because spending for investment replaces spending for consumption. To reverse the slump in saving, which starves investment and feeds consumption, thrift stimulation through long-term tax incentives for individuals and enterprises should be considered.

Encouraging savings and investment by taxing wasteful spending rather than interest or dividends, and even by replacing personal income taxes with expenditures taxes, would stimulate work incentives and boost productivity. As noted earlier, the VAT, which is collected at the various stages of production on the additions each firm makes to the value of its products and services, is a tax on consumption that encourages savings and investment and therefore long-term productivity. The implementation of the VAT may help reduce bureaucracy and stimulate employment through capital formation. High tax rates on earned income destroy personal incentives to work, reduce productivity, and may have regressive effects. Tax reductions to stimulate production may pay for themselves by creating a surge in investment and new work effort, thereby increasing tax revenue. However, if tax cuts are not matched with selective tax increases that minimally affect production incentives, budget deficits may be pushed upward. Then, tax increases may be directed to that portion of income which is actually spent. Thus, a tax cut on personal income and/or a reduction in social security payroll tax may be matched with a sales or value-added tax, which discourages consumption and encourages savings and investment, especially when the propensity to consume is high. Moreover, a system of gradually vanishing income tax credits can make the VAT or any other consumption tax fair and progressive.

Although such "right kind" of tax structure, emphasizing reduction on overspending, would not be an economic panacea, it might help pep up investment, revive productivity, combat inflation, and stimulate exports. It would most probably have an anti-inflationary and anti-recessionary function, helping solve the dilemma of simultaneous inflation and unemployment, which plagues many market economies. Moreover, faster depreciation and lower capital gains taxes give opportunities to old enterprises to renew aging facilities and to young enterprises to satisfy their modern capital appetites.[5] Even to companies with losses, there might be provisions for investment tax credit refundable or payable by the government to the companies that owe no tax. Or there might be provisions for carrying backward or forward a tax loss to apply it against taxes paid on an earlier or later profitable year. To stimulate competition and encourage initial investment in productive businesses, favorable loans and a tax structure favoring small and new employment-creating firms could also be considered by the monetary or fiscal authorities. Perhaps borrowing funds from the private sector, by the government or other public enterprises for investment purposes, may be a proper policy when private businesses are unable or hesitate to invest in long-term projects. However, if such borrowing takes place to finance further consumption, then the government competes with productive enterprises for a finite supply of lendable money, and the rate of investment will decrease while the rate of inflation will increase from this type of deficit spending.

Sometimes large amounts of collected taxes are paid back through budget outlays to subsidize production of certain goods at proper levels. In these cases policymakers cannot escape from the well-accepted principle, "If you tax something, you get less of it. If you subsidize something, you get more of it."

The income tax base is affected by the degree of employment and productivity. Technological innovation introduces computers, microelectronics, satellite communications, and robotics, among other things, which reduce the opportunities for employment mainly in clerical and office work. To cut costs, spur productivity, and control the work process, managers introduce automation technologies that displace skilled employees and limit their exercise of independent judgment and creativity. Even the jobs created by computers and high tech are mostly simplified, dull, and low-wage positions that contribute relatively low amounts of tax revenues.

Employer-paid educational benefits are usually tax exempt. The idea is that such benefits upgrade the training and the skills of the employees. However, suggested tax reforms in the United States aim at taxing such investment in human capital, along with other fringe benefits. Concerned companies, universities, and other educational institutions argue that this would hurt U.S. competitiveness, which depends largely on the competence of the working people. Moreover, if such educational benefits become taxable, they argue, many companies would move toward the use of more in-house training programs that cannot be considered as complete substitutes of school training. For although on-the-job or in-house training plays an important role in the employees' improvement of skills, it does not provide the kind of classroom cross-fertilization that comes from students working at different industries and even in diverse countries. Making these benefits taxable and cutting financial aid to students in general would discourage incentives to modern education and reduce skills needed in modern brain-driven societies.

TAXATION AND INFLATION

Intentionally or unintentionally, inflation is an alternative way of transferring resources from the private to the public sector. Depending on the elasticity of taxes with respect to price increases, the influence of inflation on taxation has a profound effect on tax revenue. However, for indirect taxes, that is, consumption taxes, the impact of inflation on public revenue is less significant. Therefore, the impact of inflation on taxation depends on the tax structure and especially on the direct tax–indirect tax ratio.

Indirect taxes, which include production or value-added taxes, tariffs, sales taxes, excises, property taxes, and social security contributions by the employers, are more or less proportional to the value of goods and services upon which they are levied. Thus, one can expect an increase in prices to bring about an increase in indirect taxes that would, most probably, not affect the real value of *ad valorem* excises and other indirect taxes.

In the case of direct taxes, inflation pushes households up the progressive rate schedule and increases nominal and real income taxes. Furthermore, inflation reduces the real value of depreciation allowances, based on historical costs, and raises the effective rate of tax on the return to savings. Although under inflation the aggregate nominal gains realized from the sale of corporate stocks may be positive and high, real gains may be very low or negative. Inflation, then, provides additional tax revenues without any changes in the related laws and regulations. This takes place through nominal increases in income and spending *pari passu* with inflation.

These tax revenues finance additional expenditures that stimulate inflation (as

long as they are not directed toward productive investment), and the public sector
keeps on expanding. For the government, then, inflation seems to be a wonderful
tax. But for individuals, it poisons incentives, melts away savings, and weakens
the link between effort and reward. It is a form of transferring real purchasing
power from the private to the public sector. Thus, for governments inflationary
financing seems to have all the attractions of an invisible "indirect" tax. It is a
form of taxation that even the weakest government can enforce and the public
finds most difficult to evade. However, as Keynes pointed out, it gradually
debauches the currency and undermines the economic system of the country.
Indeed, Lenin once said that inflation invites state controls and sounds the death
knell of capitalism.

Inflation is directly related to government policy and as such is part of public
finance. It is a disguised or implicit tax, an attractive levy extensively used by
almost all governments, especially since the 1940s. Although even before tax
levying deliberate depreciation of monetary units was used by princes and rulers
throughout history to finance wars and other public services, modern governments
also resort to the process of printing money proportionately more than the increase
in real production. This is a way of transferring real goods and services to the
public sector from people holding or using cash and people receiving less increments than the rates of inflation as a remuneration for more real goods and
services they produce.

Government authorities frequently spend more than they collect from tax
revenue and finance the difference by borrowing from the public or through
money creation. In the United States, the supply of money is regulated by the
Fed through its seven-member board, which has control over bank reserves. In
most other countries, the control over money rests with the central banks, which
are under the control of the government. When the U.S. Treasury or the government borrows from the Fed or the central bank to finance its deficit, most
frequently the result is, not higher interest rates and lower private investment
and consumption, but an increase in money supply that is higher than the increase
in real goods and services, especially if resources are fully employed or serious
rigidities exist in the economy.

Making real tax rates sensitive to inflation would also help corporations eliminate the effects of inflation on depreciation expenses and inventory estimations.
When the original acquisition or historical cost, and not the replacement cost,
is used to measure depreciation and inventories, their true value is underestimated. In both cases, lower costs enter into the accounting process and higher
taxes are paid on the inflated profits. However, outstanding debt liabilities of
the government, corporations, and individuals fall in real terms with ongoing
inflation; but the difference is not taxed, and so real gains are realized as a result
of inflation. It is questionable, though, if the inflationable favorable results of
corporate debt offset the unfavorable ones from depreciation and inventory expenses. Moreover, with the expectation of inflation, people and institutions try
to convert money into goods and real property for which prices are expected to

rise, while the values of fixed claims, such as bonds, fall and their yield rates rise. Also, interest rates rise in order to accommodate rates of inflation, and the velocity of money circulation rises as people rush to get rid of cash to avoid the impact of inflation.

For implementing fiscal measures to reduce inflation and to dwindle the power of labor, a production cost control policy may be more effective and more humane, instead of using the nineteenth-century income policies of creating slack markets and high unemployment. To move from large deficits toward balanced budgets through extensive spending cuts or tax increases may result in severe slumps, as happened in 1936–37. Using cautiously and gradually both tools and implementing selective controls on production costs may reduce deficits without penalizing the economy with disastrous recessions and depressions.

Tax Indexing

To minimize distortions on the tax system caused by inflation and to protect the taxpayers from automatic tax increases, tax indexing is contemplated from time to time. Such an automatic adjustment of tax rates is expected to benefit the taxpayers and increase economic efficiency, but it may instead perpetuate inflation. To keep tax increases tied to increases in real income, rather than to illusory increases, indexation was introduced in the United States in 1985. It was estimated that $91 billion was *not* collected in 1985–88 because of indexation.

The progressive tax on personal and corporate incomes involves higher rates on successively higher nominal money incomes. Thus, a single person with $20,000 taxable income in 1987 would have paid a tax of $3,351, or an average rate of 16.8 percent. Suppose inflation is 50 percent in a period of five years and the individual's money income increases also by 50 percent, keeping pace with inflation. Then the tax on the fifth year's taxable income of $30,000 would be $6,363, or an average rate of 21.2 percent; that is, there would be an increase from 16.8 percent to 21.2 percent, although there would be no rise in real income. On a proportional basis the individual would have paid $5,040, but with the progressiveness of income taxes he pays $1,323 more. This means a transfer of real income from the individual to the government of more than $1,500—a transfer that takes place through the invisible hand of inflation. Thus, even a temporary inflation would have a long-run effect that would not be readily corrected.

Also, the purchasing power of a personal exemption would be reduced unless increased by 50 percent to cover inflation. Likewise, if an asset was bought for $10,000 and sold for $15,000, there would be taxation on the $5,000 nominal gain although no real gain would have occurred. From these examples, it becomes obvious that in order to isolate the progressive income tax rates from the effects of inflation, an adjustment for the declining purchasing power of taxable income becomes necessary. This can be done by introducing a price-level index to make the tax rate structure inflation-proof, which, at the same time, removes the bias toward a growing public sector.

The indexing tax cuts which started in 1985 increased the $1,000-a-person exemption by 4.1 percent to $1,040 for that year. The single-taxpayer deduction rose from $2,300 to $2,390, and for joint returns the deduction rose from $3,400 to $3,540, while tax brackets were widened by 4.1 percent to allow more income to be taxed at lower rates. Social security benefits were also increased by 3.5 percent, so that the average retired person received $15 extra per month, or $449. Also, in 1985 the average elderly couple received $26 extra, or a total of $776 per month. Someone entitled to the maximum benefits who retired at age 65 in 1984 received $728 per month in 1985. Similar anti-inflationary adjustments have been made thereafter.

The present U.S. consumer price index, CPI, which can be used for tax indexing, is based on a survey of 23,000 businesses, instead of the former 18,000 retailers, and in 85 cities, instead of the former 56 cities. The spending patterns include workers, clerks, the self-employed, retirees, and the unemployed in the new all-urban consumer index, while the number of commodities includes several thousands in the base year and the current year.[6]

DISTRIBUTIONAL EFFECTS OF TAXATION

Progressive taxes, which increase proportionately more than income, are criticized as doing great harm to people's incentives and to the efficiency of resources, discouraging job-making investment. And taxes on corporate income are criticized because they discourage new ventures and lead to unfair double taxation on corporate earnings and on stockholder dividends. However, part of corporate earnings may not be distributed to stockholders but retained by the corporations (plowed-back profits), thereby not being subject to double taxation.

The progressive income tax structure diverts ever-larger shares of pretax income into taxes, thus reducing discretionary income. It discourages investments, which are required for modernization and improvement of equipment, and kills initiative. From that point of view, the use of taxes for curbing inflation may prove to be counterproductive, for it discourages investment and reduces supply in such a way that the cure may turn out to be more harmful than the disease itself. In any case, tax incentives for investment stimulation and industrial growth should not be used to shore up obsolescence and perpetuate inefficiency.

Progressive taxation may help reduce income inequalities. This can be shown by the taxation effect on income distribution in Figure 7.1. The area of inequality on the Lorenz diagram is smaller after tax than before tax. Also, the Gini ratio, that is, the distance of the after-tax Lorenz curve of inequality over the total distance below the equality (45°) line (EB/EP), or 20/80 = 0.25, is smaller than the distance of before-tax curve (EA/EP), or 40/80 = 0.50. Such a Gini ratio is estimated to be about 0.65 for the United States and other market economies. If all tax liabilities are raised by the same percentage, revenue will increase

Figure 7.1
Lorenz Curve of Inequality and Taxation Effects

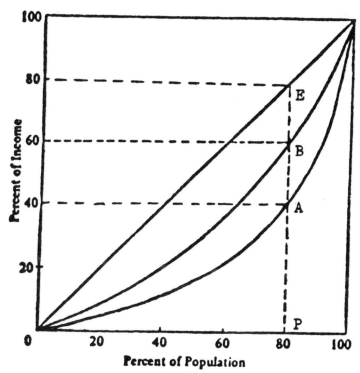

without changing the rate structure. Also, tax rates may be changed and total revenue remain the same.

To approach equitable taxation or equal sacrifice in the process of distribution of real tax burden, the government, without disturbing economic efficiency, could use a mix of direct and indirect taxes. In such an equity-efficiency trade-off, governments usually leave low incomes untaxed or even subsidize them and impose greater burdens on high incomes, tending toward an egalitarian society, at the same time imposing taxes on certain unhealthy commodities such as tobacco, alcohol, and even gasoline. However, incentives for people to work harder and to increase their income should be preserved so that the dilemma of a more egalitarian but poorer society be avoided.

Regarding the distribution of the tax burden, or the incidence of various taxes, it can be postulated that individual income taxes stay with the wage earner. Payroll taxes are paid partly by the employees and partly by employers, who usually shift them to consumers. Depending on the degree of competition, corporation income taxes fall partly on consumption, partly on employees' remuneration, and partly on capital income (mainly shareholder dividends in the short run and property ownership in the long run). Likewise, property taxes fall on homeowners (residences) or on tenants, while business property taxes fall partly on consumers and partly on property owners. The impact of excise and sales taxes falls primarily on consumers, through price raising, and that of estate and gift taxes upon donors.

Government taxes directly or indirectly affect prices and reduce real disposable income, that is, after-tax personal income adjusted for inflation. Although individual income taxes are not shiftable, changes in tax rates influence people's incentives to work and save, as do payroll taxes levied on the employees. As already pointed out, excise and sales taxes fall mainly on consumption and as such are largely regressive.[7] Depending on the elasticities of the taxed goods, relative prices of these goods change, affecting accordingly interpersonal tax distributions in different areas.

However, there exist a number of legislative loopholes and instances of tax evasion that make progressive or graduated taxes less effective in their function of reducing inequalities. To reduce loopholes and tax evasion, governments try to dig deep into high incomes but frequently with limited results. But progressive taxes take large amounts of money from frugal people and tend to reduce saving and increase consumption through a more equitable distribution. This is a process that threatens further inflation in the case of high levels of spending without equivalent high levels of production and supply.

Legislative loopholes may include exemptions on personal income, on income from interest, on dividends, on owner-occupied homes, on tax-exempt bonds, on drilling operations and some other forms of productive investment, on income averages for previous years, and on long-run capital gains.

Here one can accept what Joan Robinson pointed out in her review of Keynes's *General Theory of Employment*, that there are inherent incompatibilities of full employment and price stability that offset income distribution. The use of taxation and/or expenditures for countercyclical reasons is not effective enough in leading the economy to the plateau of full employment with no inflation or deflation. What is common in modern economies instead is the widespread dilemma of simultaneous inflation and unemployment. To subside inflation without increasing unemployment, a tax measure, among other measures, is to introduce in particular enterprises tax rebates to employees receiving salary increases below a certain percentage of expected inflation and to the firms for low price increases, thereby reducing the firms' income tax liabilities. However, this measure might create administrative problems and possible distortions in the labor market as employees try to move to firms offering higher real salaries, not because of high productivity, but because of the related rebates.

To mitigate high inequalities, the government implements fiscal and monetary measures that vary according to the political philosophy of the party in power. Such measures include progressive taxation, tax exemptions, social security and Medicare programs, subsidies and welfare benefits, mortgage interest rates determination, educational loans and aid, decentralization policies toward less-developed rural and urban regions, and the like. Those policies make income inequalities less severe than wealth inequalities.

Thus, in the United States the average chief executive's salary was $775,000 in 1984, while 30 million families had income varying from $20,000 to $40,000 and 35.3 million Americans, or 15.2 percent of the population, were classified as poor, with incomes below $5,061 per person and less than $10,178 per family of four, according to the Census Bureau. However, concentration of wealth in the United States is high. Only 2 percent of U.S. families own 50 percent of common stock, 39 percent of all bonds, and 71 percent of tax-free securities. The top fifth of Americans own more than 75 percent of personal wealth, that is, three times more than the total wealth of the bottom 80 percent.

There was not much change in the percentage share of aggregate money income by the different income groups during the last two decades. The highest fifth of households continued to absorb about 44 percent of total national income, followed by the next fifth with 25 percent, and the third fifth with 17 percent. The lowest fifth of households absorbed only about 4 percent of aggregate national income and the second fifth around 10 percent. In spite of a growing economy, the number of Americans living in poverty in 1987 totaled 32.5 million or 13.5 percent of the population; that is, for families of four incomes was less than $11,611 and for single persons less than $5,800. Some 21.4 million (10.5 percent) whites, 9.68 million (33.1 percent) blacks, and 5.47 million (28.2 percent) Hispanics lived in poverty that year. One American family in six is now headed by a single woman.

TAX REFORMS

Complexities and Efficiency

The modern U.S. income tax, which originated in the nineteenth century, was first applied mainly as a protest against raising revenues from sales taxes and tariffs. However, the many exceptions, deductions, and credits introduced later have made the tax code highly complex and inefficient. For purposes of tax advantages alone, individuals and businesses are steered to nonproductive tax shelters. On the other hand, some industries enjoy tax benefits not available to other industries, especially those in the modern high-technology sector. For these and many other reasons drastic tax reforms were suggested and implemented by the Reagan administration and the U.S. Congress.[8]

Complicated tax laws and regulations may please accountants and lawyers specializing in taxation, but they are painful and detrimental to the rest of the taxpayers, who may find it difficult to keep up with all the requirements, loopholes, and related changes. Also, politicians and public servants may find themselves in trouble because they or their accountants are not familiar with all tax legislations and their frequent changes and reforms. Candidates for public offices

may be challenged for, or accused of, tax code violations, although their mis-
demeanor may have been the result of their not knowing all the changes and
complexities of the tax system.

Frequent tax reforms make the tax system more complex by adding new
legislation and more pages to the existing numerous volumes. Indeed, since
1975, tax reform bills have added about 2,000 new pages to the basic 1954 tax
code of some 1,000 pages, plus more than 4,000 pages accompanying legislative
history by Congress. Pressure groups, some 10,000 special-interest lobbyists in
Washington, D.C., and political compromises are responsible for new loopholes.
But in many instances a loophole for one group becomes a burden for another
group or the rest of the taxpayers. Thus, tax reductions for charitable contributions, for expenses on research and development, for interest on mortgages,
and so many other cases of tax credits eventually fall on other taxpayers who
pay for the budgetary revenue required. Moreover, frequent changes regarding
exceptions and reforms in tax rules complicate decision making and provide
incentives for their manipulation by individuals and businesses.

As a result of the complicated tax system, diversion of capital into tax gim-
micks takes place, new business development is held back, and unemployment
is kept high. Many people retreat behind tax shelters while additional labor and
new investment and enterprising are discouraged. Considering these drawbacks,
it would seem reasonable to seek tax revisions toward low, simple, and fair tax
rates and a few broad exclusions that would enhance incentives to work and
productivity and reduce unemployment and idle capacity. In addition, the lab-
yrinth of the current tax code with more than 5,000 pages, plus 10,000 more
pages of IRS interpretations, would be simplified. Looking back to 1913, for
example, one will find that the original tax forms were one-page documents
only.

The main question in tax policies is how to get more revenue or at least keep
the same revenue while increasing simplicity, fairness, and economic efficiency.
It seems that any taxpayer favors tax changes as long as taxes are expected to
be reduced or at least not to be increased. Tax changes, though, mostly mean
redistributing existing tax burdens, mainly through closing loopholes and broad-
ening the tax base so that total revenue will increase, or not decline, and incentives
to work will be preserved.

Policies of simple and low tax rates aim at higher efficiency and fairness. In
addition, one can expect a great deal of bureaucratic complication and waste to
be reduced or eliminated, as well as a reduction in incentives to cheat and resort
to the underground economy. Concomitantly, many tax-preparing agencies and
persons, as well as employees of the tax authorities and tribes of lawyers and
judges, would be released to devote their energies for more productive endeavors.

A tax surcharge is also suggested as a separate sinking fund for debt retirement.
Such a deficit sinking fund, through a surcharge tax on income or, better, on
consumption, which would exist outside of the budget, would be used to buy
U.S. Treasury securities in the open market.[9] A similar measure was used by

U.S. Treasurer Alexander Hamilton to retire the large debt created during the War of Independence.

Major Changes by the Tax Reform Act of 1986

In addition to the reduction of the tax brackets and the top tax rates for personal and corporation income taxes, mentioned previously, the tax reforms of 1986 introduced the following changes:[10]

- Increases in individual exemptions to $1,900 for 1987, $1,950 for 1988, and $2,000 for 1989 and later years (up from $1,080).

- Increases in the standard deductions to $5,000 for married taxpayers filing jointly (beginning in 1988), $3,000 for single taxpayers, and $2,500 for married taypayers filing separately. Beginning in 1989, these deductions are indexed to reflect inflation. Also, persons earning $149,250 or more cannot use personal exemptions and the 15 percent tax bracket benefits. For married taxpayers filing jointly, the phasing out of these benefits begins after taxable income reaches $71,900 and is complete when income reaches $149,250; for single taxpayers, the 15 percent tax bracket benefits begin to phase out when taxable income reaches $43,150 and are completely phased out when income reaches $89,560; for married taxpayers filing separately, the income range is $35,950 to $113,300; while for heads of households it is $61,650 to $123,790. Moreover, when personal incomes exceed the above various ending levels set for the phase out of the 15 percent tax bracket, the personal exemptions also begin to erode.

- After 1986, income averaging does not exist, as does not the 10 percent deduction for the smaller income of two-earner couples.

- Beginning in 1987, all unemployment benefits will be fully taxed.

- State and local sales tax deductions are repealed beginning in 1987. Also, only those who itemize their deductions can write off their charitable donations and moving expenses; while political contributions can no longer be used for tax credit.

- Only medical expenses that exceed 7.5 percent of the adjusted gross income can be tax deductible.

- Miscellaneous itemized deductions will be deductible only to the extent that they exceed 2 percent of the adjusted gross income. They include union dues, work, clothing, unreimbursed employee business expenses, employment agency fees, job hunting expenses, and safety box rentals.

- Mortgage interest on first and second homes is still deductible.

- Consumer interest will be 100 percent deductible in 1986, only 65 percent deductible in 1987, 40 percent in 1988, 20 percent in 1989, and 10 percent in 1990; there is no deduction for consumer interest after 1990.

- Persons older than 55 years can still claim as much as $125,000 of the profit from the sale of their personal residence as tax deductible.

- Self-employed persons can deduct 25 percent of the health insurance premiums paid for themselves and their families.

- Business meals and entertainment expenses can be deducted from income by only 80 percent.
- Casualty losses are tax deductible only to the extent that they exceed 10 percent of the adjusted gross income.
- Americans working abroad can deduct $70,000 earned income, compared to $80,000 previously.

PART III

POLICY IMPLICATIONS

Countercyclical Public Policy

ECONOMIC FLUCTUATIONS AND FISCAL PROBLEMS

The main goals of the U.S. economy, which refer primarily to full employment, economic growth, price stability, balance-of-payments equilibrium, and a more equitable distribution of income, can be pursued by the proper coordination of fiscal and monetary policies. Fiscal policy is the manipulation of the governmental budget, that is, variations in expenditures and taxes for countercyclical effects in the economy. Monetary policy deals with the economy's supply of money and credit.

In previous chapters we outlined the complications that may arise from excessive market failures to stabilize the economy and bring about full employment without inflation. Growing monopolistic or oligopolistic conditions, even outside the area of public utilities and natural monopolies, require government intervention via regulations and fiscal policy measures. In many cases, though, government intervention and fiscal measures may introduce their own distortions and inefficiencies and wide disagreements may arise over whether free market forces or public policies are more beneficial to economic stability and growth.

From time to time, the economy is affected by business fluctuations. Prosperity or boom, recession or slack, depression or crisis, and revival or recovery, these are the main phases of economic fluctuations, have individual personalities from the point of view of intensity and duration, and usually do not balance each other. More or less, the economy faces a never-ending movement of ups and downs comparable to what the mythological figure Sisyphus faced when he was condemned to push a boulder up a mountain time after time, only to see it roll back down upon him.

In the upswing stage of the economy, factor imbalances and sectoral bottlenecks lead to price increases that in turn reduce the power of the monetary unit of the country and create the economic and psychological environment for the next stage of downswing movement. To avoid sharp ups and downs in the economy or to smooth out the cycles, the government implements temporary or permanent measures, which vary from time to time. Thus the Roosevelt administration introduced the New Deal in 1933, which took the United States off the gold standard and by the use of widespread monetary and fiscal measures brought about sweeping changes in the depression-racked market economy. Next, in 1962 the Kennedy administration introduced wage-price guideposts to achieve higher rates of employment and growth with stable prices. The Nixon administration introduced in 1971–74 controls (Phases I to IV) to freeze prices and wages and suspended the dollar-gold convertibility (floating dollar).

In cases of severe inflation, an effective price-wage control machinery need not be elaborate. Controls can, for the most part, be limited to the operations of the largest corporations and unions, leaving the rest of the economy to free market forces. This type of upper economic level controls would save the administration from the huge bureaucracy necessitated by detailed and largely ineffective and painful controls.

Occasionally, there are cases in which business tends to thrust itself into social fields and governments into business operations. The constructive partnership of these two institutions may be helpful for many socioeconomic and urban problems in the future. The National Corporation for Housing Partnership, Amtrak (The National Railroad Passenger Corporation), Comsat (The Communications Satellite Corporation), and many other hybrid activities on local or national levels are some of the prototypes of such operations. The establishment of mixed boards of directors, partially elected and partially appointed, with six to eight years' tenure may be one of the effective ways of management and public accountability. (Chapter 3 deals in more detail with such partnerships between the public and private sectors.)

Although there is strong criticism of the bureaucratic public sector, investment spending by the public sector, particularly in public utility projects where the private sector is unable or hesitates to invest, increases expectations of economic stimulation. These expectations arise in the same manner as the private investment, since they are based on the positive effects of the multiplier and the accelerator. In case of a slackening economy any form of public spending would have beneficial effects on the market sector demand and production by offsetting the deflationary impact of a rising propensity to save.

When the public sector devotes high proportions of spending to investment and exports, there might arise expectations for a better growth performance. Hence, it would be difficult to establish causality of a growing public sector leading to low growth performance. In many cases growth performance depends on the managerial efficiency and technological innovations affected by the decisionmakers in charge of public enterprises and the public sector in general.

Regarding the question of whether the taxpayers are willing to support government programs and a growing public sector and pay more taxes, the answer seems to be no. Frequently, governments impose taxes on individuals to finance expenditures, instead of monitoring their demand for governmental services.

However, it should be recognized that the main area of governmental activities lies in services of a general sort, such as civil administration and defense, which cannot be sold at a price to individuals and are collectively consumed. Hence, there is no automatic mechanism by which one may compare cost with benefits of government services and it is difficult to determine how far government expenditures for specific services may go.

FISCAL MEASURES TO INFLUENCE PRICES AND OUTPUT

Increase in prices is a serious economic problem for the fiscal and monetary authorities. Because of its importance, an extensive survey of its sources and cyclical effects is needed.

It seems that a limited range of price raising or inflation may be required to mobilize resources for investment. But if inflation continues for a long period, it may hamper growth. This is a danger, for entrepreneurs and investors may expect the inflationary trend to go on and thus prefer speculation and quick profits in services and short-term trading instead of long-term productive investment. Accepting the argument and some inflation is necessary to discourage hoarding and encourage investment, the question is, How much? Is an annual increase in prices of 2 percent or 3 percent endurable? And what may be the role of the public sector in keeping inflation at desirable levels and at the same time stimulating investment and growth?

Economists like W. Arthur Lewis, Gunnar Myrdal and Paul Samuelson argue that some degree of inflation helps economic growth, provided that it is kept within bounds. They seem to accept as desirable an average increase in prices of 2 percent to 3 percent per annum. Keynes also thought that inflation promotes growth by redistributing income from people with high consumption rates to producers and entrepreneurs with high rates of saving and investment. Inflation attracts resources, while deflation expels or drives them out of a certain sector, according to inflationists.

If productivity is not increased equiproportionally to wages and profits, prices will go up and people with fixed or low increments in income will be the victims. In many cases, the government, through protective legislation or arbitration, may interfere in favor of the general public and the economy as a whole. But giant oligopolistic corporations and powerful labor unions may exert pressure upon the government to side in favor of one or the other party.

Demand-Pull, Cost-Push and Structural Inflation: Measures to Curb It

When aggregate demand is higher than supply, there will be pressure on prices to rise. Such excess demand over supply may be due to an increase in population, an increase in spending by the same population (stimulated by governmental spending, increase in money supply, credit, and other expansionary measures), or by external factors like wars, floods, and similar phenomena, which tend to reduce total supply of goods and services, as they keep or increase total demand. In any case, when demand is rising more than supply, prices are going up. This is demand-pull inflation, which can be curbed by restrictive and austerity measures.

As a result of fixed wage levels and excessive social security payments practiced at times by the government, wages may be artificially high in relation to labor productivity. Very often the government, in alliance with labor unions, lays down wage rules and ultimatums to producers, regardless of the costs involved, thus stimulating cost-push inflation. This is an anomaly that may intensify the misallocation of labor and create unemployment. Producers may also, under monopolistic conditions, increase prices to earn more profits.

In addition to demand-pull and cost-push inflation, there are structural factors in the economy that may create inflation. The failure of some sectors to supply what the demand requires causes increases in prices. Factors that are chronically structured into the economy and cause price changes may include noncompeting labor groups and factor immobility, disequilibria in foreign trade, rigidities in raw material supplies and income distribution, and other sociopolitical bottlenecks. Conventional fiscal and monetary measures may be unable to restrain price increases. Structural changes in production, imports, and income distribution, and not changes in money income and demand, may sometimes be needed to correct rigidities in economic activities.

If structural rigidities are ignored, monetary and fiscal measures to curb inflation may, through restrictions in bank credit and holding down wages and prices, be directed to the symptoms of the disease, not to its real cause. They may in fact do more harm than good by depressing output and reducing employment. They may turn out to be ineffective and superficial anti-inflationary factors if the fundamental underlying structural factors continue to exist.

As Hippocrates once pointed out centuries ago, serious sickness requires strong medicine. But to take strong fiscal and monetary measures to terminate or drastically reduce inflation would cause hardship, unemployment, and possibly political and social unrest. A gradual reduction in the rate of inflation can solve the problem without causing widespread dissension.

To reduce the rate of inflation gradually several remedies may be applied depending on the causes. If it is a demand-pull inflation, then overspending should be reduced and purchasing power curtailed. This measure may require a simultaneous reduction in bank loans and in money supply, an increase in taxes, encouragement of savings (through the reduction or abolition of taxes on interest or the increase on the rate of interest banks pay to savings), or the use of an anti-inflationary budget. If it is a cost-push inflation, controls on strong unions and big corporations may be required to arrest wage-price spirals in a noncompetitive market. Such controls substitute public for private wage and price fixing.

In any case, efforts to increase the supply of goods and services should be intensified. Increase in production is always beneficial, especially in cases of structural rigidities. Such rigidities, however, manifest themselves in inelastic supplies, and it should be recognized that it is therefore difficult to change production in the short run by changes in prices.

At the same time, some changes in the distribution of income by helping the old, weak, and small, from whom inflation takes the most, and by absorbing from the affluent, big and organized, to whom inflation gives the most, may accompany some or all of the anti-inflationary measures taken. Furthermore, since the news media have the ability to spread rapidly and even exaggerate economic trends and expectations, quick and careful reaction is required in claiming and publicizing in advance anti-inflationary measures to be taken in the near future. Such a policy would restrain inflationary psychology in periods of rapid inflation.

Demand Stimulation and Price and Output Changes

After the Great Depression of the 1930s, the United States and other Western governments successfully used Keynesian fiscal policies to cure some of their economic ills, such as unemployment, low productivity, and uncompetitiveness. At times of inflationary spirals they put more emphasis to monetarism and supply-side economics; at other times, they turned to the use of fiscal policy. Sometimes they used a combination of both approaches.

As has already been noted, an effective tool used in cases of recession to stimulate income and employment is the tax cut, which was used primarily during 1962 and 1981–83. The last U.S. tax cut (a cut of some 25 percent) was also used to undo part of the inflation-induced bracket creep during the 1970s. But while the average effective tax rate, as percentage of earned personal income, declined from about 25 percent to 22 percent it still remained above the 20 percent to 21 percent of the early 1970s. On the other hand, the reduction in tax rates in 1986 was considered as revenue neutral. In any case, tax cuts and other fiscal measures have been used in the past to influence aggregate demand and increase output and employment. Along these lines, it is estimated that 3 percent in output growth is related to 1 percent reduction in unemployment (Okun's law).

Figure 8.1 shows the relationship between prices and output, which is considered to change together with employment. A higher equilibrium of output (Q) and price (P) from E to E' may be achieved by raising government expenditures, lowering taxation, or increasing the money supply. Such measures increase the aggregate demand and shift the demand curve from D to D', leading to higher employment and output (Q') but also to a higher price (P'). This is a process of demand-pull inflation that also creates more jobs as long as there is unemployment. If full employment output is reached, any additional spending leads only to inflation.

Figure 8.1
Equilibria of Output and Prices

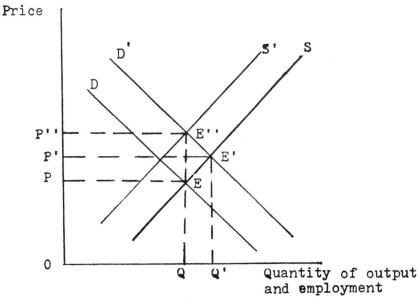

Assuming other things remain the same, given an increase in the cost of production, from a rise in wages or raw material prices, for example, the supply curve shifts from S to S' and the new equilibrium of output and price from E' to E". At this point, prices increased to P", while output decreased from Q' to Q because some people cannot afford to buy at this high price. This is the case of cost-push inflation, which leads to lower real production and less employment. New efforts by the public sector to reduce unemployment by stimulating aggregate demand would shift the demand curve further to the right. Then together with higher employment and output, prices would increase, generating a wage-price-wage spiral as one price tends to lead to another. To stop this spiral, governments from time to time resort to wage-price guideposts, that is, an increase in wages equal to the increase in labor productivity without rising price. An increase in wages that is higher than productivity may take place, though, as long as a small increase in prices is projected.

From a socioeconomic standpoint, there is pressure for additional government services in the form of higher social security payments, distribution of more welfare, higher and extended unemployment benefits, better health coverage, education improvement, better police and fire protection, and similar other social services. There is also an increasing demand for greater fringe benefits in private enterprises. Greater pensions, longer vacations, improved work conditions, and better health and life insurance coverage are claimed by people working in private firms. All these claims exercise great pressures upon prices and generate what has recently been called social inflation. Expenditures for antipollution measures or depollution equipment and the protection of the natural environment by private firms or governments are also pushing prices up.

The Dilemma of Inflation and Unemployment

As mentioned earlier, in their effort to achieve high rates of growth governments face the problem of inflationary spirals. To reconcile high employment and growth with price stability they try to apply the most suitable tools of fiscal and monetary policy. If such policy tools are not effective enough and conflicts between high employment and price stability exist, then more drastic measures, like structural reforms and wage-price controls should be set forth. Such compulsory controls have on occasion been imposed in the United States, England, and other countries in order to curb inflation and avoid extensive unemployment.

The trade-off between inflation and unemployment, that is, the decrease of the rate of inflation at the sacrifice of an increase in the rate of unemployment, seems to be verified empirically (the Phillips' curve) and accepted by policy-makers. For the United States, however, this trading-off did not materialize in the 1970s or even a little later, since both inflation and unemployment were then high. The anti-inflationary measures taken during that period brought high rates of unemployment through reduction in investment, as was expected, but they did not curb inflation. This might be due to the existence of the noncompeting groups in the U.S. economy and the sluggish adjustment in the shift of labor from industry to industry. Labor-saving technological progress and the constant increase in the labor force, as well as the increase in oil prices, might be considered additional reasons that explain the simultaneous existence of inflation and unemployment. Furthermore, prevailing inflationary psychology, various forms of social welfare, and excessive budgetary expenditures kept overall demand at high levels.

This dilemma of simultaneous inflation and unemployment, which neither the neoclassical nor the Keynesian theory can explain, led to a shift from the demand-side policy in favor of supply-side policy in the 1980s. And the question is whether or not this dilemma will appear in the future. Even though one cannot call upon the oracle of Delphi, once used in the Temple of Apollo, in ancient Greece, to make either pessimistic or optimistic predictions, one may expect similar conditions to appear in the future, especially when serious structural bottlenecks inhibit factor and product adjustments to the market forces of supply and demand.

Traditional economic theory suggests that measures to curb inflation usually lead to unemployment. But to have both inflation and unemployment at the same time is an unjustifiable condition, a strange phenomenon. This paradox, the simultaneous existence of both inflation and unemployment, which is known as stagflation, is due mainly to the imperfection of domestic markets. As they waiver between the Scylla of inflation and the Charybdis of unemployment, policymakers may deviate from traditional economic principles and adopt control measures such as wage and price freezes or rationing in order to correct the situation. In modern times, politicians and democratic governments are inclined to accept inflation but not high unemployment, since the latter is not highly correlated with reelection. Of the two evils, unemployment is the worse. It is more painful not to have a job and, therefore, have no income rather than to have a job and suffer a somewhat inflated income.

Figure 8.2 (a) shows the empirically established Phillips curve, which indicates a possible trade-off between unemployment and inflation. For example, a reduction in the rate of inflation from 8 percent to 4 percent leads to an increase in the rate of unemployment from 4 percent to 6 percent. However, if fiscal and monetary measures to curb inflation result in the expected increase of unemployment from 4 percent to 6 percent, but not to any decrease in inflation, probably because of the anticipated inflation by the public, what we can observe is an outward shift of the Phillips curve (I) to a new position (II). Another way of presenting the relationship of inflation and unemployment is to replace the Philips curve by the so-called acceleration curve, which relates the unemployment rate, not with the rate of inflation, but with the rate of change in the pace of inflation, as Figure 8.2 (b) shows.

The fact that inflationary expectations appear to play a major role in price and wage decisions makes the acceleration curve more useful than the Phillips curve for the explanation of the relationship between inflation and unemployment. This is because each specific rate of unemployment corresponds to a particular rate of change in the pace of inflation rather than to a particular rate of inflation. The trade-off is not between unemployment and inflation but between unemployment and the speed and direction of change in inflation.

The traditional application of a trade-off between unemployment and inflation, therefore, may be misleading because it may institutionalize inflation without lowering unemployment. People seem to form expectations about future price and wage behavior on the basis of their experience in the years or months just past. As wage earners find their real income eroded and employers easily yield to demands for wage increases and then jack up prices immediately, rising prices will tend to push inflation up.

If a particular rate of inflation becomes fully expected, there is a certain rate of unemployment consistent with maintaining this expectation over time; this is called the natural rate. If this natural rate is relatively high, the result is the phenomenon of slumpflation. This natural rate of unemployment depends on such things as the supply of cooperating factors combined with labor, composition of the labor force (age, race, sex), restrictions on job entry, efficiency of labor markets regarding job information and mobility, and taxation. If unemployment drops substantially below this natural rate, which for the United States is probably about 5 percent, inflation will tend to resume its upward march. Empirically,

Figure 8.2
The Stagflation Paradox

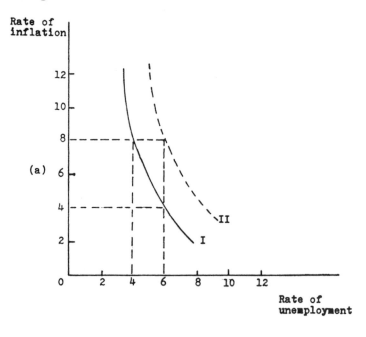

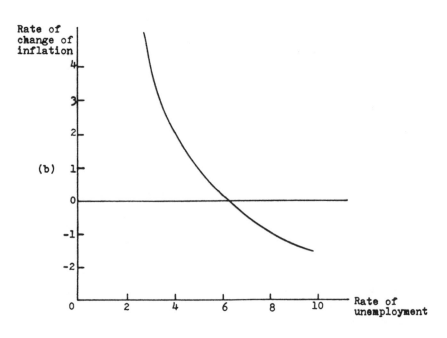

for each percentage point change in inflation there is an opposite change of about two million jobs in the United States, or roughly 2 percent of the labor force.

Inflation also affects interest rates to a large extent. A statistical correlation of these two variables for the years 1960–82, indicates a close positive relationship between them, with a regression coefficient 0.63 for the United States. This means that when inflation increases by 1 percent, interest rates increase by 0.63 percent. Although monetary policymakers sometimes determine interest rates arbitrarily, as happened to some extent in the early 1980s, they cannot deviate much from this relationship and the supportive market forces of supply and demand.

RELATIONSHIP OF GOVERNMENT SPENDING, INTEREST AND EMPLOYMENT

At times, the government uses investment and public employment programs or subsidies to provide employment as a means of alleviating both general unemployment and particular distributional inequalities in depressed sectors and regions. On many occasions when lagging demand tends to stagnate the economy and in order to avoid high unemployment, the government may resort to investment and income policies.

The government's demand for skilled personnel and its wage policies have an important influence on macroeconomic policies, budgetary considerations, and income distribution. This is particularly so for developing nations where total public sector employment averages 44 percent of nonagricultural employment, compared with 24 percent for Western developed nations. However, developed market economies have, on the average, seven general government employees per hundred inhabitants (excluding employees of nonfinancial public enterprises), in contrast to only three in developing countries. This is so because of the large agricultural sector in the latter group of countries. In the United States, there were 16.7 million public sector employees (2.9 million in federal government) in 1986, out of a 117.8 total labor force, that is, 14.2 percent only.[1]

On a per capita basis, the number of government employees rises with the rise of per capita income, especially after a certain level of income is achieved. This rise reflects a relatively greater importance of state and local government employees, regardless of the size of population. Central government employees are better paid than those in state or local governments, while nonfinancial public enterprises generally pay higher wages compared to government employees at all levels. However, average wages of employees at all levels of government are not much different than those paid by the private sector.

It would seem that job creation subsidies for hard-to-place persons have limited success. From a distributional point of view, government expenditures through supported work programs might have the same impact as through existing income maintenance systems. In many cases, though, governments resort to growing unproductive spending to reduce unemployment. However, when taxes or other revenues are available, government programs should be selected on their effi-ciency rather than their redistributive effects. Such a policy is expected in the long run to reduce the income gap ratio and the Gini coefficient of income distribution among the poor, as well as unemployment, which exerts strong influence on the popularity of parties and politicians.

Fiscal measures to stimulate the economy include increases in government expenditures and decreases in taxes. A rise in government expenditures in the form of investment, transfer payments, or other kinds of spending will increase autonomous demand and stimulate the economy. A reduction in taxes will leave taxpayers with a larger income to spend. Again, a rise in spending by taxpayers will increase aggregate demand and stimulate economic activity. In both cases, if there is unemployment in the economy, one can expect employment and production to rise. The opposite holds true when expenditures are reduced and taxes are raised.

Also, aggregate demand is affected by liquidity preference functions. Ac-cording to the Keynesian prescription, if people prefer less liquidity, they will release and use idle cash balances and so aggregate demand will increase. This is another form of stimulation of the economy. And vice versa, if people prefer more liquidity, they will reduce spending, and so aggregate demand will decline.

The relationship between interest rates and national output or product, when planned spending equals income that is, when aggregate supply equals aggregate demand, can be shown with the IS curve in Figure 8.3, which explains the goods market equilibrium schedule. The IS curve shows the equilibrium points of investment (I), at different rates of interest, and saving (S), at different levels of income. Thus, the lower the interest rate, the more the investment and the higher the income. The higher the income, the more the saving for investment financing. The steepness of the negatively sloped IS curve depends on how sensitive investment spending is to changes in the interest rate or return to investment.

The money market equilibrium, or the upsloping LM schedule (liquidity pref-erence function), is derived by the demand for money (L) curve, at different levels of the interest rate, and the money available at various levels of income and a given money supply fixed by the monetary authorities. With the level of income rising, the need for transactions money rises and the amount left over (supply of money, M) declines.

At the equilibrium level of income, saving (S) is equal to investment (I), while at the money market equilibrium supply of money (M) and demand for money or loans (L) are equal. The investment-saving (IS) curve in Figure 8.3 shows the level of national income when intended (ex ante) saving and intended in-vestment are adjusted to be equal. The lower the interest rate, the less people want to save and the more corporations and entrepreneurs want to borrow and invest. The demand for loans and supply of money (LM) curve shows the equilibria of the money market at different interest rates and income levels.

Different interest rates are associated with different income levels. At equi-

Figure 8.3
The Relationship of Interest, Income, Unemployment, and Inflation

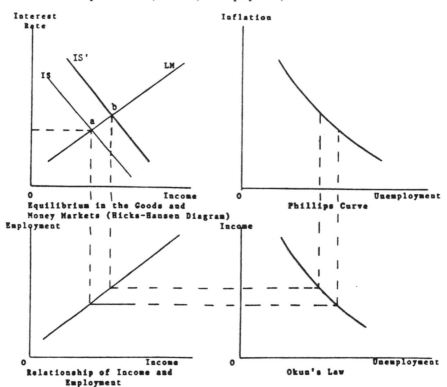

librium point *b*, the shift in the IS curve to a new position IS', mainly because of government spending, leads to a higher interest rate and higher income, compared to equilibrium at point *a*. Depending on the labor-intensive method of production introduced, this leads to more employment and, ceteris paribus, to less unemployment but higher inflation. This is shown in the Okun's law curve, which relates income or production and unemployment, on the one hand, and the Phillips curve, which relates unemployment with inflation, on the other hand.

The points where the IS and LM curves meet indicate the interest rates and the levels of income at which both the saving-investment market and the money market are at equilibrium. Expansionary fiscal policies, through an increase in public expenditures or a decrease in taxes, would shift the IS curve outward, increasing, income but also raising interest rates. However, an expansionary monetary policy would shift the LM curve outward, but then interest rates would be lower and national income higher. Therefore, all things being equal, a monetary easing would keep interest rates down, stimulate investment, and increase income and employment toward the full employment level of the economy.

When people are trying to save much but investors want to invest little, a downturn in the economy and an increase in unemployment is expected. In such a case, the government can fill the gap by stepping up spending, that is, by increasing the budget deficit. However, easy money may be preferable because it reduces interest rates and stimulates investment, while large budget deficits will increase interest rates and discourage new investment. Easy-money policy may be implemented through buying government securities by the Fed in an open market. This provides the banks with more money available for loans, reduces interest rates, and stimulates investment. The opposite is true when the Fed sells securities to the general public to cool off high demand in the economy and reduce inflation. Likewise, when the Fed increases interest rates, demand for loans declines, inflation is reduced, but unemployment rises. Empirically, such economic changes occurred during 1980–82 when interest rates were increased up to 21 percent and a severe recession followed, increasing unemployment from 7 percent to 12 percent but reducing inflation from 13.5 percent to around 5 percent.

AGGREGATE FISCAL POLICY

Monetarism and classical economics alone may not solve the problems of inflation or recession. Fiscal policy and Keynesian demand-side measures and, at times, wage and price controls may also be needed to limit severe recessions or fight inflations and propel the economy toward real growth. Monetary policy relies heavily on velocity, the movements of which are difficult to predict, and interest rates, which may easily plunge investment and lead the economy to severe recessions when they are high. Classical economists assume a perfectly competitive economy with no long-term contracts, no unions and other restrictions, in which prices and wages dance to the market drumbeats of supply and demand toward full employment. From a Keynesian perspective, though, there are doubts that the economy operates in an auctionlike or competitive fashion. On the contrary, there exist institutional features or bottlenecks and the market cannot regulate itself smoothly and reliably.

The following sections of this chapter present the results of governmental spending and taxation upon national income with diagrams and equations. Additional spending generates a multiple increase in income (multiplier effect). Additional income, in turn, generates additional investment (accelerator effect). The interactions of the multiplier and the accelerator propel the economy forward when they are positive and backward when they are negative.

Figure 8.4 shows that a $5 trillion spending for consumption (C) leads to an equal amount of national income (Y), as the consumption function (line C) indicates. An additional spending for investment (I) of $0.4 trillion creates a new equilibrium of spending and income (Y = C + I) and pushes national income or output to $6 trillion. That is, each dollar invested adds $2.5 more

Figure 8.4
National Income (Y) Determination with Government Expenditures (G)

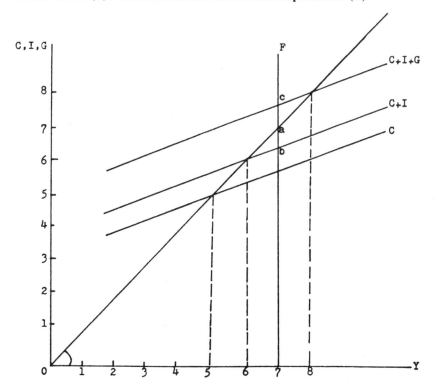

income to the economy, which means that the multiplier (k) is equal to 2.5 (or k = ΔY/ΔI = 1.0/0.4 = 2.5).

Here, full employment (F) in the economy can be achieved at an income or production of $7 trillion. The difference between actual income and potential or full-employment income (7 − 6 = 1) is lost income or output due to unemployment. If there is no additional spending, the economy faces what Keynes called chronic unemployment, which is equal to this difference. The resultant gap, *ab*, is called the deflationary gap. An additional spending by government (G) to point *a* will push total spending to $7 trillion and lead the economy to a full-employment equilibrium of aggregate demand and supply, where total spending is equal to total earning (C+I+G = Y). This will be ideal position of the economy, with full employment and stability.

However, if governmental spending is more than that required for the full employment level, an inflationary gap *ac* would be created and the increase in national income from $7 trillion to $8 trillion is an increase in prices or inflation; that is, it is an increase in nominal, not real, income and production.

On the other hand, in Figure 8.5 the equilibrium of investment and government spending (I + G) with the saving and taxation level (S + T) at $600 billion is

Figure 8.5
Equilibrium Level of Income with Increased Government Expenditures

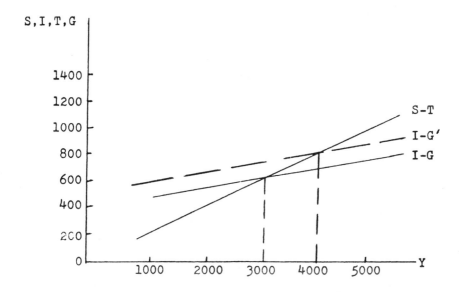

associated with a national income (Y) of $3,000 billion. If the government spending rises to a new level (I + G') at $800 billion, the new equilibrium income will be $4,000 billion. In this case, the government spending multiplier is 5 (or $\Delta Y/\Delta G = 1,000/200$). This means that, other things being equal, each additional dollar spent by the government leads to five dollars of additional income. However, it is difficult to measure the time required for the multiplier to work to the full extent, although for practical and comparative reasons annual changes of income are related to annual changes in spending (the notion of the multiplier effect).

Moreover, a reduction in government expenditures will lead to a shift of the I + G curve at a lower level of equilibrium income. Therefore, fiscal policy measures intended to reduce aggregate demand and inflation through a reduction in nominal income would reduce government spending. On the contrary, when the policy is to stimulate the economy and increase employment, more government expenditures should be injected into the economy.

Similarly, a change in taxes will lead to a multiple change in national income. Figure 8.6 shows that a tax cut leads to higher national income. The shift of the S + T curve, through a tax cut of $100 billion to a new one, S + T', results in an increase in national income (Y) from $3,000 billion to $3,400 billion. The tax multiplier, therefore, is equal to 4 (or $\Delta Y/\Delta T = 400/100$). The opposite result is expected in the case of an increase in taxes, through a shift in the S + T curve to the left and the establishment of a new equilibrium at a lower level of income.

Figure 8.6
Equilibrium Level of Income with Tax Cut

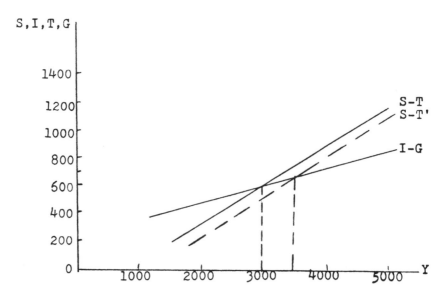

The Multiplier Effect

At equilibrium, total national income (Y), which is channeled into consumption (C), saving (S), taxation (T), and imports (M), is equal to total production or output, which is the result of spending for consumption, investment (I), government expenditures (G), and exports (X). That is,

$$C + S + T + M = C + I + G + X$$

If imports are equal to exports (balance-of-trade equilibrium) and taxes are equal to government expenditures (balanced budget), then

$$S + T = I + G$$

If government expenditures is larger than taxation (G>T); that is, if there is a deficit in the budget, then saving should be greater than investment (S>I), so that sufficient extra private saving would be available to finance the budgetary deficit and preserve equilibrium, because

$$T + (S - I) = G$$

The investment multiplier (k), which can be defined as the change in income as a result of a change in investment, $k = \Delta Y / \Delta I$, assuming other things remain the same, is equal to $1/(1-c) = 1/s$, where c is the marginal propensity to consume (MPC $= \Delta C/\Delta Y$) and s is the marginal propensity to save (MPS $= \Delta S/\Delta Y$).[2]

A change in government expenditures (ΔG) would produce a change in income similar to that from a change in investment. Therefore,

$$\Delta Y/\Delta G = 1/(1 - c) \text{ or } \Delta Y = \Delta G/(1 - c)$$

For example, if the marginal propensity to consume is 0.80, a change in government spending of $10 billion for transfers or other expenditures would change income by $50 billion; that is, $10/(1 - 0.80) = 10/0.20 = 50$ and the spending multiplier is equal to 5. This means that each additional dollar spent by the government would create five dollars of additional income through the responding process in the economy by consumer groups receiving additional income.

However, a change in taxation (T) of the same amount as a change in investment or government expenditure is expected to result in a smaller change in income and in an opposite direction. A part of the rise in taxation would be absorbed by a decrease in saving and the remainder by a decrease in consumption or aggregate demand. Thus, an increase in taxes would reduce demand by c times the rise in taxes, or

$$\Delta Y = -c\Delta T/(1-c)$$

and the tax multiplier ($\Delta Y/\Delta T = k_t$) is

$$k_t = -c/(1-c) = -c/s$$

where c is the marginal propensity to consume and s the marginal propensity to save. Thus, a decrease in taxes by $10 billion, assuming a marginal propensity to consume (c) equal to 0.80, would increase income by $40 billion, not $50 billion (as the equivalent increase of government expenditures would do). That is,

$$\Delta Y = \frac{-c(-\Delta T)}{1-c} = \frac{-0.80(-10)}{1-0.80} = \frac{8}{0.20} = 40$$

Thus, the effect of a tax cut on aggregate demand would depend on how much would be absorbed by saving and how much would be directed to spending. The tax cuts of 1981 and 1986, which affected primarily high-income people, had most probably not increased much consumption in the short run because high-income people have low marginal propensity to consume.

Considering the result of tax absorption by saving and, therefore, the effects on consumption, we can derive the tax multiplier as follows:

$$k_t = \frac{1}{1-c(1-t)} = \frac{1}{1-c+ct}$$

Assuming a marginal propensity to consume (c) of 0.75 and a marginal propensity to tax (MPT $= \Delta Y/\Delta T =$ t) equal to 0.20, then the tax multiplier would be

$$k_t = \frac{1}{1-0.75+(0.75)(0.20)} = \frac{1}{0.25+0.15} = \frac{1}{0.40} = 2.5$$

For example, a tax decrease by $40 billion would lead to an increase in national income of $100 billion, and vice versa for a tax increase.

Stabilization Policy

The problem of economic stabilization preoccupied many economists throughout history. Some two centuries ago Adam Smith thought that a more equitable distribution of income was necessary for a large market so that the whole economy can take full advantage of specialization and economies of scale. "No society can surely be flourishing and happy, of which the far greater part of the members are poor and miserable."[3] However, it is doubtful that Smith wanted to stress the social aspect of the distribution of income or the problem of defective demand, which Malthus, Marx, and Keynes emphasized later, or that he wanted government intervention to bring about such a more equitable distribution of income through taxation or other fiscal and welfare measures. Along these lines, Thomas Malthus argued that in a competitive economy, overproduction or a general glut of the market could occur when an effectual demand for produce becomes less than the supply. To this argument of partial market failure, which was contrary to Say's law that supply creates its own demand and there can never be shortages or gluts in a competitive market, no suggestions for public sector intervention or other remedies were made. It was John Keynes far later who introduced the policy of government spending to stimulate income and employment and avoid economic crises.

John Stuart Mill, on the other hand, thought that the laws of production are physically determined, whereas the laws of distribution are manmade. From that point of view, the role of government may be considered as more effectual on matters of economic stabilization and income distribution than production. He felt that the government should take upon itself the function of protecting the general interest and that the best state for human nature is that in which, while no one is poor, no one desires to be richer.[4]

Many fiscal and monetary measures Keynes suggested in his system of governmental intervention were applied in several countries, including the United States, but it is questionable whether these measures and tools are responsible for the inflationary bias the United States and other countries practiced during the post-World War II years. However, in many instances, lack of skills and cooperant factors, market limitations, and bottlenecks in particular sectors and industries make such policy prescriptions result in rises in money incomes and prices instead of increases in real output and employment. One cannot use public sector spending to increase consumption and stimulate development in economies where there are inelastic supplies and scarcity of available resources.

Moreover, the public sector or government spending may be needed for reasons of economic stabilization. In the United States and other economies, a high proportion of national income is expected to be saved, primarily because of increases in the institutionalization of savings in the form of contractual obligations, such as pension fund contributions and insurance premiums, as well as increases in corporate savings. Such a trend to save more would lead to less private spending, less demand, and less income and employment unless offset by public sector spending. In addition, generous incentives and other measures to stimulate investment and other forms of spending are provided by governments during periods of sluggish demand.

The tax cuts and other stimulative measures introduced before 1987 led to the rapid growth of the stock market at rates far higher than the growth of the economy. This illusory growth of the stock market provoked the market plunge in October 19, 1987. The Dow Jones industrial average fell 508 points, losing 23 percent of its value in one day, compared to 12.6 percent loss in the crash of October 29, 1929. Financial deregulation, the domination of stock trading by mutual funds and pension funds, program trading, and the growing corporate buyouts have encouraged quick return and discouraged long term productive investment. Thus the overoptimistic euphoria resulted in the crash of the stock market and the subsequent pessimistic expectations of a recession or even depression. Similar conditions may occur again, unless corrective countercyclical measures are taken by fiscal and monetary policymakers.

The use of tax and expenditure policies by the government to achieve full employment, price stability, and economic growth have attained great importance in the three previous decades. Underutilization of the labor force and of the capital stock involves waste and inequities. One of the main goals of fiscal policy is to avoid such waste and inequities through demand stimulation, production incentives, and replacement of welfare by workfare.

However, changes in the structure of the labor force, with larger proportions of females and young people, occur. Therefore, a certain rate of unemployment of, say, up to 5 percent may be permitted. Such a "natural" rate of unemployment may be the result, of job changing (frictional unemployment), that is, when people are in a transitional period seeking new employment. Also, retraining may be required because of structural changes in the economy. Likewise, a reasonable rate of inflation of, say, up to 3 percent may be considered as desirable for purposes of discouraging hoarding and encouraging investment. Therefore, economic policies aiming at less than 5 percent unemployment and no more than 3 percent inflation are more reasonable and realistic than a simultaneous zero unemployment (where everybody has a job) and zero inflation. As explained earlier, though, this is difficult to achieve and a trade off between unemployment and inflation usually takes place.

Fiscal policy as a stabilization tool often conflicts with other objectives in the economy, primarily with those of monetary and growth policies. Moreover, coordinating the timing of governmental policies is a difficult task in the political process. It takes time to recognize a fiscal problem and then to implement needed actions, as well as to observe and evaluate related responses. In a decentralized economic system, such as that of the United States, there are administrative and legislative delays in implementing tax and expenditure measures in stabilization and growth policies, as there are in monitoring the effectiveness of such measures. However, there are certain fiscal parameters with built-in flexibility that work automatically without discretion as to time and magnitude. Such built-in or automatic stabilizers include unemployment benefits, progressive taxation, indexing, retirement benefits, pensions, and similar fiscal variables that exist and work alone without having the government change them through new legislation or regulations. As such, they cushion the amplitude of cyclical fluctuations and tend to stabilize the economy.

A distinction between the long-run roles of government policies and their short-run stabilizing roles in the economy seems to be absent in popular and political discussions. In the short run, cyclical measures may be used to reduce the market failures of recessions and help adjust disposable and spendable income to permanent income. To reduce inflationary pressures, easy fiscal policy may be accompanied by tight monetary policy in a fine-tuning process, so that real interest rates and currency appreciations would not be excessive, domestically and internationally.

On the contrary, in order to keep high employment targets, tight fiscal policies may require easier monetary policy and increases in exports. Nevertheless, disciplined fiscal management should recognize structural budget deficiencies and accept the need for pursuing "natural" rates of unemployment and reasonable inflation rates. Moreover, stimulatory budget policies and counterbalancing monetary policies should encourage investment in the human and physical capital for long-run growth in the economy.

Table 8.1 demonstrates the successive changes of income (ΔY) generated by an initial amount of government expenditures (ΔG). Additional income created is partially spent for additional consumption and partially saved and presumably invested through financial institutions. Depending on the marginal propensity to consume, the initial government spending generates a multiple amount of income. This is known as the government spending multiplier ($\Delta Y/\Delta G$), which in our example (assuming a marginal propensity to consume 0.80) is equal to 5. This means that each additional dollar of government spending generates five additional dollars of income. Moreover, assuming that the resulting savings are channeled into investment, an additional amount of capital investment from the incremental incomes (induced investment) is generated. This is known as the accelerator ($\Delta I/\Delta Y$), which in our example is equal to 0.20. This additional

Table 8.1
Government-Spending Multiplier

ΔG	ΔC	ΔY	ΔS= ΔI
100	—	100	—
	80	80	20
	64	64	16
	51.20	51.20	12.80
	40.96	40.96	10.24
	32.77	32.77	8.19
	26.22	26.22	6.55
	. . . . .	. . . . .	. . . . .
	. . . . .	. . . . .	. . . . .
	400	500	100

investment would bring into operation a similar multiplier and another accelerator, and so on. The interactions of the multiplier and the accelerator contribute to economic fluctuations, resulting in booms when they are positive and slumps when they are negative. However, in case these tools are positive, real income and employment would increase up to the level of full unemployment. Thereafter, additional spending would increase only nominal income, generating a rise in prices or inflation.

9

Budget Deficits and Public Debt

BUDGET DEFICITS AND THEIR FINANCING

Problems of Borrowing

Budgetary deficits, that is, excesses of government expenditures over revenues, and their financing play a significant role in economic policies concerning employment, inflation, and growth. Depending on the way they are financed (through borrowing, taxation, or money creation), they influence, savings, investment, income distribution, and price changes.

Among the arguments in favor of deficit spending are that

1. it stimulates the economy and increases income and employment in cases of recession and depression;
2. it is not a serious problem because it is a debt we owe to ourselves;
3. it solves short-run needs of the government, which through its power of taxation can raise revenue, later, to finance the resulting debt.

Among the arguments against deficit spending are that

1. it turns out to be a burden on future generations;
2. there are tax limitations for its financing;
3. it is used primarily for consumption and is financed mostly through savings that would be used for investment;
4. it is no longer a debt we owe to ourselves since other nations have begun to finance such debts.

One of the serious problems with large government borrowing is that it crowds out productive enterprises for the limited funds available for loans. This leads to an increase in interest rates, because the demand for loanable funds is higher than the supply.

Governments can stimulate growth through expenditures. They may finance the construction of roads, hydroelectric dams, irrigation plants, housing, and other long-term and short-term productive projects. In addition, spending on education, health facilities, sewage, communications, and other public utilities helps economic growth directly or indirectly. Subsidizing productive enterprises or investing in projects that hasten production are more preferable from the viewpoint of output growth and price stability. However, the government should reduce or eliminate additional spending if the economy is approaching full employment of the factors of production and if inflation is anticipated.

As has already been noted, when annual governmental spending is higher than total revenue, a budgetary deficit results. To cover the difference, the government usually borrows either from the banks or from the public. This measure is extensively used by many governments as a means of stimulating demand and creating additional employment. Table 9.1 shows that federal deficits have increased dramatically in recent years. From a small surplus ($0.3) billion in 1960, such deficits increased to $2.8 billion in 1970, $73.8 billion in 1980, $207.8 billion in 1983, and $221.2 billion in 1986.

Governmental borrowing from central and commercial banks tends to increase prices more than borrowing from the general public. Borrowing from the public, by selling securities, is more preferable because it absorbs income and reduces inflationary pressures. Government deficits that accompany or replace hoarding may drive prices up, unless excess capacity exists. To attract people to buy securities, governments can offer high interest rates, introduce tax exemptions, assure their acceptability as collaterals for loans, provide a ready market (probably in the banks) for liquidation at any time, and even guarantee payment in gold or issue lotteries.

Increase in charges for a number of financial services provided by the government are considered as an additional measure to reduce budget deficits. They include farm credit, export loan guarantees, and home mortgage insurance. These charges, which are expected to add about $4 billion in revenue per year, would be paid by the agencies and individuals involved. However, usually politicians and interest groups affected by such charges show stiff opposition. The main source of revenue from such services would be the fee increases for the Federal Housing Authority (FHA), with a total of about 5 million mortgages insured, and the Veterans Administration with some 6 million loans guaranteed. In both cases, the fee required to be paid by the customers to the government for insured loans is expected to be 5 percent instead of the 3.8 percent and 1 percent paid so far. Other institutions affected are the Student Loan Marketing Association and the Export-Import Bank, which guarantees loans for foreigners buying U.S. goods.

Table 9.1
Federal Budget Receipts, Outlay, and Deficits, Selected Years, 1929–89 (billions of dollars)

Fiscal Year	Receipts	Outlays	Surplus or Deficit (−)
1929	3.9	3.1	3.3
1933	2.0	4.6	− 2.6
1939	6.3	9.1	− 2.8
1940	6.5	9.5	− 2.9
1941	8.7	13.7	− 4.9
1942	14.6	35.1	−20.5
1943	24.0	78.6	−54.6
1944	43.7	91.3	−47.6
1945	45.2	92.7	−47.6
1946	39.3	55.2	−15.9
1947	38.5	34.5	4.0
1948	41.6	29.8	11.8
1949	39.4	38.8	0.6
1950	39.4	42.6	− 3.1
1951	51.6	45.5	6.1
1952	66.2	67.7	− 1.5
1953	69.6	76.1	− 6.5
1954	69.7	70.9	− 1.2
1955	65.5	68.4	− 3.0
1956	74.6	70.6	3.9
1957	80.0	76.6	3.4
1958	79.6	82.4	− 2.8
1959	79.2	92.1	−12.8
1960	92.5	92.2	.3
1961	94.4	97.7	− 3.3
1962	99.7	106.8	− 7.1
1963	106.6	111.3	− 4.8
1964	112.6	118.5	− 5.9
1965	116.8	118.2	− 1.4
1966	130.8	134.5	− 3.7
1967	148.8	157.5	− 8.6
1968	153.0	178.1	−25.2
1969	186.9	183.6	3.2
1970	192.8	195.6	− 2.8
1971	187.1	210.2	−23.0
1972	207.3	230.7	−23.4
1973	230.8	245.7	−14.9
1974	263.2	269.4	− 6.1

Table 9.1 Continued

Fiscal Year	Receipts	Outlays	Surplus or Deficit (−)
1975	279.1	332.3	−53.2
1976	298.1	371.8	−73.7
1977	355.6	409.2	−53.6
1978	399.6	458.7	−59.2
1979	463.3	503.5	−40.2
1980	617.1	590.9	−73.8
1981	599.3	678.2	−78.9
1982	617.8	745.7	−127.9
1983	600.6	808.3	−207.8
1984	666.5	851.8	−185.3
1985	734.1	946.3	−212.3
1986	769.1	990.3	−221.2
1987	854.1	1,044.6	−150.4
1988*	909.2	1,055.9	−146.7
1989*	964.7	1,094.2	−129.5

*Estimates

Note: Through fiscal year 1976, the fiscal year was on a July 1–June 30 basis; beginning October 1976 (fiscal year 1977), the fiscal year is on an October 1–September 30 basis.
Source: *Economic Report of the President*, 1988, p. 337.

If the economy is at a prosperity stage of the cycle with inflation, government borrowing or higher taxation may be a proper way of undoing inflation. However, in the case of a lagged economy, government borrowing or additional taxation will stifle further economic activity, businesses will diminish inventories and reduce production, and unemployment will rise. A proper fiscal policy prescription, then, is to increase taxes or to borrow monies during the upswing stage of an inflationary economy. These monies will then be spent for investment or debt payment during the downturn of a recessionary economy.

The government's growing appetite for borrowing money to finance large deficits swamps credit markets and leads to higher debt and ever-growing interest costs paid by the government every year. Such interest payments by the government have been rising in the United States at a rate of about 20 percent per year over the last decade compared with 15 percent for income-transfer programs and 11 percent for the entire budget. This means that large debts perpetuate the problem of further deficits via growing interest costs and the burden on future generations becomes heavier. Moreover, because of deficit financing, high interest rates also drain funds from other nations as individuals and corporations shift monies to where they can get high returns. This means revaluation of the currency of the country with high interest rates and deterioration of its term of trade, as happened in the United States in the 1980s.

Figure 9.1
Demand and Supply of Loanable Funds

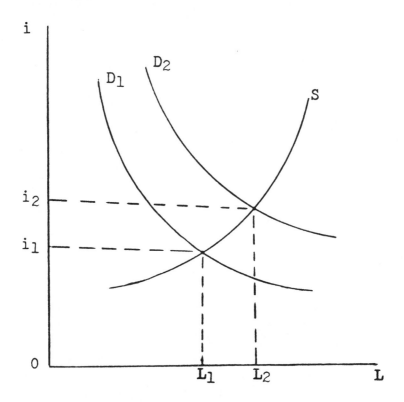

Effects of Government Borrowing on Loanable Funds

During periods of high deficit spending, a huge inflow of money into the economy occurs that stimulates demand of consumer goods. To respond to high aggregate demand, which is rising further through the spending multiplier, entrepreneurs and managers will seek to borrow money in order to expand production and sales. However, high real interest rates, resulting from the government's ravenous appetite for deficit financing, will prevent the private sector from expanding. This is so because of the high demand for funds stimulated by government spending. Therefore, aggregate supply will be less than demand thus causing prices of commodities and services to go up. Such inflationary trends, which are intensified by high capital cost, can dampen economic recoveries and perpetuate unemployment.

Figure 9.1 shows a shift in demand of loanable funds (L) by government borrowing from D_1 to D_2 and the consequent increase in the interest rate (i). Ceteris paribus, such an increase in demand for loanable funds by the government from L_1 to L_2 would increase interest rates from i_1 to i_2. The increase in the supply of such funds might come from domestic or from foreign sources, mainly because of higher interest rates. If the supply of loanable funds is inelastic, less money will be available for loans and interest rates will increase even more. If it is completely inelastic (vertical supply curve), the upward shift of demand curve for loans by the public sector will result in far higher interest rates, since the supply would be fixed.

If borrowing takes place for long-term productive investment in equipment, material, or skills, then future production will provide additional income, perhaps more than enough to repay principal and pay interest on the loan. Such a borrowing for investment was practiced in the United States and elsewhere during the nineteenth century with good results. However, borrowing for consumption increases today's consumption and reduces future consumption by a larger amount. Because of this, larger future sacrifices will be required to pay for present consumption beyond our means.

Some of the borrowing by the U.S. Treasury to finance budget deficits may be from foreign sources. When foreigners buy dollars with their currencies in order to acquire government securities, they tend to bid the price of the dollar up. Then budget deficits are associated with net flows of world capital into the United States, the value of the dollar rises on foreign exchange markets, and foreign trade deficits increase as imports become cheaper and exports dearer. Also, U.S. banks and investors may turn to domestic opportunities created by government borrowing, instead of lending or investing abroad, especially to financially unstable debtor nations. This reduces the supply of dollars abroad and intensifies the rising price of the dollar.

As noted previously, foreign companies, institutions, and individuals invest in U.S. government securities. Already about 17 percent of the debt is owned by foreigners. This helps alleviate the problem of a domestic clash between business and government borrowing. It also reduces the upward pressure of interest rates, but it can lead to problems in the future. To pay off internal debts the government can borrow more, increase taxes, or print additional money, but it cannot print foreign currencies.

These are proposals that if the federal government sells its $280 billion loan portfolio to private investors, it can break the deficit without ripping the economy apart and igniting social unrest. The privatization of these loans, which could be sold below their face values, might generate more than $150 billion to be applied to future deficits. Of the outstanding loans, 18 percent are for agriculture, 16 percent for foreign aid, another 16 percent for rural electrification, 12 percent for housing in rural areas, 7 percent for housing in urban areas, 4 percent for education, 4 percent for the Small Business Administration (SBA), and 11 percent for loans to other businesses. In addition to these outstanding loans, similar future loans, estimated to be about $40 billion annually in the forthcoming years, may also be sold to the private sector in a gradual manner so that flooding the market and disposing of them at amounts far below their face value will be avoided.

Other assets and governmental functions suggested to be transferred to the private sector include public housing; airport terrain; mail services; gold (worth $81 billion); oil, gas, and coal reserves (worth more than $600 billion); federal structures ($300 billion), equipment ($400 billion), and inventories ($200 billion); mortgages ($203 billion); miscellaneous financial assets ($95 billion); and even the Tennessee Valley Authority and the Bonneville Dam. Ironically, some critics ask to sell all government buildings, including the Capitol and the White House, and in turn rent them if needs exist for their use.

Such large-scale privatization of government assets and services may provide sufficient funds to balance the budgets in the near future and even to reduce or wipe out the debt. However, in the long run, the rent and the prices the government would have to pay to the private sector might be larger than the revenue collected from such sales. Bureaucrats may be less efficient than private managers, but rents and prices to be charged may be higher under the principle of profit maximization prevailing in private sector economics. Again, taxpayers would pay the difference.

Moreover, budget deficits tend also to "crowd in" investment because they stimulate consumer and investment spending. It seems, then, that the question of "publicness" versus "privatization" would remain for many years to come. Nevertheless, it depends on the consumption and investment components of government spending whether the current or the future period would enjoy more benefits.[1] Thus, spending on consumption reduces capital accumulation and growth, while spending on investment yields future goods and services that increase productivity and suppress inflation.

DEFICITS AND INTEREST RATES

Budget deficits and public debt can be repaid through surplus in the budget, which is unusual, or, as noted earlier, through printing new money at rates higher than the rates of real growth. This last case is an inflationary process in which nominal interest rates rise. If budgetary deficits persist and no additional money is issued to finance them, then real interest rates will go up, reflecting an ever-increasing debt in a noninflationary economy. Through a synchronized fiscal and monetary policy and prudent debt management, deficits may be reduced and interest rates may be held down, so that the cost of capital formation may remain low. Similar deflationary actions in the domestic economy may keep prices and costs down and satisfy stabilization needs.

Current and expected huge federal deficits result in high interest rates and crowd out of the credit markets other borrowers for home mortgages, corporate investment and consumer spending. Borrowing huge amounts of money every year, the U.S Treasury has turned into an addicted spender, thus becoming less sensitive to interest rates. However, private and business borrowing for capital formation is highly sensitive to soaring interest rates. Deficit spending is largely not used for investment, while its financing shoves other investors aside. This results in a slow down of noninflationary growth.

Large budget deficits are customarily the result of large government expenditures that normally stimulate the economy and in cases of booms may intensify inflation. To offset excessive stimulus from deficit spending and to moderate inflation, high interest rates and other fiscal and monetary measures are usually introduced. This is what happened to the United States in the early 1980s when the prime interest rate was raised to 21 percent and that of U.S. Treasury bills to 15 percent. High interest rates, in turn, make reduction of budget deficits difficult. The results of the 1981 U.S. tax cut and investment incentives only neutralized somewhat the effects of higher interest rates.

The harm from deficits may not be serious in the immediate future. Most of the damage deficits cause is subtle, long run, and indirect. They depress investment, penalize exports, and sap long-term economic growth. For short-run political reasons, administrations in power may hesitate in or dislike the raising taxes or lowering expenditures to reduce deficits, but we and our children will eventually pay dearly for high deficits. In such instances of enjoy now, pay later, government budgets are designed to avoid pain and exploit short-term gains but let the future go hang. Budget deficits overburden future generations and thus may be considered a form of "fiscal child abuse."

Moreover, large deficits and high interest rates make government securities attractive to foreign investors and drive interest rates further up as demand for currency to invest in these securities increases. Directly or indirectly, foreigners are financing half or more of the budget deficits. Even when foreigners put their money into corporate bonds or bank deposits, funds are available in the U.S. market. As will be explained in the next chapter in more detail, these trends drive up the exchange value of the currency and impede the competitive status of U.S industries. Such a currency overvaluation is similar to levying taxes on exports and subsidizing imports, thereby deteriorating the balance of trade.

To narrow budgetary deficits and to reduce or avoid inflation, effective income policies may be needed as a supplement to fiscal and monetary policies. Such income policies to gear average wage increases to the average rate of increase in productivity may also mitigate recessions and reduce unemployment in hard-pressed sectors of the economy.

To finance budget deficits, bonds and notes may also be sold in Eurodollars, Euroyens, and other currencies in the Eurobond market, where big corporations, banks, and governments raise large amounts of money ($135.5 billion in 1985 alone). This market may be attractive especially when interest rates are comparatively low. In addition, the flow of foreign capital into the United States to buy government securities and other assets has increased dramatically in recent years. Thus, international investment slowly and certainly enter all the sectors of the national economy, including the public finance sector.

Empirical research indicates however, that there is no positive association, or at the most a very weak one, between U.S. budget deficits and nominal interest

rates.[2] The use of discretionary policy in the determination of interest rates by
the Fed, along with price controls to repress inflation and other government fiscal
measures, may be considered responsible for affecting changes in interest rates
independently of changes in budgetary deficits. This became obvious in periods
of high deficits, as, for instance, during the years 1861–66 (Civil War), 1917–
20 (World War I), and 1941–46 (World War II). Had interest rates not been
pegged and had prices and other variables not been controlled, most probably
there would, ceteris paribus, be a positive correlation of deficits and interest
rates. Such correlations, in turn, are expected to affect capital accumulation and
economic growth, as explained previously.

Along Ricardian reasoning, one may argue that the financing of government
spending through taxes or borrowing has no serious effect on wealth once discounted future tax liabilities are considered. However, although empirical findings indicate no strong relationship between deficits and short-term interest rates,
larger deficits are associated with higher long-term interest rates.[3] For example,
interest-sensitive spending for home construction and business plant and equipment is largely affected by variations in long-term rates.

After the Great Depression, fiscal actions (taxing and spending) played a
substantial role on real economic activity. On a number of occasions tax cuts
were used for expansionary reasons. As noted earlier, when there is slack capacity
in the economy, tax cuts are used to raise total demand of goods and services;
this in turn, results in higher levels of real output. Moreover, cutting marginal
tax rates discourages efforts in seeking tax shelters and increases incentives to
work and invest, which may bring larger budgetary revenue and lower interest
rates.

John Maynard Keynes, calling himself a Cassandra who would never influence
the course of events in time, suggested that in cases of unemployment, increase
in total demand through government spending or tax cutting would be needed,
even if this meant temporarily increasing budget deficits. Monetary policy is
supposed to support such fiscal policy. But economics does not live in a vacuum.
In the real political world government spending and tax cutting seem rather, to
lead to budget deficits, inflation, and high interest rates. On the other hand,
Michael Kalecki predicted some 40 years ago that forthcoming ''political business cycles'' would make governments vacillate between fears of inflation and
fears of unemployment.[4] In the dilemma of stagflation, simultaneous unemployment and inflation, politicians usually resort to fiscal policy measures that
make huge budget deficits and high interest rates acceptable if not respectable.

Assuming other things remain the same, as the budget deficits rise, real interest
rates rise (as they do when investment demand increases), private saving declines,
or the money supply grows at rates less than the real economic growth. Such
interest rates are crucial in decisions on capital formation in new plants and
equipment to propel economic expansion.

With deficits expected to be high in the coming years, chances are that interest
rates will go up; and with a growing mountain of debt, interest costs are expected

to grow at a faster rate than the debt itself. To deal with this trend, a change in the economic policy mix toward a tighter fiscal policy and an easier monetary policy is needed. In a less than full employment economy, this may lower interest rates without generating inflation and prevent long-run instability and the erosion of the economy's productive capacity, which the growing national debt may bring about.

In the mid–1970s, the federal deficits required about a third of the net national savings, while in the 1980s soaked up about two-thirds of that pool. To keep up interest payments alone, the government spends about $150 billion per year. One out of five dollars the U.S. government spends is a dollar borrowed. And this takes place in a period when the nation is not engaged in war and the economy is in a good position. One can imagine what would happen in cases of recessions or depressions, which periodically visit the U.S. and other flexible market economies. Again, such swollen deficits would be demanding their big share of whatever domestic and foreign savings are available. As a result, competition for limited funds would increase and the cost of borrowing, that is, the interest rate, would follow suit; productive investment and technological innovations would shrink, industrial production would decline, and unemployment would rise. The alternative might be easy money and credit and probably runaway inflation, as has happened, for instance, in Latin American countries, which chase their own tails in ever-increasing spirals of inflation and soaring indebtedness. Another alternative, which has been used extensively in the 1980s in the United States, is inflow of foreign capital for financing budget deficits.

Although budget deficits are undesirable, they are not disabling. They are not expected to lead to a disaster, an economic catastrophe. Budget deficits are primarily a domestic problem that concerns the government of the country and its citizens. As the budget deficits pile up and the governmental debt increases, more savings are absorbed from the private sector to be used by the public sector. It is true that under such conditions more and more interest is paid to holders of bonds and other government securities, but macroeconomically such interest payments are channeled back into the economy. The interest received may be reused by the securityholders to buy more bonds, to save in banks, or to use for other forms of investment. Thus, from the standpoint of aggregate economics we need not fear as long as the money from interest remains within the economy.

The main question in such a debt accumulation arises: How is the borrowed money spent by the government? If it is spent for consumption, as is mostly the case, and not for job-creating direct investment, the growth of the economy may not be as high as it would be if the money remained with the private sector and was used for investment. From another perspective, a growing debt means that the government increasingly infiltrates the economy.

In the long run high budget deficits and large interest payments present great problems to the stability and growth of the country. They seriously affect domestic and even international economic conditions. Although it is desirable to run deficits in time of depressions and severe recessions in order to increase

Figure 9.2
Deficit, Surplus, and Full-Employment Budget

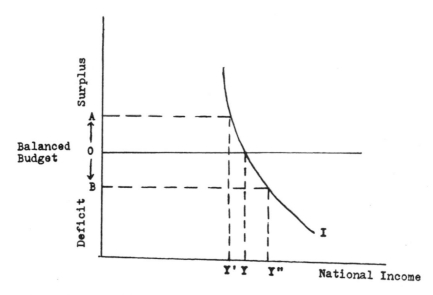

aggregate demand and boost the economy, to do that in times of high employment and prosperity is only inviting trouble. The annual deficit's dangerous feature and its damage to the economy, difficult to measure in the short run, is that it may lead to higher taxes, slower growth, and a reduction in living standards in the long run. The longer politicians put off reacting to the huge deficits, the worse their painful consequences will be. Policymakers must not continue to exploit the gains of the present while neglecting the future. They must try to build the present without heavily mortgaging the future.

BALANCED BUDGET AND THE GRAMM-RUDMAN-HOLLINGS ACT

In an optimal economy there is a balanced budget related to full employment. Restrictive or expansionary fiscal measures may lead to deviations from such a full employment, or optimal, budget. Figure 9.2 shows that an expansionary budget policy results in an increase in national income from Y (full employment income) to Y" and to a budget deficit (OB). On the contrary, a restrictive budget policy results to a decrease in national income from Y to Y' and to a budget surplus (OA).

However, because of inflexibility in the labor market and other bottlenecks in the economy, there may be deficits in the budget and, at the same time, unemployment and inflation. Therefore, discretionary fiscal policies should consider the existence of such bottlenecks and accept that the economy is at full employment with a "natural" rate of unemployment, say 5.1 percent, and a certain rate of inflation, say 3 percent. A reduction of unemployment to 5.4 percent was achieved in 1988, but mainly through the replacement of high-paying jobs with more low-paying jobs. Policymakers can then use practical fiscal measures to implement budget changes, departing from the potential full employment level of the economy, and to consider the dilemma of simultaneous unemployment and inflation at higher than the natural rates.

Balancing the Budget

Suggestions to correct large budget deficits include reductions in expenditures or freezing in the overall spending, as well as tax reforms. Reduction of expenditures in social programs becomes more and more difficult as the programs become entrenched, and so proposals are promulgated to eliminate such programs. This recalls the solution of Alexander the Great applied to the Gordian Knot, which was to cut the knot because there was no way to untie it. Thus, analogous to the case of the Procrustian bed, the solution suggested is to chop off social programs if they do not fit the tax base.

It should be realized that it is difficult to implement constitutional amendments to correct the budget deficit in a short period of time because of the safety net requirements of many social programs. That is why perhaps more years will be needed for the gradual reduction and complete elimination of budget deficits. Any exemption to the principle of zero deficit would require qualified or more than simple-majority voting in both houses. As it is argued, such a constitutional amendment would solve our deficit dilemma through the political process and thereby impose long-overdue fiscal discipline in federal government. However, automatic budget cuts during a recession could plunge the economy into a deeper slump.

A portion of budget deficits may be the result of subsidization or aid to enterprises and banks that have failed the market competitive test and their revenues have fallen to less than the costs of their operations. Government regulations and controls may be considered as another source of deficits because of the high administrative expenditures that can be associated with them and the largely unjustified stifling of productive investment arising from them. In such government bureaucracies there are interest groups certainly concerned with doing the job assigned to them by society. Frequently, though, they do that in a bureaucratic and inefficient way. Policy recommendations to fine-tune the economy by budgetary deficits, at times, turn out just to stultify the economy through perpetuating self-serving bureaucracies. However, in the case of high unemployment deficit spending can be a significant stimulant to a sagging economy.

Another element contributing to budgetary deficits is that near the end of the fiscal year a number of ministries and other government agencies rush to spend their unspent allotments. Such a bureaucratic waste may take place not only to avoid future cuts but also to increase the possibility of additional procurements in consecutive fiscal years. As a result of a ''spend it or lose it'' philosophy, many public agencies are busy spending on activities and projects of dubious importance, such as buying unnecessary furniture or employing contractors and consultants to advise them how to spend or prepare studies for future projects that may never be implemented.

Such excessive end-of-year spending may cease when proper incentives are provided for responsible managers who are left with unspent appropriated funds. Other measures may include the assurance that monies unspent at the end of the fiscal year can be used partially or totally toward expenses of the following year. The permission to carry forward unspent money would eliminate penalties for having failed to spend allocated public funds. Moreover, such savings should not be used as a guide to budgetary cuts in the agencies concerned during later years. Instead, appropriate rewards must be introduced to encourage the savings, toward the end of each fiscal year, which may lead to a reduction in taxation and/or a decrease in inflation.

Also, deficits may appear in public enterprises and other state and local institutions dealing with urban transportation, electricity, railways, airlines, and water distribution. There are usually two main reasons for deficits in such public enterprises: First, prices are kept at low levels for political reasons; second, public enterprises are stuffed with excessive personnel to accommodate unemployed constituencies of the politicians or other persons in power. As a result, administrative costs remain high, revenues are low, and the deficits are growing.

For an effective operation, the management of public enterprises needs to be independent of political pressures and the control of the central or local governments, which means that more decentralization may be needed. Moreover, periodic price adjustments of their products or services are needed to match the general rate of inflation and increases in costs.

The Gramm-Rudman-Hollings Act

To reduce deficits and eventually to wipe them out, the Balanced Budget and Emergency Deficit Control Act of 1985 was passed by the U.S. Congress and signed into law by President Reagan. This is known as the Gramm-Rudman-Hollings Law (from the names of the three senators who introduced this piece of legislation, Phil Gramm, Republican from Texas, Warren Rudman, Republican from New Hampshire, and Ernest Hollings, Democrat from South Carolina). It provides for gradual deficit reductions to $180 billion in the fiscal year 1986, $144 billion in 1987, $108 billion in 1988, $72 billion in 1989, $36 billion in 1990 and zero in 1991.

Concerns have been expressed over the constitutionality of certain provisions of the law, which have been challenged in the courts. The law's ''automatic pilot,'' which mandates across-the-board spending cuts on the basis of budget forecasts by three federal agencies, impinges on Congress's authority and on the power of the executive. These three agencies are the President's office of Management and Budget (OMB), the Congressional Budget Office (CBO), and the General Accounting Office (GAO), which is of disputed lineage. According to this law, the OBM and the CBO jointly, or separately if they disagree, submit their budget estimates to GAO, which accepts or revises them and issues a final deficit prediction. The president must then order the spending cuts according to a prescribed formula. If the deficit exceeds the above annual limits by more than $10 billion, Congress and the president get 30 days to enact new expenditure and tax bills. Large welfare programs, along with social security and veteran's benefits, are protected from automatic slashes. In addition, a 2 percent ceiling on the annual reductions is placed on half a dozen other social programs, including Medicare and other health projects for the poor, while some types of military spending will have to absorb half of whatever automatic cuts are ordered.

Critics of this law of automatic deficit reduction say that it is arbitrary and violates the spirit and the word of the Constitution regarding the separation of legislative, executive, and judiciary powers for the Constitution states that expenditures of the public's money shall be voted by Congress and approved by the President. Yet with this most recent legislation a deus ex machina was created for automatic budget cuts regardless of the national needs. The law seems to be depriving the government of needed flexibility and encouraging the use of tricks by the government, rendering its intent meaningless. Such tricks may include impounding funds by the president (from other programs), raising budget revenue by selling some of its land and other assets or leasing oil fields, providing "tax expenditures" through tax credits to businesses or tax reductions and exemptions to individuals for state and local taxes and interest on certain bonds, and also providing loan guarantees or increasing social security benefits for which the outlays lie some time in the future.

Moreover, there is the danger that the restrictive measures to balance the budget may lead the economy into a severe recession or perhaps a depression. A similar phenomenon could be observed during the years of the Great Depression, when the Federal Revenue Act of 1932 raised the tax rates (the top-bracket rate was increased from 24 percent to 63 percent). However, tax revenues were not raised to close the budget deficits, which remained $2.6 billion in 1933, despite the substantial increase in tax rates and the federal expenditure cuts by 1.3 percent in that year. On the contrary, private spending was restricted, aggregate demand declined, unemployment rose to a record 24.9 percent, and deflation was aggravated as prices declined.

To help reduce the deficit quickly, the Reagan administration planned in 1985 to sell government assets and to introduce the privatization of federal activities. It looked for a way to sell the FHA, established in 1934, to abolish the ICC formed in 1887, to sell the Bonneville Power Administration, created in 1937, and to withdraw support for the Agricultural Extension Service, which was created in 1914 to provide scientific knowledge to farmers.

From the viewpoint of economic stability and growth, drastic cuts of deficits will take much out of the economy and may bring on severe recessions. High deficits in World War II, reaching 25 percent of GNP stimulated the economy, and helped bring high rates of economic growth in later years. Although large at face value, today's deficits are running at 4–5 percent of GNP. However, gradual reduction of such budget deficits matched with an easing monetary policy, would keep low interest rates and encourage economic growth. Moreover, such growth would increase government revenue and reduce budget deficits.

NATIONAL DEBT AND ITS COMPOSITION

The accumulation of annual budgetary deficits comprises public debt. Governments with such debt expect to reduce it through surpluses in their budgets when the economy is at prosperous stages. Given that surplus realization is a rare phenomenon for almost any government, the deficits continue to accumulate, the debt becomes larger, and the total interest paid to service it increases. This internal debt, which shows the amount the government owes mostly to its citizens and domestic institutions, is different from the external debt, which shows how much the nation owes to foreigners.

From a national macroeconomic point of view, the public debt is not a frightening factor because it is a domestic economic issue that can be dealt with effectively by the government in the long run. Nevertheless, the continuous rise of the debt requires more taxes or further deficits to provide the necessary revenue for interest payments and puts heavier burdens on later generations. Furthermore, it means more and more government involvement in the economy, which might be undesirable politically.

There have been only seven small surpluses in the United States budgets since 1931 and one (in 1969) during the last 25 years. To follow a policy of budget surpluses in order to reduce or wipe out the debt will be difficult if not impossible in the foreseeable future. Moreover, such a policy may have depressing effects on the economy. Whereas, in periods of unemployment budget deficits may in fact act as stimulus in the economy, as past experiences indicate.

Historically and in terms of absolute dollars, the federal debt outstanding was changed from $75.5 million in 1791 to $127.3 million in 1816. Then, from $0.4 million in 1836 it increased to $2,755.8 million in 1866 and declined to $961.4 million in 1893, only to increase again gradually to $24.3 billion in 1920 and then to decline to $16.2 billion in 1930.[5] Thereafter, it has grown from $50.7 billion in 1940 (about half of the GNP) to $260.1 billion in 1945, at the end of World War II (about 130 percent of the GNP), and $2,355.3 billion in 1987. During the last three decades the federal debt has tripled while other kinds of debts have risen far more sharply. Thus, residential mortgage debt has climbed nearly 20-fold to about $1.2 trillion and consumer loans 19-fold (about $310 billion) during the same period. Also, the corporation debt amounted to $1.6 trillion in 1985. The federal debt of 1988, about $2.5 trillion, is more than double than that of 1981.

Table 9.2
Federal Debt, Selected Fiscal Years, 1929–89 (billions of dollars)

Fiscal year	Gross Federal debt (end of period)		Gross national product	Debt as percentage of GNP
	Total	Held by the public		
1940	50.7	42.8	95.8	53.4
1945	260.1	235.2	212.4	122.5
1950	256.9	219.0	266.8	96.3
1955	274.4	226.8	386.4	71.0
1960	290.9	237.2	506.7	57.3
1965	323.2	261.6	672.6	48.1
1970	382.6	284.9	990.2	38.6
1975	544.1	396.9	1,522.5	35.7
1980	914.3	715.1	2,670.6	34.2
1981	1,003.9	794.4	2,986.4	33.6
1982	1,147.0	929.4	3,139.1	36.5
1983	1,381.9	1,141.8	3,321.9	41.6
1984	1,576.7	1,312.6	3,686.8	42.8
1985	1,827.5	1,509.9	3,943.4	46.3
1986	2,130.0	1,746.1	4,192.5	50.8
1987	2.355.3	1,897.8	4,408.7	53.4
1988*	2,581.6	2,025.1	4,705.8	54.9
1989*	2,825.3	2,152.1	5,023.3	56.2

*Estimates

Note: Through fiscal year 1976, the fiscal year was on a July 1–June 30 basis; beginning October 1976 (fiscal year 1977), the fiscal year is on an October 1–September 30 basis.

Source: U.S. Department of the Treasury, Office of Management and Budget, and U.S. Department of Commerce (Bureau of Economic Analysis).

Looking at the past, one will observe that the U.S. federal government was in debt virtually from the time it was founded, in 1789. Treasury Secretary Alexander Hamilton and the Federalists initiated a sinking fund to pay off the debt. The Jeffersonians (1800) thought that debt is a mortgage on the nation's future held by well-born creditors and the rich. That is why they abhorred public debt. The Swiss-born Treasury Secretary Albert Gallatin, who served both Thomas Jefferson and James Madison, accelerated repayment of what he called "the national curse of growing and perpetual debt."[6] As a result, the national debt shrank from $123 million in 1817 to zero by 1834. However, three years later, the government issued $10 million notes to finance growing expenditures and the debt-free golden age ended.

Table 9.2 shows the growing size of the federal debt, which has taken alarming dimensions in recent years. From 17.0 billion in 1929 and $22.5 billion in 1933 it reached $50.7 billion in 1940, $256.9 billion in 1950, $290.9 billion in 1960, $382.6 billion in 1970, $914.3 billion in 1980, and as high as $2,355.3 billion in 1987. However, as a percentage of GNP it was kept relatively constant for the last decade, although it started growing in the very recent past. Table 9.3, on the other hand, indicates the composition of the federal debt in government securities (bills, notes, bonds).

Figure 9.3 demonstrates the holders of federal debt. United States government accounts hold 22 percent of the total debt; individual citizens, 14 percent; foreign holders, 17 percent; the Fed, 13 percent; commercial banks and savings banks, 11 percent and 8 percent, respectively; and corporations, only 2 percent. It is expected that the flow of capital funds from other countries into the United States will continue and the proportion of debt held by foreign holders will increase. As a result, interest payments abroad will gradually increase, thus draining the available funds for domestic investment.

By June 1985 outstanding foreign holdings of marketable U.S. Treasuries totaled $201.3 billion, compared to roughly $100 billion in 1980. In 1984 alone, net foreign purchases of U.S. Treasury notes, bonds, and bills totaled $25.5 billion. Japan purchased the largest amount ($6.4 billion), followed by Britain ($6.1 billion), oil-producing nations ($2.2 billion) and Switzerland ($1.1 billion). Foreigners prefer U.S. securities because they enjoy high interest rates (3–4 percent higher than in Japan alone) and a large, dynamic, liquid, and safe market.

As a proportion of GNP, though, the federal debt has shrunk since 1945. In real terms, the value of the debt and therefore the real liability of the government is reduced implicitly by inflation. Thus, when inflation is 10 percent, a deficit of $100 billion in a debt of $1 trillion does not change the real value of total debt.

Moreover, about one-third of the total debt belongs to the government itself, particularly to the Social Security Trust Fund, the Civil Service Retirement Fund, the Federal Reserve, and various other government trust funds. Interest payments on the part of the debt held by the government are received back by the government. In reality they are accounting or paper transactions of the same institution, without serious budgetary implications.

The use of government debt for lasting investment, such as highways and ports, benefits not only the present economy, through the multiplier and accelerator effects, but also the future generations who will use these long-term investment projects. In cases of recessions and depressions and, along the Keynesian fiscalism, any kind of deficit spending helps stimulate the economy and reduce unemployment. The success of the massive spending in World War II that pulled the U.S. economy out of the Great Depression is an example frequently used by economists and politicians. However, deficit spending may make sense in periods of economic slack to provide work for workers and facilities that remain idle, but megadeficits in periods of economic boom create serious problems in draining from the market financial resources that could be directed to private investment.

The severe recession of 1981–82 and the decline in inflation that followed it, as well as the income tax cuts of about 25 percent at that time, kept tax revenue

Table 9.3
Interest-Bearing Public Debt Securities by Kind of Obligation, 1967–87 (billions of dollars)

End of Year	Total interest-bearing public debt securities	Marketable				Nonmarketable				
		Total	Treasury bills	Treasury notes	Treasury bonds	Total	U.S. Savings bonds	Foreign government and public series	Government account series	Other
1967	322,286	210,672	58,535	49,108	97,418	111,614	51,213	1,514	56,155	2,731
1968	344,401	226,592	64,440	71,073	91,079	117,808	51,712	3,741	59,526	2,828
1969	351,729	226,107	68,356	78,946	78,805	125,623	51,711	4,070	66,790	3,051
1970	369,026	232,599	76,154	93,489	62,956	136,426	51,281	4,755	76,323	4,068
1971	396,289	245,473	86,677	104,807	53,989	150,816	53,003	9,270	82,784	5,759
1972	425,360	257,202	96,648	113,419	49,135	168,158	55,921	18,985	89,598	3,654
1973	456,353	262,971	100,061	117,840	45,071	193,382	59,418	28,524	101,738	3,701
1974	473,238	266,575	105,019	128,419	33,137	206,663	61,921	25,011	115,442	4,289
1975	532,122	315,606	128,569	150,257	36,779	216,516	65,482	23,216	124,173	3,644
1976	619,254	392,581	161,198	191,758	39,626	226,673	69,733	21,500	130,557	4,833
1977	697,629	443,508	156,091	241,692	45,724	254,121	75,411	21,799	140,113	16,797
1978	766,971	485,155	160,936	267,865	56,355	281,816	79,798	21,680	153,271	27,067
1979	819,007	506,693	161,378	274,242	71,073	312,314	80,440	28,115	176,360	27,400
1980	906,402	594,506	199,832	310,903	83,772	311,896	72,727	25,158	189,848	24,164
1981	996,495	683,209	223,388	363,643	96,178	313,286	68,017	20,499	201,052	23,718
1982	1,140,883	824,422	277,900	442,890	103,631	316,461	67,274	14,641	210,462	24,085
1983	1,375,751	1,024,000	340,733	557,525	125,742	351,751	70,024	11,450	234,684	35,593
1984	1,559,570	1,176,556	356,798	661,687	158,070	383,015	72,832	8,806	259,534	41,843
1985	1,812,010	1,360,179	384,220	776,449	199,510	460,831	77,011	6,638	313,928	63,255
1986	2,122,684	1,564,329	410,730	896,884	241,716	558,355	85,551	4,128	365,872	102,804
1987	2,347,750	1,675,980	378,263	1,005,127	277,590	671,769	97,004	4,350	440,658	129,758

Note: Through fiscal year 1976, the fiscal year was on a July 1–June 30 basis. Beginning October 1976 (fiscal year 1977), the fiscal year is on an October 1–September 30 basis.
Source: U.S. Department of the Treasury.

Figure 9.3
Holders of Federal Debt

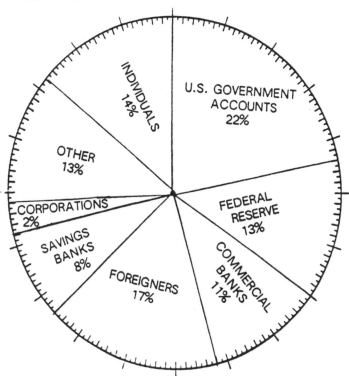

Source: U.S. Department of the Treasury.

relatively low and budget deficits and the debt at high levels. Like the reduction of nuclear proliferation, reduction or elimination of the deficit has become a long-term and difficult problem. It is an albatross around the neck of the government.

Much has recently been made of the large U.S. deficits and debt. At any rate, adjustments of conventional measures of government assets and liabilities to include inflation and assets accumulation may change the picture of budget deficits and the real value of net debt. Such adjustments and the distinction between current and capital accounts in the budget, so that financial and real assets accumulation are considered, may reveal a secular decline in the private sector's net claims on the federal government.

From that perspective, the federal high-employment budget (currently calculated for an unemployment level of 5.1 percent) may be viewed as more frequently in surplus than in deficit in the years since World War II, especially in periods of significant inflation. This, in turn, suggests that tight money has not been the only tool in town to slow inflation in recent years, for fiscal contraction in real terms has also played a role in the anti-inflationary game.

To many, the recent magnitude of federal deficit and the debt is a serious problem for the economy. However, in real terms, or in constant dollars, both the federal deficit and the debt are far less than in nominal terms. Then, the conventional measure of the deficit and the debt can be misleading in periods of significant inflation and high and fluctuating interest rates. In such periods, adjustments are to be made to incorporate changes in market rates of interest (par-to-market adjustment) and changes in prices (nominal-to-real adjustment).[7] Furthermore, the federal government's debt of $2.36 trillion in 1987 may be offset by its roughly $2 trillion in real assets and $1 trillion loans, gold, securities, cash, trust funds, and other financial assets.[8]

Interest payment to nongovernment institutions and domestic and foreign individuals and corporations, though, is growing so fast that it may be the most uncontrollable item in the budget.[9] It increased from $49 billion in 1978, with an average interest rate of 7.12 percent, to $52 billion in 1980 at 9.03 percent interest, $111 billion in 1984, and about $150 billion in 1985. To pay these growing amounts of interest, the government has to raise taxes or borrow again to service previous borrowings, and so on.

STATE AND LOCAL GOVERNMENT DEBT

What has been said about federal debt applies also to state and local government debt, except for the power to create money and to monetize the debt, which belongs exclusively to the national government. As long as state and local governments cannot monetize their debt, their risk of default is higher than the federal government's and higher interests should be paid. State and local governments usually borrow money to finance investment in ports, sports stadiums, large bridges and tunnels, school buildings, hospitals, and other public projects. To secure intergenerational equity, the debt burden should be distributed and amortized throughout the time the facility is used up. Thus, the costs of public investment are spread so that they are related to the benefits gradually received by the beneficiaries of the investment.

Since the 1940s, state as well as local government debts, as percentages of GNP, followed a more or less declining trend. Out of the total public debt, state governments hold about 10 percent and local governments about 20 percent, while the federal government holds the rest. Table 9.4 shows rapid growth of state and local debt during the twentieth century.

Individual states have different debt obligations. Thus, general obligation debt per capita in 1981 varied from $769 for Indiana to $1,090 for California, $1,231 for Michigan, $1,571 for Pennsylvania, $2,051 for New Mexico, $2,528 for New York, and $3,233 for Wyoming. During the same year, the average American was in debt $1,500, or 14.2 percent of his or her personal income.[10] Federal debt per capita was $8,825 in 1986.

Table 9.4
State and Local Government Debt
(selected years, billions of current dollars)

Year	Total	State	Local
1902	2.1	0.2	1.9
1927	14.9	2.0	12.9
1940	28.3	3.6	16.7
1950	24.1	5.3	18.8
1960	70.0	18.5	51.4
1970	143.6	42.0	101.6
1976	239.9	79.6	160.3
1985*	771.3	257.1	514.2

*estimated

Source: U.S. Department of Commerce, Bureau of the Census, *Historical Statistics of the United States, Colonial Times to 1970, 1975*, pp. 1117–20; and *Survey of Current Business*, various issues.

DEBT MANAGEMENT AND ECONOMIC POLICY

Coordination of debt management and overall economic policy goals is an important issue in advanced economies. The U.S. Treasury wants to finance and refinance its debt with low cost and to structure it on a long-term basis. Countercyclical or stabilization and redistributional policies, though, may require different approaches. For example, in case of high unemployment and recession, absorption of market funds to finance debt would deprive other borrowers and would raise interest rates. This would be detrimental to investment financing in the productive sector of the economy and delay revival.

It is proper to sell securities when the economy is at an upswing, or in the prosperity stage, and to absorb money and then spend it when the economy is at a downswing, or in a recessionary stage. This is a policy to reduce inflation when the economy is hot and increase employment when the economy is slow. An inverse policy would have opposite results. However, low interest rates, desired by the U.S. Treasury, prevail mainly during economic slacks and troughs,

Table 9.5

Maturity Distribution and Average Length of Marketable Interest-Bearing Public Debt Securities Held by Private Investors, 1967–87 (billions of dollars)

End of Year	Amount outstanding privately held	Maturity Class					Average Length	
		Within 1 Year	1 to 5 Years	5 to 10 Years	10 to 10 Years	20 Years and over		
		Millions of dolars					Years	Month
1967	150,321	56,561	53,584	21,057	6,153	12,968	5	1
1968	159,671	66,746	52,295	21,850	6,110	12,670	4	5
1969	156,008	69,311	50,182	18,078	6,097	12,337	4	2
1970	157,910	76,443	57,035	8,286	7,876	8,272	3	8
1971	161,863	74,803	58,557	14,503	6,357	7,645	3	6
1972	165,978	79,509	57,157	16,033	6,358	6,922	3	3
1973	167,869	84,041	54,139	16,385	8,741	4,564	3	1
1974	164,862	87,150	50,103	14,197	9,930	3,481	2	11
1975	210,382	115,677	65,852	15,385	8,857	4,611	2	8
1976	279,782	151,723	89,151	24,169	8,087	6,652	2	7
1977	326,674	161,329	113,219	33,067	8,428	10,531	2	11
1978	356,501	163,819	132,993	33,500	11,383	14,805	3	3
1979	380,530	181,883	127,574	32,279	18,489	20,304	3	7
1980	463,717	220,084	166,244	38,809	25,901	22,679	3	9
1981	549,863	256,187	182,237	48,743	32,569	30,127	4	0
1982	682,043	314,436	221,783	75,749	33,017	37,058	3	11
1983	862,631	379,579	294,955	99,174	40,826	48,097	4	1
1984	1,017,488	437,941	332,808	130,417	49,664	66,658	4	6
1985	1,185,675	472,661	402,766	159,383	62,853	88,012	4	11
1986	1,394,275	506,903	467,348	189,995	70,664	119,365	5	3
1987	1,445,366	483,582	526,746	209,160	72,862	153,016	5	9

Source: U.S. Department of the Treasury.

while high interest rates are associated with high performance of the economy. It seems, therefore, that debt financing by the U.S. Treasury is sometimes at odds with the stabilization policy of the monetary authorities.

Maturities of U.S. Treasury securities vary from 91-day to 1-year bills, 1-year to 10-year notes, and bonds with maturities above 10 and up to 35 years. The average maturity is about 3 years. The majority of securities, about 80 percent in fact, is marketable. Table 9.5 demonstrates in detail the maturity of the marketable interest-bearing debt. Bills are sold at a discount and pay no interest, while notes and bonds, which pay an annual interest, are redeemable at par at maturity. Nonmarketable securities can be held only by the initial buyer, mainly trust funds, such as social security, foreign governments, and individuals (savings bonds).

To lengthen the maturity of federal debt securities, the U.S. Treasury uses the process of advance financing, in which securityholders can exchange their securities for newly issued ones at higher interest rates, regardless of their maturities. Another technique of debt financing, which may prove to be satisfactory for the United States, as it has been in other countries, notably the United Kingdom, is the issuance of nonmaturing securities known as consols. In this type of perpetual-debt securities, the government will pay only interest to the debtholders or their heirs, but not the debt itself. In short, deficits are financed by permanent borrowing without an obligation to redeem the debt.

The distributional effects of debt financing are not too serious because owners of debt have relatively high income. They buy securities mostly from their savings, which can receive the same interest, more or less, elsewhere. Thus, the receivers of debt interest are not expected to change their spending much while consumption behavior and their marginal propensity to consume are expected to remain about the same. With an income distributional neutrality, the debt burden is symmetrical when the goods financed with the debt are divided among the people in proportion to tax payments to service the debt. If, on the contrary, tax payments to service the debt are not proportional to debt interest payments, then there is created an asymmetry or distributional non-neutrality between tax and interest payments to service the debt. In such a case, an economic unit may, for example, receive $1,000 interest from government securities and pay $600 or $1,200 taxes for the financing of the debt services.

Intergenerational Implications

Considering intergeneration equity from debt financing, it becomes obvious that with a growing public debt future generations are facing a heavier burden that the present generation, except when public borrowing is used to finance capital formation. The present generation enjoys public services financed by borrowing while future generations are expected to pay the cost.[11] In other words, debt creation merely delays tax payments to a later time. However, when the debt is refunded at maturity through borrowing again, only the interest payments require additional taxes. But interest may also be refunded, together with the maturing debt, as is customary presently, and the debt accumulation continues.

When the debt is held domestically, macroeconomically we owe it to ourselves, as long as both taxpayers and recipients of interest belong to the same nation. There would be distributional problems, though, when the group of taxpayers is mostly a different one from that of the recipients of interest. In addition, tax disincentives could occur. Tax finance of interest and possibly amortization is likely to fall on consumption. However, loan finance tends to fall on saving and investment, thereby reducing economic growth.

Borrowing, that is, the creation of public debt, relies upon a voluntary basis of exchange, while taxation implies a politically determined coercion or compulsion. It finances public services without reducing current real wealth of individuals, as taxation is doing. The interest on debt tends to transfer purchasing power from the taxpayers to the holders of bonds and other government securities. If these persons belong to the same group, there are no serious distributional problems. Otherwise, the burden of debt financing falls on taxpayers who do not receive interest from debt instruments.

As indicated earlier, owners of the federal debt may be government units, consumers, businesses, and foreigners. In the first case the lending unit lends the money back to itself. In other cases where consumers, businesses, and foreigners lend the money, interest is paid by the government to these economic units. It would seem that the public sector (federal, state, and local governments) has an advantage over the private sector (consumers and businesses) in collecting taxes to pay back and to service the debt. Thus, the greater power of the public sector to carry debt should lead to gradual reallocation of resources in favor of the public sector and against the private sector. Moreover, federal or central governments have the power to issue money, but state and local governments have not. However, as long as the lenders are economic units in the country, there is no problem of outflow of interest payments, as would be the case with foreign lenders. In the latter instance, taxes collected from the domestic economy are used to pay debt interest to foreign holders of the debt, and, assuming other things to be the same, equal amounts of the country's resources are withdrawn.

The U.S. federal debt at the end of 1984 was $1.6 trillion. With an interest rate of 10 percent annually and no other primary deficit, it was estimated that the debt would be $2.56 trillion in five years.[12] Current deficit reports of the U.S. Treasury seem to verify this trend.

Even with an increasing industrial productivity of 4 percent annually, as it grew in the middle of the 1980s as a result of the cyclical rebound, the budget deficits and the federal debt will continue to grow. With projected high military budgets for the coming fiscal years and indexation of the individual income tax (which started in 1985), along with the cost-of-living index of social security benefits, the federal debt will keep on growing. On the other hand, assuming that inflation averages 4 percent annually, indexation would reduce tax revenues to about $60 billion annually. This means that tax increases and/or spending cuts are expected to achieve a balanced budget and stop the growth of the national debt. Along these lines, the Balanced Budget Act of 1985 could lead to further cuts in social programs.

There seems to be a negative relationship between the ratio of public debt to GNP and the ratio of capital stock to GNP. As the first ratio rises, the second ratio declines. As the federal debt increases, capital investment in plant, equipment, housing, and other productive assets is expected to decline for the private sector as well as for state and local governments. To attract people to acquire more government securities, higher interest rates must be offered. Ceteris paribus, this would push up the cost of borrowing money for capital formation. Therefore, the argument that economic growth would eventually reduce the public debt seems to put the cart before the horse. Economic growth requires new investment which, in turn, requires low capital cost, that is, low interest rates. Then low interest rates can be achieved with a large supply of loanable funds in the market, as long as they are not drained by debt financing. Of course, there is always the possibility of borrowing from the rest of the world to finance deficits. However, heavy reliance upon this source may be risky, especially in periods of recession.

Debt Retirement

Public debt can be retired through budgetary surplus, that is, by using tax revenue over and above government expenditures, or through money creation. Compared to private businesses, governments, national or local, have the advantage of raising taxes. Private companies without surplus revenue can retire their debt through bankruptcy. Moreover, national or federal, not local, governments have the power to issue money and can finance deficits and retire the debt partially or totally by expanding the money supply. The federal government can "borrow" from the central bank in exchange for bonds and other debt instruments. This process of debt monetization, or disguised money creation, transfers purchasing power to the government; and, depending on employment conditions, this may lead to inflation.

To prevent inflation, the government can sell securities to the public and use the revenue to retire securities held by the Fed. These securities are used to back Federal Reserve notes, the main U.S. currency, and are exchanged in the open market, mainly for countercyclical reasons. The nominal interest paid to the Central Bank and indirectly to commercial banks is usually small; and the debt, financed through concealed money creation, is "fake," not real, debt. In cases of severe recessions, outstanding public debt can be monetized by the government to increase income and employment.

If the debt is used to finance public investment, future returns on such investment may provide the needed funds to finance debt retirement. Provisions, though, should be made to avoid the replacement or offsetting of private with public investment. On these grounds, it can be suggested that capital expenditures be separated from current expenditures in government budgets. Servicing and amortization of debt, used to finance long-term public projects, can be made through the gradual returns on such investment projects.

To limit federal debt, Congress has from time to time imposed debt ceilings. Such ceilings were gradually uplifted from $11.5 billion in 1917 until they reached more than $2 trillion in 1986; they are raised periodically to match the real figures. The idea is to discourage excessive federal spending. Yet this device has proven to have limited success in the long run.

10

International Aspects of Public Finance

INTERNATIONAL REPERCUSSIONS OF U.S. FISCAL POLICY

Subsidies and other fiscal policy measures are frequently used by the United States and many other countries to stimulate industrial production and to increase exports. In many instances, though, industrial and agricultural expansions create unneeded and duplicative projects with high proportions of idle capacity that threaten to initiate slumps on a worldwide scale. To reduce unemployment and to increase income and public revenue, governments try to implement such policies as investment tax credit, faster write-offs of capital assets, and similar changes, all of which will speed economic growth and grasp foreign markets.

As U.S. spending, relative to foreign spending, rises through expansionary government policies, domestic demand is pumped up, relative to foreign demand, and the current accounts are worsened. On the other hand, U.S. fiscal deficits, financed by sales of bonds and other government securities, tend to overvalue the exchange rate by raising real interest rates, which attract capital inflows, appreciating the dollar and worsening the current account balance. It would seem, therefore, that fiscal deficits, domestic demand pressures, and real exchange rates are closely interlinked and tend to rise together with deficits in current accounts.

Capital inflow from abroad, which maintains U.S. investment at a good level, affects and is largely affected by public finance policies. About 40 percent of all current net investment is financed by foreign capital. If foreign investors became unwilling to continue such financing and funds from abroad shrink, real investment rates will decline and fiscal measures will have to change. This unprecedented inflow of capital has increased total foreign assets in the United

States to about $1.5 trillion and has made the country the largest net debtor nation in the world (with more than $400 billion debt to other countries).

Foreign funds, arriving rapidly (at the speed of a telex) in the United States from Europe, Latin America, Asia, and the Arab countries for security and high earnings, help mitigate the problem of budget deficits and foreign trade deficits. However, from an international point of view, U.S. deficits help the economic recoveries in other countries and stimulate the entire world economy. It looks like a stimulative Keynesian policy on the international scale.

Rising profits and high real interest rates in the U.S. economy have attracted large amounts of foreign capital and have helped relieve domestic financial markets and budget deficits, exacerbating, though, the country's obligation for future interest payments to service the growing external debt, along with amortization. However, if the flow of foreign capital stops, as foreigners reach limits on funds available, or reverses itself for different economic and political reasons, then interest rates would go further up and deficit financing would be a serious problem.

Yet high interest rates due to high budget deficits in the United States force other countries to keep their interest rates high or face capital flight and massive currency depreciations. Therefore, a decline in interest rates, which could come from a reduction in budget deficits and coordination of policies with other nations, could be the major remedy of widespread contraction that threatens to cripple the economies of many countries.

From time to time, budget appropriations are needed for contributions to the International Monetary Fund (IMF), the World Bank, and other institutions, which provide loans and advice to the countries concerned. Because delinquent debtor countries are cut off from private bank loans, IMF seems to be the last resort of borrowing. But IMF needs higher contributions by its member countries to be able to function in a worldwide credit crisis. Thus, an increase in the U.S. contribution to the IMF by $8.4 billion, in addition to the current annual contribution of $14.6 billion has been appropriated by Congress in the mid–1980s. Such financial support would help not only debtor countries but also U.S. commercial banks that have extended risky loans in their efforts to increase their profits by recycling petrodollars to developing countries, many of which have large debts. A similar credit trap occurred in the 1840s, when nine U.S. states suspended interest payments on their debts to European banks. The same thing happened also during the Great Depression of the 1930s and may happen in the near future if corrective measures are not taken.

To help avoid a worldwide credit and monetary crisis, the U.S. government could support the establishment of a multilateral agency to buy up foreign debt at a discount or to reschedule long-term payments at low interest rates. This would be beneficial to U.S. and Western exports and world trade. It would also bail out U.S. and other banks engaged heavily in foreign loans, thereby reducing the pressure on the federal budget.

In spite of the arguments that budget deficits are immoral, prevent recoveries, and cause inflation and national bankruptcy, such deficits became common in many countries and continue to pile up debts. Fiscal virtue and the golden rule of budget balancing became remote concepts or empty slogans. On the contrary, growing debts from annual deficits absorb domestic and foreign savings and crowd out private investment.

From the point of view of capital flows, the introduction of an interest equalization tax, that is, a tax on outflows of capital to offset the interest gap, may be appropriate. Such a tax, though ineffective, was applied in the 1960s by the United States and is contemplated presently in Japan and Western Europe.

Although budget deficits were higher than trade deficits in the early 1980s, it is expected that foreign trade deficits will rise faster than the structural budget deficits and that the drag from trade deficits will outweigh the stimulus of budget deficits. To deal with this imbalance, domestic economic policies should be designed in light of their impact on foreign trade and international relations. Modern nations should acknowledge the close links of domestic economies to the world economy, particularly on matters of investment, fiscal measures, and currency fluctuations.

RELATIONSHIP BETWEEN BUDGET AND FOREIGN TRADE DEFICITS

Alarming Twin Deficits

In addition to the chronic federal budget deficit is the U.S. trade deficit, which is equally alarming. Since 1893 and until 1970, that is, for 77 consecutive years, the United States enjoyed a surplus in its merchandise trade with the rest of the world. However, since 1971 the United States has had deficits in foreign trade, especially with Japan, Canada, Germany, Britain, France, and Italy and even with Brazil, Mexico, Singapore, and Korea.

The U.S. budget deficits, and the relatively high interest rates they have produced in the past, are blamed for the huge trade deficits. Yet the merchandise deficits are going up although interest rates have come down somewhat. Even with a weak dollar, the United States had foreign trade problems. Although some complaints that unfair trade practices of other nations may be justified, the globalization of the economy and severe international competition may be considered the main reasons for the U.S. trade deficits.

Nevertheless, greater private saving, which will pay future taxes for debt servicing, may offset increased government borrowing and interest rates without affecting investment. This may be so if budget deficits are not large in relation to the rate of economic growth. On the other hand, higher taxes, which are required to pay interest on a large debt, have distorting market effects and impose a dead weight burden on the economy. Moreover, the financing of budget deficits through capital imports, practiced largely by the Reagan administration in the 1980s, led to pressure by special interests and politicians to deploy protectionist measures in favor of particular U.S. industries. Such measures included tariffs (motorcycles, cheese, textiles), trigger prices (steel), corporate bailouts (Chrysler, Lockheed), quotas (auto, textiles), government allocation of private credit, and other policies to protect certain industries from going off the cliff. Perceptively, the adoption of a prop-up-the-losers policy may lead to the erosion of U.S. competitiveness and to "a strategy for failure and lemon socialism."[1]

A good foreign trade policy requires a sound budgetary policy, which can be achieved through taming budget deficits and reducing interest rates, both of which make the economy and the nation vulnerable to foreign competition. Such competition is damaging to certain industries and sectors that require government support, as happened, for example, with the agricultural subsidies for 1985–88. This, in turn, keeps budget deficits high, thus maintaining high trade deficits so that the country enters a vicious circle of domestic and foreign sector deficits. Given this interactive cycle, it may be that deficit reduction and eventual budget balancing will preoccupy economic policy for the years to come.

The huge U.S. budget and foreign trade (twin) deficits as well as the growing dependence on capital inflow make the country turn inward and lose its international economic dominance. Like Britain after 1890, the United States is gradually losing its position as the lender of last resort. This may lead to a financial crisis similar to those of 1873, 1890, and 1929, which produced deep depressions. Jointly with Western Europe and Japan, however, the United States can yet play the role of an important borrower and lender of last resort, so that a global economic equilibrium can be sustained. In a sense, the financial underpinning of global expansion can be a symbiotic mixture of U.S. hedonism, oriental thrift, and the European balancing force.

The U.S. government spends sizable amounts of money to defend other Western countries (some $120 billion a year for Western Europe alone). This allows other governments, including Japan, to use tax savings to subsidize their exports and compete with the United States. A reduction of such spending for the defense of allied advanced countries and the sharing of their responsibilities would permit reductions in budget and trade deficits and/or transfer of funds toward the developing debtor nations.

In short, budget and trade deficits will predominate economic thinking for years to come. Debtor countries will continue to face serious problems of paying back maturing debts and interests and will repetitively ask for new loans or debt rescheduling. But, as Swiss bankers stress, loans should never be given for interest payment because debts would pile up without the possibility of repayment. A liquidity crisis might thus be concealed under a thick financial ice upon which the world economies are skating. Growing domestic and foreign debts, as well as leveraged buyouts, index futures, junk bonds, and other financial instruments, will continue to create unstable economic conditions.

The U.S. budget deficits have acted like a worldwide mega-Keynesian stimulus as other countries have stepped up their exports to the United States and increased their economic growth. It seems that the United States uses foreign saving to stimulate its economy and, in turn, to end recession for foreign countries as well. It assembles energy from all over the world and feeds energy to the rest of the world.[2] However, in the long run a growing portion of production should be devoted every year to service the debt which is incorporated in the exported iou's. It should be pointed out, of course, that about 30 percent of U.S. imports come from U.S. corporations operating abroad.

A gradual correction of budgetary imbalances and a smooth landing of the dollar could restore financial and economic stability in both the U.S. and the international markets. It seems that while budget deficits generate employment, trade deficits export jobs, especially in manufacturing.

To harmonize diverging national policies toward foreign investment and taxes, an international code of government behavior and business ethics may be needed. Common customs duties, antitrust policies, transportation rates, benefits, and taxation may be included in such a harmonized code. Technological progress and robotization in our supersonic era make the world smaller and the corporation bigger so that very soon we may emphasize, not independent fiscal policies, but unified international policies.

The Romance of Budget and Trade Deficits

Excessive government expenditures and fiscal deficits play a significant role in external trade deficits and vice versa. When budget deficits are financed in inflationary ways, as has frequently happened in the past, demand for foreign products increases and trade deficits rise. In many instances, reductions in trade deficits are the results of reduced fiscal deficits. On the other hand, when trade deficits rise, the main reasons are increases in government spending and budget deficits.

The gap between national savings and investment (or that between domestic income and expenditure) is related to the foreign trade position. Therefore, external trade deficits can affect and be affected by policies that change net private sector savings and those that influence government deficits. From that point of view, economic policies to reduce trade deficits must be consistent with domestic targets. They should include fiscal policies that will diminish budgetary deficits through changes in tax rates and government expenditures and alter private saving and investment behavior primarily through changes in interest rates and exchange rates. In addition, exogenous factors may affect internal fiscal deficits and external trade deficits. They include changes in the terms of trade, fluctuations in foreign demand, and sociopolitical disturbances. Nevertheless, there seems to be a high correlation between changes in domestic budget deficits and changes in external trade deficits. This means that improvements in the foreign trade position are related to improvements in the government budget position.

As Figure 10.1 indicates, foreign trade deficits follow the trend of the budget deficits. This became obvious after 1969 and especially after 1973, when both

Figure 10.1
The Relationship of Budget Deficits and Trade Deficits (billions of dollars)

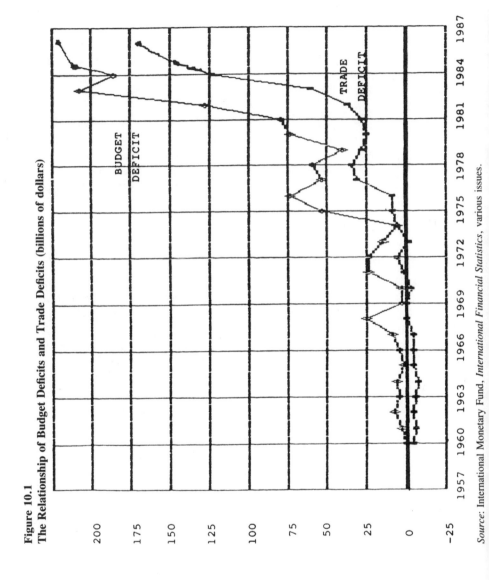

Source: International Monetary Fund, *International Financial Statistics*, various issues.

variables followed a dramatic upward trend.[3] If this trend continues for long, the U.S. economy will have to pay out large amounts of interest and dividends, instead of collecting them (as it has done for the last 65 years). Then political power and international influence would be unfavorably affected by such a change in economic power and the dollar could be undermined, forcing fiscal and monetary policies that might have worldwide destabilizing effects.

To promote greater currency stability in the world, major Western nations try to conclude a new monetary agreement that could give the IMF a significant role in coordinating related domestic policies. Through a new International Open Market Committee, the IMF could set "target zones" for exchange rates and then encourage countries to adopt fiscal and monetary policies for their implementation. Such coordinated policies would stop certain currencies, notably the dollar, from changing drastically and ease the debt repayment problems of debtor nations.

A regression analysis of trade deficits on budget deficits shows a close relationship of the two variables for the period 1960–86. The regression coefficient, 0.45, indicates that for each dollar change in the budget deficit there is a 0.45 dollars change in foreign trade deficit.

Although correlation does not establish causality, this statistical result shows that when budget deficits in the United States increase by a certain percentage, trade deficits increase by almost half of that percentage and vice versa. Therefore, reductions in budget deficits are expected to bring about reductions in foreign trade deficits. Also, persistence of deficits in the governmental budget, caused by spending that has been higher than taxation, could perpetuate trade deficits. This means that a growing federal debt could increase foreign debt as well.

The statistical results of the correlation of budget and trade deficits are satisfactory. The fit of the regression is good. The corrected coefficient of determination is high ($\bar{R}^2 = 0.752$), indicating that the budget deficit is a good explanatory variable of the trade deficit. On the other hand, the Durbin-Watson (D-W) statistic (1.76) is high enough to exclude serial correlation, and the result should be interpreted with confidence.

For a further review of the relationship between trade deficit and a few of the most important variables affecting it, multiple regression analyses were conducted for the years 1960–86. The dependent variable was the trade deficit. The independent variables were the budget deficit, gross national product, inflation, and unemployment.

Comparatively speaking, the regression coefficient of foreign trade deficit on budget deficit (0.38) for 1960–86 was higher than that on private consumption (0.061), inflation (0.036), and GNP (0.021); while the regression coefficient of trade deficit on unemployment was far higher (7.73).[4] This means that for the United States a change of 1 percent in unemployment was associated with a change of 7.73 percent in trade deficit. Also, a unit change in budget deficit was associated with 0.38 units in trade deficit and so on for the other variables.

The corrected coefficient of determination in this multiple regression was high

($\bar{R}^2 = 0.826$), indicating a very good correlation. However, the Durbin-Watson statistic (D-W) at 5 percent level of significance was not high enough to signify the nonexistence of serial correlation, and the results should be interpreted with caution.

SIMILARITIES AND DIFFERENCES BETWEEN FOREIGN TAXATION AND CUSTOMS DUTIES

Impacts of Tax Differences

In recent years many countries have enacted legislation concerning tax exemptions or tax reductions to attract foreign investment. Also, international tax treaties have been concluded between the major capital-importing and capital-exporting countries to promote such investment. However, different tax systems still in existence inevitably distort allocation. They create opportunities for foreign investors to maximize net profits after taxes by departing from the optimal allocation of resources on a before-tax basis.

Consequently, international treaties and laws, which eliminate tax differences and promote uniformity and equality, are of great importance for the efficient allocation in production and distribution. Furthermore, the existence of tax inequalities leads to self-defeating policies, since foreign corporations will prefer investment in privileged countries. Actually governments compete to attract investments in their countries by offering advantages in the form of tax exemptions, employment benefits for foreign personnel, and easy capital repatriation. Thus, developing and developed countries, one after another, adopt favorable tax measures and favor investment by foreign corporations. In making tax concessions, however, care must be taken not to give foreign firms extensive competitive advantages over existing domestic firms. Presently, the U.S. Congress is considering the placement of limitations on foreign acquisitions of certain U.S. industries, which are increasing rapidly because of the dollar devaluation.

Domestic taxation draws instant attention from the taxpayers and the fiscal policymakers. But taxation on foreign earnings appears to be of remote importance, even though it may have serious long-term repercussions upon the economy. Corporations with overseas earnings are customarily taxed by two countries: the foreign country where earnings take place and the country in which the citizens or corporations receiving the earnings belong. Here two main principles of taxation must prevail: tax equity, that is, all the citizens and corporations with the same income should pay the same amount of tax; and tax universality, that is, taxes should be paid on all income earned.

Many countries have enacted laws with credit provisions. Thus, the U.S. tax law provides for tax credit for income taxed in another country. The tax credit permits companies and citizens to subtract from their U.S. tax on income earned abroad the amount of tax they paid to a foreign country on the same income. Thus, assuming that the foreign tax on $100 income earned abroad was $30 and given that the highest U.S. tax liability is $34 (34 percent on taxable corporate income), then only $4 should be paid to the U.S. government.

The problem of double taxation, that is, taxation on the same income by the host country and by the home country, is not a new phenomenon. Prior to 1918, foreign income taxes were allowed by Congress to be deducted from gross income earned in other countries. After 1918, taxes paid abroad by U.S. corporations with foreign branches were permitted to be deducted from the U.S. tax liability, thus becoming a tax credit. In 1921, the foreign tax credit was extended to cover corporations that owned a majority of voting stock in a foreign subsidiary. After 1951, the tax credit was further liberalized to cover corporations that own 10 percent or more of the voting stock of a foreign subsidiary from which they receive dividends. The idea was to spread the U.S. system, to increase trade, and to replace aid. As a result of foreign tax credit, it is estimated that the U.S. government collects only about 6 percent of the taxable foreign-derived income, while foreign governments collect 40 percent to 50 percent on the same taxable income. Moreover, by juggling their books, so to speak, and arranging their worldwide income distribution, big corporations frequently manage to pay little or no domestic income taxes.

Multinational corporations are affected by taxation abroad in their allocation of management and service costs and the adjustment of transfer prices by tax authorities. However, Western industrial (OECD member) countries have agreed that enterprises operating in their territory and controlled by nationals of another member country should be treated as domestic enterprises in like situations. At times, royalties paid by a company to a host country on oil or other products might be converted to income taxes and be subtracted from U.S. taxes. This means a transfer of tax revenue from the United States to the host country without affecting the company.

The foreign tax credit provision is criticized on the ground that it is a loophole in favor of the companies investing abroad. It is claimed that taxes paid to another country on income earned abroad should be deducted from the total income, not from the U.S. tax liability. Thus, in our previous example of $100 taxable income abroad, at the highest bracket the U.S. tax would be $23.80, ($100 - $30).34, instead of $4.

Arguments to repeal the U.S. foreign tax credit intend to treat taxes paid to another government in the same way as taxes paid to different states within the United States. However, the supporters of the foreign tax credit argue that the U.S. system is such that the federal government does not have the power on the individual states to regulate state taxes and that in some states, such as Texas, Nevada, Washington, and Wyoming, there are no corporate income taxes. Furthermore, it was calculated by the National Foreign Trade Council that the substitution of an income deduction for the tax credit would increase the effective tax rate, but the difference of tax collection would not be significant. In addition, the argument that the elimination of the tax credit would increase exports and employment at home does not seem to be persuasive. On the contrary, it may be argued that multinational manufacturing companies have expanded U.S. exports and employment faster than manufacturing firms in general.

Restricting foreign operations through heavier taxation upon firms investing abroad would probably lead to the elimination of present and future markets and the loss of efficiency from greater comparative advantages, as well as the loss from more dynamic management and further technological advances. The use of foreign sources for the financing of these firms and the increase in total earnings from operations abroad are additional reasons of support of foreign ventures. Some countries, such as Canada, Germany, and the Netherlands, do not even tax foreign earnings of their multinational companies, while France and Japan have very small tax rates on dividends from abroad.

Personal income tax exemptions for foreign personnel, especially managers and technicians, have been introduced by many countries, rich and poor, to promote capital investment and foreign ventures.[5] Furthermore, aside from the United States, developed countries such as Germany and the United Kingdom have introduced measures of deferring tax liabilities on profits abroad until repatriation, thus encouraging reinvestment.

Tax deferral, which prevails in some developed countries including the United States, means that taxation is levied on dividends remitted to the country. This is a form of an interest-free loan from the government to the corporations, which then will reinvest profits in low-tax countries to defer tax payments until their liquidation. Efforts to eliminate the tax deferrals for the sake of tax neutrality and improvement in the balance of payments have been largely ineffective.

Transfer-price manipulation, or price adjustment, is another device used between parent companies and their affiliates to save taxes or to repatriate more profits than the amounts permitted. A number of firms are accused or charging their affiliates exorbitant prices in order to reduce taxes and primarily to shift profits, which have been frozen in other countries, and bring them back to the home country. To achieve a fair income tax policy, negotiations between governments and companies involved have been enacted periodically.

As a means of reducing the capital flight, some countries from time to time impose interest equalization taxes on purchase of foreign stocks, bonds, and other liquid assets. On the other hand, companies investing abroad borrow large amounts of funds from host-country banks, exporting small amounts of currencies from the home countries. As a matter of fact, there are complaints that multinational corporations drain domestic financial resources and deprive local entrepreneurs of their main source of investment financing, in addition to the fiscal advantages they enjoy.

Moreover, when a company borrows money and treats the interest it pays as a domestic expense although its operations are largely abroad, it can reduce domestic profits and claim tax credits for the whole amount of interest paid. This encourages investment abroad by U.S. multinationals and intensifies complaints by labor unions that jobs are exported. For that reason and for more tax revenue, proposals have been made to change the law so that related expenses are split or allocated between domestic and foreign operations.

Effects of Customs Duties

Although tariffs and other free trade restrictions are in the domain of international economics, their growing importance on domestic fiscal policies requires a brief review here. In taxed imports, through tariffs or customs duties, foreign suppliers have to sell their products at lower net prices, affecting domestic policies on subsidies, employment, and bankruptcies. The burden of product taxes is thus shifted to foreigners. Such a shifting runs counter to the international equity principle, according to which each country should pay its own taxes. However, other countries whose products are taxed use the principle of retaliation and impose their own taxes on products they import. The results of such protectionistic policies are higher prices and lower quantities of products exchanged.

Similar changes in prices may take place through taxes on exports, which burden foreign consumers. Countries that enjoy monopolies or oligopolies in natural resources or products and dominate export markets may impose export taxes, thereby increasing the cost of exports. Again, the foreign consumers will pay more, free trade will be restricted, and conflicts among countries may arise, unless such policies are in harmony through mutual understanding or international agreements among the governments concerned.

The government can use customs duties to collect revenue and, at the same time, to protect domestic production and employment, especially in infant industries. The amount of revenue from tariffs and the degree of protection depend on the elasticities of supply and demand for the commodity imported. The higher the elasticity of demand for imports, the more the decrease in the quantity of imports and the less the revenue from customs duties. The same holds true for the elasticity of supply.

Figure 10.2 shows the supply and demand for a commodity that is produced partly domestically (PA) and is partly imported (AG) to cover total demand (PG). When a tariff PP' per unit is introduced, total demand would be reduced to P'F, domestic production would be increased to P'E, and imports would be reduced to EF. The government would collect total revenue BCFE (revenue effect), that is (EB) × (EF). The triangle ABE measures the benefits of tariffs to the producers (protective effect), while the triangle CGF measures the sacrifice to the consumers (consumer effect) because of higher prices due to tariffs. Domestic producers produce more output by AB and consumers demand less output by CG as a result of tariffs. The rectangle PP'BE represents payment of subsidies to domestic producers, which can be considered as an income transfer from the consumers to the producers of the import-competing good considered.

Changes in relative prices of internationally exchanged products and the effects of tariffs can be explained by what Alfred Marshall called offer curves or re-

Figure 10.2
Government Revenue from Customs Duties

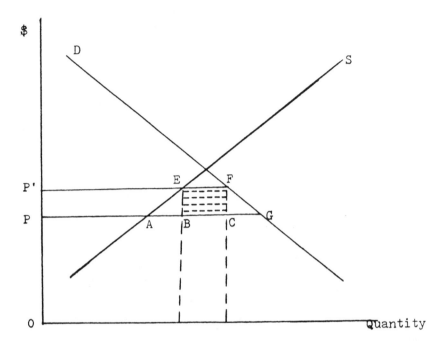

ciprocal demand curves, which are presented in Figure 10.3. The reciprocal demands between two countries establish the terms of trade, which are affected by domestic costs, as John Stuart Mill suggested. Thus, the offer curve of country X (say Japan) indicates how much wheat the country demands from another country Y (say the United States) in exchange for steel at different prevailing prices, and vice versa for country Y. After successive trade transactions between the two countries, the two offer curves meet at the equilibrium point, E, where the amounts of wheat offered and steel demanded by country Y equal the amounts of steel offered and wheat demanded by country X. That is the point where the reciprocal demands of the two countries are equal. The price ratio, which is measured by the slope of the ray OA, shows the terms of trade.

As a result of tariffs imposed by country X on the import of wheat, the same ton of wheat is exchanged with more steel (1.3 tons). This means that X's terms of trade deteriorated by 30 percent in favor of Y's because of a relative change in the demand against country X and in favor of country Y due to tariffs on the imports of wheat. The new price ratio, OB, reflects the shift of the exchange ratio from 1.0 ton of steel per ton of wheat to 1.3 tons of steel for the same ton of wheat.

Some governments provide budget subsidies for certain products that can be unloaded to other countries at prices below the cost of production. To retaliate,

Figure 10.3
Changes in Terms of Trade Due to Tariffs Imposed by the Government

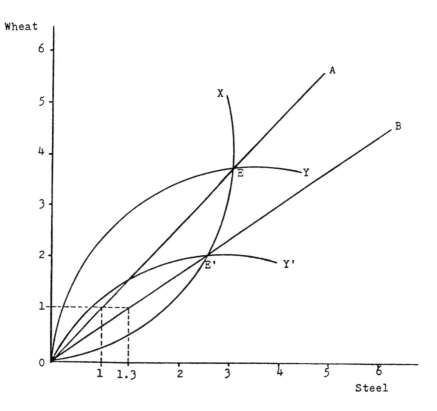

other nations use antidumping and countervailing duty measures. Such subsidies and antidumping policies restrict free and fair trade among nations and increase the possibilities of protectionism, in addition to budgetary expenditures needed to pay for subsidies. Among the products subsidized are textiles and primarily steel. Steelmakers in the United States complain against Japan and the EEC and ask for quota restrictions; the Japanese complain against South Korea; EEC steelmakers, against Romania and Brazil; and those in developing countries, against industrial countries, accusing them of trying to keep the ''new boys''— the third world producers—off the world markets.

To avoid protectionism and trade wars, many steelmakers and other producers ask for multilateral agreements among interested nations similar to that of cotton textiles in the 1960s, which allows developed countries to restrict textile imports from developing countries. However, steel users and primarily automakers and construction industries object to such agreements, which protect inefficient domestic manufacturers and push up prices. For the government, though, such agreements lead to less unemployment and more tax revenue.

An unwise policy of protectionism in the 1930s exacerbated the Great Depression of that period. Throughout the 1920s U.S. exports increased, as did private loans to finance such exports to other countries. After the crash of 1929, average tariffs were raised to 40 percent (Smoot-Hawley Law of 1930). Foreign firms could not sell their products to the United States and could not collect dollars to pay their loans. The tariffs of the 1930s walled out competition and walled in inefficiency. They cut back imports but they reduced exports as well. The result of this beggar-my-neighbor policy of protectionism reduced world industrial production by about 30 percent and increased unemployment by more than 25 percent, while world trade in manufactured goods declined by more than 40 percent and overall government revenue from tariffs was reduced.

For some commodities, effective tariffs are already high in the United States. Thus, for clothing and fabrics tariffs are 40 percent of the value of the commodities imported; for milk, cheese, and butter, 37 percent; for cigars and cigarettes, 113 percent; for plant, vegetable, and olive oil, 18 percent; and so on. Similar and even higher tariffs prevail in Japan and the EEC countries. Tariff reductions and improvement in trade with the poor nations would allow reduction in the U.S. aid (some $7.4 billion in 1986), which is a burden on the budget, and stop their cry of "trade, no aid."

EFFECTS OF FISCAL POLICIES ON FOREIGN DEBTS

National economic policies and fiscal policies in particular not only affect changes in domestic deficits and debts but also have repercussions on the debts of other countries. Measures on multinational corporations and mergers, rules and regulations to minimize government distortions of capital and technology transfers, and controls on foreign exchange rates and financial transactions influence and are influenced by fiscal and monetary policies in other nations. Technical and financial assistance, government guarantees for bank loans, the absence of tax discrimination, and international agreements for business protection and economic cooperation affect world trade and play a significant role on changes in economic and social conditions in other countries.

The need for international fiscal cooperation and coordination of demand policies requires that the tax equity and tax neutrality principles of public finance be extended from an interindividual to an international level. Government aid and capital transfers among nations should consider the principles of efficient allocation and income distribution in a way of raising economic growth, in the long run, without debt accumulations. Along these lines, investment in sectors and regions with low capital-output ratios is expected to receive priority in capital formation, subsidies, and other incentive policies. In low-income regions and nations, where the private sector hesitates or is unable to undertake the construction of needed infrastructural facilities, the public sector has an important role to play in allocating resources and training people, especially in the early stages of development. However, state enterprises and the public sector in general are responsible for large budget and trade deficits, which bring about big foreign debts.

Laxity in fiscal and monetary discipline, structural rigidities, and biased growth strategies in rich and poor countries, as well as the rise in protectionist sentiment, are some of the factors responsible for huge external debts and the financial dependency of mainly third world countries.

To avoid a worldwide financial crisis and to soften economic shocks, which could lead to fiscal and social disruptions, an expanded role of the IMF has been introduced. Such a role includes the introduction of fiscal performance clauses, ceilings on budget deficits, restrictions on bank credit to the public sector, and controls on public enterprise pricing policies. In more practical terms, debt rescheduling and refinancing include provisions that debtor countries introduce austerity measures to balance their public budgets, deflate their economies, and reduce or eliminate balance-of-trade deficits.

Empirical evidence suggests that a one percentage point increase in the ratio of fiscal deficit to GNP would cause a deterioration of the current account by about half a percentage point.[6] Therefore, from the point of view of domestic policy, fiscal restraints, together with currency adjustments, can be applied in order to keep the current account balance from worsening. Urgent priority, therefore, is to reduce the budget deficit, which was $155.1 billion plus a surplus of $97 billion transferred from Social Security, civil service and military retirement funds in 1988.

To prevent an international economic crunch from foreign loan defaults, especially from Latin American countries, the United States has to adjust its budget deficits. This pressure from a possible foreign credit crunch is expected to be severe in the foreseeable future because a number of countries are close to the brink and look perilous, for both economic and political reasons.

Continuation of high interest rates because of large budget deficits in the United States aggravates the world debt crisis and threatens widespread protectionism. Countries with large debts, such as Brazil, Mexico, Argentina, Poland, Yugoslavia, Romania, Chile, Peru, Turkey, and the Philippines, ask for long-run debt rescheduling with lower interest rates and other loan fees.[7] The alternative may be widespread defaults and large-scale bankruptcies of creditor banks. More than 800 banks are owed money by Brazil alone. They include large banks such as Chase Manhattan, Morgan Guaranty Trust Company, and Citibank. It would seem, then, that poor people abroad and banks and taxpayers at home share a common interest to stimulate international trade and avoid a world financial crisis. Thus domestic fiscal and monetary policies become more and more intertwined with international economic policies.

Whether we commend or condemn the U.S. fiscal policy, the net capital inflow is not all a simple direct result of the budget deficits and the increase in national debt. In addition to the demand for U.S. government securities, the inflow of foreign funds reflects also a significant increase in private sector deposits and investment in stocks, bonds, and other financial instruments. On the other hand, U.S. banks have started reducing lending to financially unstable developing nations. This has reduced the supply of dollars abroad and contributed in making the United States a net international borrower. A U.S. fiscal discipline, then, would help world economic growth and lead nations toward a socioeconomic convergence.

According to Vassily Leontief, the Nobel Prize winner for economics in 1973, the cost to U.S. taxpayers of propping up friendly "authoritarian" countries and combating hostile "totalitarian" regimes in developing countries with large debts is expected to increase.[8] On the other hand, record deficits have propelled U.S. debts to high levels and are used to pay for themselves. Under such a heavy burden, the government might be unable to rescue defaulting debtor nations and U.S. banks.

Notes

CHAPTER 1

1. There are 82,688 government units, including the federal government, 50 state governments (with Alaska and Hawaii since 1959), the District of Columbia, 3,041 counties, 16,748 townships, 19,083 municipalities, 28,733 special districts, and 15,032 school districts.

2. Jean Jacques Rousseau, *The Social Contract*, translated by Charles Frankel (New York: Hafner Publishing Company, 1947), Book I, 5–8.

3. More on the relationship between externalities and resource allocation in Arthur C. Pigou, *The Economics of Welfare* (London: Macmillan, 1932).

4. The next chapter deals with Pareto's optimality. For a more detailed study, see Vilfredo Pareto, *Cours d'Economie Politique* vol. I, II (Lausanne: 1896–97).

CHAPTER 2

1. Plato, *Laws*, v. 736.

2. Aristotle, *Ethics*, ix, 8. Also, Earnest Barker, *The Political Thought of Plato and Aristotle* (New York: Dover, 1959), 390–400.

3. Saint Thomas Aquinas (1225–74), a theologian, adapted Aristotle's philosophy to Christian doctrine in his writings, primarily in *Summa Theologica*.

4. Thomas Mun (1571–1641) was the main proponent of mercantilism; and François Quesnay (1694–1774) and Robert Turgot (1727–81) of physiocracy. For a historical review, see Carolyn Webber and Aaron Wildavsky, *A History of Taxation and Expenditure in the Western World* (New York: Simon and Schuster, 1986), chap. 4.

5. Adam Smith, *An Inquiry into the Nature and Causes of the Wealth of Nations*, E. Cannan, ed. (New York: Modern Library, 1937), 423.

6. Ibid. 653–89.

7. Friedrich List, *The National System of Political Economy*, translated by S. Lloyd (New York: Longmans, Green, 1904), 143.

8. However, there is no indication of a withering away of the state, as suggested. Instead the state remains strong and government controls on the economy prevail in all countries that are practicing extensive public sector ownership.

9. More discussion in John Maynard Keynes, "The End of Laissez-Faire," in his *Laissez-Faire and Communism* (New York: New Republic, 1926); and his *General Theory of Employment Interest and Money* (New York: Harcourt, 1936).

10. For predictions concerning such economic developments, see Alvin Hansen, "Economic Progress and Declining Population Growth," *American Economic Review* (March 1939): 1–15; and his *Economic Issues of the 1960s*, (New York: McGraw-Hill, 1960), 44–45.

11. John Kenneth Galbraith, *The New Industrial State*, 2nd ed. revised (Boston: Houghton Mifflin, 1971), chap. 19.

12. Vilfredo Pareto, *Cours d'Economie Politique*; and Joseph Schumpeter, "Vilfredo Pareto," *Quarterly Journal of Economics*, LXIII, no. 2 (May 1949).

13. A deeper analysis in Arthur C. Pigou, *A Study of Public Finance*, 3rd ed. (London: Macmillan, 1951); and his *The Economics of Welfare*, (London: Macmillan, 1932); also Antony Atkinson and Nicholas Stern, "Pigou, Taxation and Public Goods," *Review of Economic Studies*, *41*, (1974): 119–28.

14. Externalities, which cause prices to diverge from true opportunity costs of resources, are explained in William J. Baumol, and Wallace E. Oates, *The Theory of Environmental Policy* (Englewood Cliffs, N.J.: Prentice-Hall, 1975); and Lawrence Ball, "Externalities from Contract Length," *American Economic Review* (September 1987): 615–25.

15. For a review of the fable of the apples and the bees, see Steven Cheung, "The Fable of the Bees: An Economic Investigation," *Journal of Law and Economics* (April 1973): 11–33.

16. For related legal and other cases, see Ronald H. Coase, "The Problem of Social Cost," *Journal of Law and Economics* (October 1960): 1–44.

17. Further analysis in James M. Buchanan, "An Economic Theory of Clubs," *Economica* (February 1965); G. Brennan and M. Flowers, "All 'Ng' Up on Clubs?: Some Notes on the Club Theory," *Public Finance Quarterly* (April 1980); and Todd Sandler and John Tschirhart, "The Economic Theory of Clubs: An Evaluative Survey," *The Journal of Economic Literature*, *18* (December 1980).

CHAPTER 3

1. The limits of the central authority were supported by the Stoic and Epicurian philosophers (fourth century B.C.), as well as by Thomas Hobbes (1588–1679), John Locke (1632–1704), and Jean Jacques Rousseau (1717–78), in addition to classical economists mentioned earlier.

2. Adolph Wagner, *Financzwissenschaft*, 3rd ed. (Leipzig: 1890). For empirical findings in a number of countries, see Solomon Fabricant, *The Trend of Government Activity in the United States since 1900* (New York: National Bureau of Economic Research, 1952); and Harry Oshima, "Shares of Government in Gross National Product for Various Countries," *American Economic Review* (June 1957). Also Warren Nutter, *Growth of Government in the West* (Washington, D.C.: American Enterprise Institute, 1978).

3. Arthur C. Pigou, *A Study of Public Finance*, 3rd ed. (London: Macmillan, 1951), 31.

4. Alan T. Peacock and Jack Wisemen, *The Growth of Public Expenditures in the United Kingdom* (New York: National Bureau of Economic Research, 1961).

5. Richard A. Musgrave, *The Future of Fiscal Policy: A Reassessment* (Leuven, Belgium: Leuven University Press, 1978), 18.

6. William J. Baumol, "Macroeconomics of Unbalanced Growth," *American Economic Review* (June 1967).

7. Milton Friedman, *From Galbraith to Economic Freedom* (London: Institute of Economic Affairs, 1977). For cases of denationalization or privatization in China and other countries, see Emanuel S. Savas, *Privatization: The Key to Better Government* (New York: Chatam House, 1988).

8. Self-employed shopkeepers increased in China from 140,000 in 1978 to more than 7.5 million in 1984. Wheat production more than doubled in seven years to 81 million tons in 1984. Christopher Wren, "China Undergoing a New Revolution," *New York Times*, April 24, 1984, A6. Also Richard Critchfield, "Aristotle, Deng, and China's Peasants," *New York Times*, November 16, 1985, 27.

9. Adam Smith, *An Inquiry into the Nature and Causes of the Wealth of Nations*, E. Cannan, ed. (New York: Modern Library, 1937), 284.

10. John Stuart Mill, *Considerations on Representative Government* (London: Routledge, 1905), 114; and Charles Lindblom, *Politics and Markets* (New York: Basic Books, 1977), chap. 24.

11. Joseph Schumpeter, *Capitalism, Socialism and Democracy*, 3rd ed. (New York: Harper Colophon Books, 1975), 205. For some review lessons in Europe, see J. Carby-Hall, *Worker Participation in Europe* (London: C. Helm, 1977), chap. 3; and Nicholas V. Gianaris, *The Economies of the Balkan Countries* (New York: Praeger, 1982), chap. 4.

12. Martin Weizman, *The Share Economy*, (Cambridge, Mass: Harvard University Press, 1984), chap 8; and William Serrin, "Employee Owned Companies and Their Fates," *New York Times*, December 30, 1984, E3. Also, Corey Rosen, Katherine Klein, and Karen Young, *Employee Ownership in America: The Equity Solution* (Lexington, Mass.: Lexington Books, 1985), chap. 2; and Keith Bradley and Alan Gelb, "Employee Buyouts of Troubled Companies," *Harvard Business Review* (September–October 1985): 121–30.

13. It is estimated that federal regulations in the United States are responsible for 12 percent to 21 percent of the slowdown in the growth of labor productivity in manufacturing; while reductions in the ratio of capital to labor are responsible for 15 percent; and the average cyclical impact, from 0 to 15 percent. Gregory Christainsen and Robert Haveman, "Public Regulations and the Slowdown in Productivity Growth," *American Economic Review*, Proceedings, *71*, no. 2 (May 1981): 320–25.

14. In Plato's *Republic*, decisions concerning the state were to be made by the philosopher kings, that is, an intellectual and experienced elite; while under Pericles' rule (fifth century B.C.), the majority of citizens made such decisions (Athenian democracy).

15. Knut Wicksell, *Vorlesungen über Nationalökonomie* (1901), published in English as *Lectures in Political Economy*, Lionel Robbins, ed. (1934), 77–78. More on public finance in his *Finanztheoritische Untersuchungen* (Studies in Finance Theory, 1896).

16. *New York Times*, March 5, 1984, E1; and *New York Times*, September 21, 1985, 27. In relation to this, differences in annual incomes, which vary from $7,000 to $22

million, and high concentration of wealth in the United States (0.5 percent of the population owns 20 percent of national wealth) are expected to influence political trends in the country.

17. Thomas D. Lynch, *Public Budgeting in America* (Englewood Cliffs, NJ: Prentice-Hall, 1979), chap. 1; and Anthony B. Atkinson and Joseph E. Stiglitz, *Lectures on Public Economics* (New York: McGraw-Hill, 1980), 294–329.

18. For single-peaked and multiple-peaked voting in fiscal choices see Kenneth J. Arrow, *Social Choice and Individual Values* (New York: Wiley, 1951); and James Buchanan and Gordon Tullock, *The Calculus of Consent* (Ann Arbor, MI: University of Michigan Press, 1962), 323–40.

19. Duncan Black, "On the Rationale of Group Decision-Making," *Journal of Political Economy*, 56, (1948): 23–34; and his *The Theory of Committees and Elections* (Cambridge: Cambridge University Press, 1958). Also H. R. Bowen, "The Interpretation of Voting in the Allocation of Economic Resources," *Quarterly Journal of Economics*, 58, (November 1943): 27–48.

20. Further discussion in Edward Gramlich, *Benefit-Cost Analysis of Government Programs* (Englewood Cliffs, NJ: Prentice-Hall, 1981); and Peter Sassone and William Schaffer, *Cost-Benefit Analysis: A Handbook* (New York: Academic Press, 1978).

21. Charles Stuart, "Welfare Costs per Dollar of Additional Tax Revenue in the United States," *American Economic Review* (June 1984): 352–62.

CHAPTER 4

1. For the EEC countries (average of Britain, France, Germany, Italy), general government expenditures increased from 35 percent in 1960 to 36 in 1970 and 54 percent of national income in 1983.

2. Ernst Engel, the German economist, argued about a century ago that consumer budgets change as income changes, with declining portions of food expenditures and greater outlays for sundries as income increases. For related empirical results, see George J. Stigler, "The Early History of Empirical Studies of Consumer Behavior," *Journal of Political Economy* (April 1954).

3. More details in Nicholas V. Gianaris, *Greece and Yugoslavia: An Economic Comparison* (New York: Praeger, 1984), 54–60. For comparisons with other Balkan countries, see Nicholas V. Gianaris, *The Economies of the Balkan Countries: Albania, Bulgaria, Greece, Romania, Turkey, Yugoslavia* (New York: Praeger, 1982), 58–78.

4. The GNP in current dollars increased from $18.7 billion in 1900 to $265.1 billion in 1950 and $4,163.3 in 1986; while the consumer price index (1967 = 100) increased from 31.5 in 1900 to 72.1 in 1950, 116.3 in 1970, and 298.4 in 1983. U.S. Department of Commerce, Bureau of the Census, *Historical Statistics of the United States* (1975): 1110–18; *Statistical Abstracts of the United States*; and *Economic Report of the President*, various issues.

5. In addition to farm subsidies, primarily in the form of payment to farmers to reduce the acres they cultivate per year, it is expected that the government would pay more to bail out farmers with large debts, which are estimated to be $215 billion.

6. In the fiscal year 1984 total transfer payments absorbed 40.6 percent of total federal expenditures, purchase of goods and services 33.2 percent, net interest 12.8 percent, grants-in-aid to state and local governments 10.6 percent, and subsidies to government

enterprises 2.8 percent of federal outlays. Joint Economic Committee, *Economic Indicators* (September 1985): 34.

7. Mismanagement and excessive price charged for military procurement contribute also to large U.S. defense expenditures. Among other overcharged prices, Uncle Sam paid $7,417 for a 3¢ alignment pin and $2,043 for a six-sided nut that costs 13¢ at the store. Arthur Schlesinger, Jr., "Closing Down the Pentagon Follies," *New York Times*, September 28, 1984.

8. Adam Smith, *An Inquiry into the Nature and Causes of the Wealth of Nations*, E. Cannon, ed. (New York: Modern Library, 1937), 689.

9. Thus, the board of education of New York City has shown 18 year inventories of Turkish towels, $4.5 million in unused schoolbooks, a 23-year supply of foam rubber softballs, and a 48-year supply of eight-cent postcards. *New York Times*, September 14 and 28, 1984.

10. Films and books, such as *Triage*, and master plans, such as those of Hitler in his Third Reich or Lycurgus in ancient Sparta, proposed burning nursing homes and their inhabitants or exterminating elderly people regardless of their religious or ethnic backgrounds. B. Levin and A. Arluke, "Our Elderly's Fate," *New York Times*, September 29, 1983, A31.

CHAPTER 5

1. A similar classification of tax rates was introduced recently in the United States. Nicholas V. Gianaris, "Greeks Had a Word for Regan Tax Plan," *New York Times*, January 1, 1985, A26. Also, Aristotle, *The Athenian Constitution*, VII, 4, and VIII; and Augustus Boeckh, *The Public Economy of Athens* (New York: Arno Press, 1976), 494–510.

2. Other sources of revenue were those from aliens' duties (*metoikion*) and rents from public buildings, as well as from mines of silver in Lavrion, near Athens. See *Xenophon's Works*, translated by C. Ashley and others (Philadelphia: Thomas Wardle, 1843), 681–91.

3. Adam Smith, *An Inquiry into the Nature and Causes of the Wealth of Nations*, E. Cannan, ed. (New York: Modern Library, 1937), 777–79.

4. Ibid., 821.

5. David Ricardo, *Principles of Political Economy and Taxation*, (1817), chap VI.

6. Henry George, *Progress and Poverty*. (New York: Modern Library, 1938), Book III.

7. For a thorough analysis, see Karl Marx, *Capital*, vol. 3 (New York: International Publishers, 1967), chaps. 28, 29; and Richard A. Musgrave, "Theories of Fiscal Crises: An Essay in Fiscal Sociology," in H. Aaron and M. Boskin, eds., *Economics of Taxation* (Washington, D.C.: Brookings Institution, 1980), 361–90.

8. In the case of income tax, the marginal rate of substitution (MRS) of commodity x for commodity y is equal to the marginal rate of their transformation (MRT), or the ratio of the marginal cost of these commodities is equal to their price (P) ratio ($MRS_{xy} = MRT_{xy} = P_x/P_y$). However, in the case of the excise tax, the $MRS_{xy} = P_x (1 + t_x)/P_y = MRT_{xy}$, where t is tax rate.

9. More information in Carl Eakin and Ann Witte, *Beating the System: The Underground Economy* (Boston: Auburn House, 1982).

10. Vito Tangi, "The Underground Economy in the United States: Annual Estimates, 1930–80," International Monetary Fund, *Staff Papers* (June 1983): 282–303.

11. For the calculation of the ten-year average propensity to tax (APT) the total amount of general government receipts or taxes (T) during the ten-year period is divided by the total national income (Y) during the same period. That is,

$$APTi = \sum_{i=1}^{i=10} Ti \left/ \sum_{i=1}^{i=10} Yi \right.$$

For the estimation of the marginal propensity to tax (MPT), the difference in tax revenue (ΔT) is divided by the difference in national income (ΔY), during the time intervals considered. More specifically,

$$MPTi = \Delta Ti/\Delta Yi$$

12. Statistical regressions of total (general government) taxes (TT) on private consumption (PRC), imports (IMP), and inflation (INF), 1950–83, revealed that inflation was a better explanatory variable of changes in total taxes, compared to private consumption and imports. Thus,

$$TT = a + b\ INF = 3.3 + 8.9\ INF, (R^2 = 0.990)$$

That is, a 1 percent increase in inflation was associated with an almost 9 percent increase in total taxes. The coefficients for IMP and PRC were 3.7 and 0.6, respectively. For the EEC the inflation coefficient was 5 and those of imports and private consumption were 1.5 and 0.7, respectively.

13. More on local financing in John Metzer, Jr., ed., *Capital Financing Strategies for Local Governments* (Washington, D.C.: International City Management Association, 1983).

14. In order to protect the environment, the Clear Air Act (1970), the National Environmental Policy Act (1971), and other laws were passed. More information in Allen Kneese and C. Schultze, *Pollution, Prices and Public Policy* (Washington, D.C.: Brookings Institution, 1975), chaps. 5–7.

CHAPTER 6

1. More discussion on the issue in Nicholas Stern, "Optimum Taxation and Tax Policy, International Monetary Fund, *Staff Papers* (June 1984): 339–78.

2. John Stuart Mill, *Principles of Political Economy*, vol. 2 (New York: Collier and Son, 1900), 308.

3. A regression analysis of indirect taxes on private consumption for the period 1950–83 was used to determine the slope and its reliability. Similar regressions of indirect taxes on imports, as well as on inflation, were also used for the same period. Thus, the slope of the regression line for private consumption was 0.14 for the United States. This means that, on the average, an increase in private consumption by $100 is related to an increase in government revenue from indirect taxes by $14. However, imports, with a slope of 0.83, were more important in explaining indirect taxes; and inflation, with a slope of 2.12 were even more important ($R^2 > 0.940$ in all cases).

4. The tax rates on personal income for the year 1987 for married couples filing joint returns were as follows:

Taxable income		Tax rates (percent)
Over	*But not over*	
$0	$3,000	11.0
3,000	28,000	15.0
28,000	45,000	28.0
45,000	90,000	35.0
over	90,000	38.5

The same five personal tax rates prevailed for all other categories of taxpayers (married persons filing separate returns, single individuals, heads of household, and estate and nongrantor trusts) at different income brackets. More details in Commerce Clearing House, *Explanation of Tax Reform Act of 1986* (Chicago: Commerce Clearing House, 1986), 15–19.

5. The members of OPEC collected $250 billion from oil in 1980. Saudi Arabia alone amassed $97 billion. In 1983, though, the oil revenue of OPEC dropped to $140 billion and was reduced further thereafter. In 1988 the price of oil was around $16 per barrel compared to as high as $34 in 1980.

6. United States Department of Health and Human Services, Social Security Administration, *History of Social Security* (Washington, D.C.: Government Printing Office, 1988), 2–4.

7. Commerce Clearing House, *Explanation of Tax Reform Act of 1986*, 101.

8. Alan Amerback, "Corporate Taxation in the United States," *Economic Activity*, vol. 2 (Washington, D.C.: Brookings Institution, 1983), 451–513.

9. Wassily Leontief, "What It Takes To Preserve Social Equity," *New York Times*, February 1, 1985, A29 and D1; and Joseph Pechman, *Federal Tax Policy*, 5th ed. (Washington, D.C.: Brookings Institution, 1987), chap. 5.

10. David Ricardo, *Principles of Political Economy and Taxation*, 1817, reprinted in Leonard Abbott, *Masterworks of Economics* (New York: McGraw-Hill, 1973), 31. For the regressiveness of the property tax, see Charles McLure," The New View of Property Tax," *National Tax Journal* (March 1977).

11. For empirical results see Nicholas V. Gianaris, *Economic Development: Thought and Problems* (West Hanover, Mass: Christopher Publishing House, 1978), chaps. 8, 9; and "The International Differences in Capital Output Ratios," *American Economic Review, 60* (June 1970): 456–77.

12. For a renewed interest in consumption taxes, see related papers in Joseph Pechman, ed., *What Should Be Taxed: Income or Expenditure?* (Washington, D.C.: Brookings Institution, 1980); also see Nicholas Kaldor, *An Expenditure Tax* (London: Allen and Unwin, 1955).

13. Among the more than 30 countries that adopted the VAT in the 1960s and 1970s, including the EEC, Norway, Sweden, Israel, Korea, and almost all Latin American and Central American countries, only in four did the VAT have a major impact on inflation. See A. Tait, *The Value-added Tax* (New York: McGraw-Hill, 1972); and "Is the Introduction of Value-added Tax Inflationary?" *Finance and Development* (June 1981): 38–42. See also, Nicholas V. Gianaris, "Indirect Taxes: A Comparative Study of Greece and the EEC," *European Economic Review, 15* (1981): 111–17.

14. For valuable comments on tax substitution, see the articles in Carl Shoup, ed.,

NOTES

Fiscal Harmonization in Common Markets (New York: Columbia University Press, 1967). For comparisons of U.S. taxes with those of the EEC countries, see Organization for Economic Cooperation and Development, *Revenue Statistics, 1965–86* (Paris: OECD, 1987), chaps. 1, 2. Also, Joseph Pechman, ed., *World Tax Reform: A Progress Report* (Washington, D.C.: Brookings Institution, 1988), 95–147, 219–36.

15. Nicholas V. Gianaris, *Economic Development: Thought and Problems*, 228–32. Also, Richard Goode, *Government Finance in Developing Countries* (Washington, D.C.: Brookings Institution, 1984), chap. 5.

CHAPTER 7

1. Dean Leimer and Selig Lesnoy, "Social Security and Private Saving: New Time-Series Evidence," *Journal of Political Economy*, June 1982, 606–29; and Martin Feldstein, "Social Security and Saving: The Extended Life Cycle Theory," *American Economic Review, Proceedings* 66, no. 2 (May 1976): 77–86. Also Robert Eisner, "Social Security, Saving and Investment," *Journal of Macroeconomics* (Winter 1983): 1–19; and Albert Ando and Franco Modigliani, "The 'Life Cycle' Hypothesis of Saving: Aggregate Implications and Tests," *American Economic Review* (March 1963): 55–84.

2. For more detailed statistics, see Gary Klott, "Supply-Side Claims Doubled," *New York Times*, September 18, 1984, D1, 6.

3. Keith Marsden, "Taxes and Growth," *Finance and Development*, September 1983, 40–43. Also Barry Bosworth, *Tax Incentives and Economic Growth* (Washington, D.C.: Brookings Institution, 1984); and Martin Feldstein, ed., *The Effects of Taxation on Capital Accumulation* (Chicago: University of Chicago Press, 1987).

4. For the usefulness of ICOR (v) in projecting investment (j) requirement for economic growth (g), that is j = gv, see Nicholas V. Gianaris, "International Differences in Capital-Output Ratios," *American Economic Review* (June 1970): 465–77; and his "Projecting Capital Requirements in Development Planning," *Socioeconomic Planning Sciences, 8* (1974). Also Richard Musgrave, *Fiscal Systems* (New Haven: Yale University Press, 1969), 222–26.

5. However, if corporations increase their financial assets or withhold profits instead of investing in real assets, such tax incentives may not prove much effective. A number of firms use savings or borrow money, through junk bonds or leverage buyouts, to acquire other companies, instead of investing in new plants and equipment.

6. For the United States, consumer prices increased annually, on the average of 2.1 percent, in the 1950s, 2.8 percent in the 1960s, and 7.9 percent in the 1970s (with 12.4 percent in 1980, 8.9 percent in 1981, around 4 percent annually until 1985, 1.1 percent in 1986, and 3.8 percent in 1987). For the EEC, the percentages increased 3.5, 3.7, and 10.6 (with 14.5 in 1980 and lower than 10 after 1984), respectively. Germany had the lowest and Italy the highest rate of inflation from the four large EEC countries. International Monetary Fund, *International Financial Statistics*, various issues.

7. More discussion on tax distribution by income groups in Joseph Pechman and Benjamin Okner, *Who Bears the Tax Burden?* (Washington, D.C.: Brookings Institution, 1976). Also, Edgar Browings and William Johnson, *The Distribution of the Tax Burden*, (Washington, D.C.: American Enterprise Institute, 1979).

8. Tax reforms have been introduced by Senator Bradley of New Jersey and Representative Gephardt of Missouri, both Democrats, as well as Senator Kasten of Wisconsin and Representative Kemp of New York, both Republicans and supply-side advocates.

9. For arguments in favor of taxes on those who use resources (consumption) and not on those who save and invest, see Thomas Hobbes, *Leviathan* (London: J. M. Dent and Sons, 1934), chap 30, 184; and Nicholas Kaldor, *An Expenditure Tax* (London: Allen and Unwin, 1955), 5.

10. More details in Commerce Clearing House, *Explanation of Tax Reform Act of 1986* (Chicago: Commerce Clearing House, 1986), 5–14; Paul N. Strassels, *The 1986 Tax Reform Act* (Homewood, Ill.: Dow Jones–Irwin, 1986), XI–XIX; and Roscoe Egger, Jr., *The Price Waterhouse Guide to New Tax Law* (New York: Bantam Books, 1986), 3–78.

CHAPTER 8

1. United States Government, Bureau of Labor Statistics; and P. Heller and A. Tait, "Government Employees and Pay: Some International Comparisons," *Finance and Development, 20*, no. 3 (September 1983): 44–47.

2. Dividing the equation $\Delta I + \Delta C = \Delta Y$ by ΔY, we have

$$\Delta I/\Delta Y + \Delta C/\Delta Y = \Delta Y/\Delta Y$$

and $\quad\Delta I/\Delta Y = \Delta Y/\Delta Y - \Delta C/\Delta Y = 1 - c$

Reversing both parts of the equation, we have

$$\Delta Y/\Delta I = k = \frac{1}{1-c} = \frac{1}{s}$$

because $c + s = 1$ and $s = 1 - c$.

3. Adam Smith, *An Inquiry into the Nature and Causes of the Wealth of Nations*, E. Cannan, ed., (New York: Modern Library, 1937), 79.

4. John Stuart Mill, *Principles of Political Economy* (London: Longmans Green, 1926), 978.

CHAPTER 9

1. For more information, see Roger Kormendi, "Government Debt, Government Spending, and Private Sector Behavior," *American Economic Review* (December 1983): 994–1010.

2. The regression of interest rate (i) on budget deficit (BD) for the years 1960–84 gave the following results (with t-values in parentheses):

$$i = 5.93 - 0.05BD \qquad \bar{R}^2 = 0.60 \qquad D - W = 0.804$$
$$(590)$$

This means that an increase in BD by 1 percent is associated with 0.05 percent change in i. Also Martin Feldstein and Otto Eckstein have found a weak but statistically significant association between nominal interest rates and U.S. deficits. See their article "The Fundamental Determinants of the Interest Rate," *Review of Economics and Statistics, 52,* (November 1970): 363–75. For little or no evidence of such an association see Paul Evans, "Do Large Deficits Produce High Interest Rates?" *American Economic Review* (March 1985): 68–88. Also, Paul Wachtel and John Young, "Deficit Announcements and Interest Rates," *American Economic Review* (December 1987): 1007–12.

3. For empirical support, see Gregory Hoelscher, "New Evidence on Deficits and Interest Rates," *Journal of Money, Credit and Banking* (February 1986): 1–17.

4. Michael Kalecki, *The Theory of Economic Dynamics*, (London: Allen and Unwin, 1954). For pessimistic predictions for the 1990s see Ravi Batra, *The Great Depression of 1990* (New York: Dell Publishing 1987), chap. 7.

5. United States Department of Commerce, Bureau of the Census, *Historical Statistics of the United States, Colonial Times to 1970*, (Government Printing Office, 1975): 1117–18.

6. Alexander Hamilton, the first Secretary of the Treasury, said in Congress, "A national debt, if it is not excessive, will be to us a national blessing. It will be a powerful cement of our union." However, Thomas Jefferson opined that "a national debt is always a national curse, that grinds down the many and benefits only the few."

7. The market value of the financial assets of the U.S. government was $707 billion, some $115 billion more than par. Gold was $141 billion greater than that reported in U.S. Treasury accounts of $42 per ounce. Robert Eisner and Paul Pieper, "A New View of the Federal Debt and Budget Deficits," *American Economic Review* (March 1984): 11–29.

8. For related discussion see Michael Roskin, "Federal Government Deficits: Some Myths and Realities," *American Economic Review, Papers and Proceedings* (May 1982): 296–303; and Robert Eisner, *How Real Is the Federal Deficit?* (New York: Free Press, 1986).

9. For the relationship of deficits with interest, taxation and spending, see Roger Kormendi, "Government Debt, Government Spending, and Private Sector Behavior," *American Economic Review* (December 1983): 994–1010; and Robert Barro, "On the Determinants of the Public Debt," *Journal of Political Economy* (October 1979): 940–71.

10. United States Bureau of the Census, *Governmental Finances and Current Population Report*, various issues; and United States Department of Commerce, *Survey of Current Business*, various issues.

11. For intergenerational implications of the debt, see James Tobin, "The Burden of the Public Debt," *Journal of Finance* (December 1965): 679–82; Franco Modigliani, "Long-run Implications of Alternative Fiscal Policies and the National Debt," *Economic Journal* (December 1961): 730–55; James Buchanan, *Public Principles of Public Debt* (Homewood, Ill.: Richard D. Irwin, 1958); and the articles in M. Ferguson, ed., *Public Debt and Future Generations* (Chapel Hill: University of North Carolina Press, 1964).

12. Nicholas V. Gianaris, "$D_s = 1.59 (1 + 0.1)^5$ Or, Deficit Going Up," *New York Times*, October 9, 1984, A32; and Charles McLure, Jr., *The Value-added Tax: Key to Deficit Reduction?* (Lanman, MD: American Enterprise Institute, 1987).

CHAPTER 10

1. Martin Bailey and George Tavlas, "Dollar Appreciation, Deficit Stimulation and the New Protectionism," *Journal of Policy Modeling* (February 1985).

2. Total world trade is about $2 trillion per year while capital flows are about $30 trillion or 15 times of total goods and services exchanged. From the total foreign-held assets in the United States (about $1.5 trillion), close to half belongs to the Europeans, one-fifth to Canadians, one-fifth to the Japanese, and more than 10 percent to the Latin Americans. About $350 billion are private deposits in U.S. banks, $200 billion private

portfolio holdings (stock and bonds), $200 billion foreign government holdings, and the rest primarily direct investment. The U.S. Treasury made the inflow of funds easier by dropping the 30 percent withholding tax on interest paid to foreign investors and allowing anonymous purchase of securities by foreigners.

3. Such close relationships of budget and trade deficits can be observed in other countries as well, particularly in Argentina, Greece, Mexico, and Morocco. World Bank, *World Development Report* (New York: Oxford University Press, 1985), 62–63.

4. The regression equation was as follows (with t-values in parentheses):

$$TD = 0.21 + \underset{(1.96)}{0.38} \quad BD + \underset{(0.13)}{0.021} \quad GNP + \underset{(0.22)}{0.036} \ INF + \underset{(3.03)}{7.73} \quad UNM$$

$$\bar{R}^2 = 0.826 \qquad D-W = 1.59$$

Where TD is the trade deficit, BD the budget deficit, GNP the gross national product, INF inflation, and UNM unemployment. Other important variables affecting trade deficits are real exchange rates and U.S. aggregate demand over world demand.

5. In the United States, personal income tax exemption for Americans working abroad was reduced from $80,000 to $70,000 per year by the Tax Reform Act of 1986. For tax comparisons with other nations, see Michael Glautier and Frederick Bassinger, *A Reference Guide to International Taxation* (Lexington, Mass.: Lexington Books, 1987), 165–214.

6. Empirical results in Mohsin Khan and Malcolm Knight, "Sources of Payments Problems in LDCs," *Finance and Development* (December 1983): 2–5. For problems of development financing, see Nicholas V. Gianaris, *Greece and Turkey: Economic and Geopolitical Perspectives* (New York: Praeger, 1988), chap. 6.

7. About $400 billion, out of a total of more than a trillion dollars of all developing nations, is the debt of the Latin American countries alone (some $113 billion for Brazil, more than $100 billion for Mexico and so on). More details in World Bank, *World Debt Tables 1985/1986* (Washington, D.C.: World Bank, 1987); and Christ Carvounis, *The Foreign Debt/National Development Conflict* (New York: Quorum Books, 1986), 95–138.

8. Vassily Leontief, "For a Marshal Plan II," *New York Times*, September 19, 1983, A19. There are proposals to convert part of the debt of developing countries into equity ownership (debt-for-equity plans). In addition, the U.S. government is willing to provide guarantees for discounted debt bonds of Mexico and perhaps of other countries.

Bibliography

Amerback, Alan. "Corporate Taxation in the United States," *Economic Activity*. Washington, D.C.: Brookings Institution, 1983.

Ando, Albert, and Franco Modigliani. "The 'Life Cycle' Hypothesis of Saving: Aggregate Implications and Tests." *American Economic Review*, March 1963.

Aquinas, Thomas, Saint. *Summa Theologica*. New York: Benzinger Bros., 1947–48.

Aristotle. *The Athenian Constitution*, VII, 4, and VIII.

———. *Ethics*, ix, 8.

Arrow, Kenneth J. *Social Choice and Individual Values* (New York: Wiley, 1951).

Atkinson, Anthony B. and Joseph E. Stiglitz. *Lectures on Public Economics* (New York: McGraw-Hill, 1980).

Atkinson, Anthony B., and Nicholas Stern. "Pigou, Taxation and Public Goods." *Review of Economic Studies, 41*, 1974.

Bailey, Martin and George Tavlas. "Dollar Appreciation, Deficit Stimulation and the New Protectionism." *Journal of Policy Modeling*, February 1985.

Ball, Lawrence. "Externalities from Contract Length." *American Economic Review*, September 1987.

Barker, Earnest. *The Political Thought of Plato and Aristotle*. New York: Dover, 1959.

Barro, Robert. "On the Determinants of the Public Debt." *Journal of Political Economy*, October 1979.

Batra, Ravi. *The Great Depression of 1990*. New York: Dell Publishing, 1987.

Baumol, William J. and Wallace E. Oates. *The Theory of Environmental Policy*. Englewood Cliffs, NJ: Prentice-Hall, 1975.

———. "Macroeconomics of Unbalanced Growth." *American Economic Review*, June 1967.

Black, Duncan. "On the Rationale of Group Decision-Making." *Journal of Political Economy, 56*, 1948.

Boeckh, Augustus. *The Public Economy of Athens*, New York: Arno Press, 1976.

Bosworth, Barry. *Tax Incentives and Economic Growth*. Washington, D.C.: Brookings Institution, 1984.

Bowen, H. R. "The Interpretation of Voting in the Allocation of Resources." *Quarterly Journal of Economics, 58*, November 1943.

Bradley, Keith, and Alan Gelb. "Employee Buyouts of Troubled Companies." *Harvard Business Review*, September–October 1985.

Brennan, G., and M. Flowers. "All 'Ng' Up on Clubs?: Some Notes on the Club Theory." *Public Finance Quarterly*, April 1980.

Browings, Edgar, and William Johnson. *The Distribution of the Tax Burden*. Washington, D.C.: American Enterprise Institute, 1979.

Buchanan, James M. "An Economic Theory of Clubs," *Economica*, February 1965.

———. *Public Principles of Public Debt*. Homewood, Ill.: Richard D. Irwin, 1958.

Buchanan, James, and Gordon Tullock. *The Calculus of Consent*. Ann Arbor, MI: University of Michigan Press, 1962.

Carby-Hall, J. *Worker Participation in Europe*. London: C. Helm, 1977.

Carvounis, Christ. *The Foreign Debt/National Development Conflict*. New York: Quorum Books, 1986.

Cheung, Steven. "The Fable of the Bees: An Economic Investigation." *Journal of Law and Economics*, April 1973.

Christainsen, Gregory, and Robert Haveman. "Public Regulations and the Slowdown in Productivity Growth." *American Economic Review, Proceedings, 71*, no. 2, May 1981.

Coase, Ronald H. "The Problem of Social Cost." *Journal of Law and Economics*, October 1960.

Commerce Clearing House. *Explanation of Tax Reform Act of 1986*. Chicago: Commerce Clearing House, 1986.

Critchfield, Richard. "Aristotle, Deng and China's Peasants." *New York Times*, November 16, 1985, 27.

Eakin, Carl, and Ann Witte. *Beating the System: The Underground Economy*. Boston: Auburn House, 1982.

Egger, Roscoe, Jr. *The Price Waterhouse Guide to New Tax Law*: New York: Bantam Books, 1986.

Eisner, Robert. *How Real Is the Federal Deficit?* New York: Free Press, 1986.

———. "Social Security, Saving and Investment." *Journal of Macroeconomics*, Winter 1983.

Eisner, Robert, and Paul Pieper. "A New View of the Federal Debt and Budget Deficits." *American Economic Review*, March 1984.

Evans, Paul. "Do Large Deficits Produce High Interest Rates?" *American Economic Review*, March 1985.

Fabricant, Solomon. *The Trend of Government Activity in the United States Since 1900*. New York: National Bureau of Economic Research, 1952.

Feldstein, Martin, ed. *The Effects of Taxation on Capital Accumulation*. Chicago: University of Chicago Press, 1987.

———. "Social Security and Saving: The Extended Life Cycle Theory." *American Economic Review, Proceedings*, 66, no. 2, May 1976.

Feldstein, Martin, and Otto Eckstein. "The Fundamental Determinants of the Interest Rate." *Review of Economics and Statistics, 52*, November 1970.

Ferguson, M., ed. *Public Debt and Future Generations*. Chapel Hill: University of North Carolina Press, 1964.

Friedman, Milton. *From Galbraith to Economic Freedom*. London: Institute of Economic Affairs, 1977.

Galbraith, John Kenneth. *The New Industrial State*, 2nd ed. revised. Boston: Houghton Mifflin, 1971.

George, Henry. *Progress and Poverty*. New York: Modern Library, 1938, Book III.

Gianaris, Nicholas V. "The Instability of the Incremental Capital-Output Ratio." *Socio-Economic Planning Sciences, 3*, August 1969.

———. "International Differences in Capital-Output Ratios." *American Economic Review, 60*, June 1970.

———. "Projecting Capital Requirement in Development Planning." *Socioeconomic Planning Sciences, 8*, 1974.

———. *Economic Development: Thought and Problems*. West Hanover, Mass.: Christopher Publishing House, 1978.

———. "Fiscal Policy: Greece and the EEC." *Spoudai, 15*, January–March 1980.

———. "Indirect Taxes: A Comparative Study of Greece and the EEC." *European Economic Review, 15*, 1981.

———. *The Economies of the Balkan Countries: Albania, Bulgaria, Greece, Romania, Turkey, Yugoslavia*. New York: Praeger, 1982.

———. "$D_5 = 1.59 (1 + 0.10)^5$ Or, Deficit Going Up." *New York Times*, October 9, 1984, A32.

———. *Greece and Yugoslavia: An Economic Comparison*. New York: Praeger, 1984.

———. "Greeks Had a Word for Regan Tax Plan." *New York Times*, January 1, 1985, A26.

———. *Greece and Turkey: Economic and Geopolitical Perspectives*. New York: Praeger, 1988.

Glautier, Michael, and Frederick Bassinger. *A Reference Guide to International Taxation*. Lexington, Mass.: Lexington Books, 1987.

Goode, Richard. *Government Finance in Developing Countries*. Washington, D.C.: Brookings Institution, 1984.

Gramlich, Edward. *Benefit-Cost Analysis of Government Products*. Englewood Cliffs, NJ: Prentice-Hall, 1981.

Hansen, Alvin. *Economic Issues of the 1960's*. New York: McGraw-Hill, 1960.

———. "Economic Progress and Declining Population Growth." *American Economic Review*, March 1939.

Heller, Peter, and Alan Tait. "Government Employees and Pay: Some International Comparisons." *Finance and Development, 20*, no. 3, September 1983.

Hobbes, Thomas. *Leviathan*. London: J. M. Dent and Sons, 1934.

Hoelscher, Gregory. "New Evidence and Interest Rates." *Journal of Money, Credit and Banking*, February 1986.

International Monetary Fund. *International Financial Statistics*. Various issues.

Kaldor, Nicholas. *An Expenditure Tax*. London: Allen and Unwin, 1955.

Kalecki, Michael. *Theory of Economic Dynamics*. London: Allen and Unwin, 1954.

Keynes, John Maynard. *General Theory of Employment Interest and Money*. New York: Harcourt, 1936.

———. "The End of Laissez-Faire." In his *Laissez-Faire and Communism*. New York: New Republic, 1926.

Khan, Mohsin, and Malcolm Knight. "Sources of Payments Problems in LDCs." *Finance and Development*, December 1983.

Klott, Gary. "Supply-Side Claims Doubled." *New York Times*, September 18, 1984, D1, 6.

Kneese, Allen, and C. Schultze. *Pollution, Prices and Public Policy*. Washington D.C.: Brookings Institution, 1975.

Kormendi, Roger. "Government Debt, Government Spending, and Private Sector Behavior." *American Economic Review*, December 1983.

Leimer, Dean, and Selig Lesnoy. "Social Security and Private Saving: New Time-Series Evidence." *Journal of Political Economy*, June 1982.

Leontief, Vassily. "For a Marshall Plan II." *New York Times*, September 19, 1983, A19.

————. "What It Takes To Preserve Social Equity." *New York Times*, February 1, 1985, A29 and D1.

Levin, B. and A. Arluke. "Our Elderly's Fate." *New York Times*, September 29, 1983, A31.

Lindblom, Charles. *Politics and Markets*. New York: Basic Books, 1977.

List, Friedrich. *The National System of Political Economy*, translated by S. Lloyd. New York: Longmans, Green, 1904.

Lynch, Thomas D. *Public Budgeting in America*. Englewood Cliffs, NJ: Prentice-Hall, 1979.

Marsden, Keith. "Taxes and Growth." *Finance and Development*, September 1983.

Marx, Karl. *Capital*, Vol. 3. New York: International Publishers, 1967.

McLure, Charles. "The New View of Property Tax." *National Tax Journal*, March 1977.

————. *The Value-added Tax: Key to Deficit Reduction?* Lanman, MD: American Enterprise Institute, 1987.

Metzer, John, Jr., ed. *Capital Financing Strategies for Local Government*. Washington, D.C.: International City Management Association, 1983.

Mill, John Stuart. *Principles of Political Economy*. New York: Collier and Son, 1900.

————. *Considerations on Representative Government*. London: Routledge, 1905.

Modigliani, Franco. "Long-run Implications of Alternative Fiscal Policies and the National Debt." *Economic Journal*, December 1961.

Musgrave, Richard, A. *Fiscal Systems*. New Haven: Yale University Press, 1969.

————. *The Future of Fiscal Policy: A Reassessment*. Leuven, Belgium: Leuven University Press, 1978.

————. "Theories of Fiscal Crises: An Essay in Fiscal Sociology." In H. Aaron and M. Boskin, eds., *Economics of Taxation*. Washington, D.C.: Brookings Institution, 1980.

Nutter, Warren. *Growth of Government in the West*. Washington, D.C.: American Enterprise Institute, 1978.

Organization for Economic Cooperation and Development (OECD). *National Accounts*. Paris: OECD, various issues.

————. *Revenue Statistics*, 1965–86. Paris: OECD, 1987.

Oshima, Harry. "Shares of Government in Gross National Product for Various Countries." *American Economic Review*, XLVII, no. 3, June 1957.

Pareto, Vilfredo. *Cours d'Economie Politique*, vol. I, II. Lausanne: 1896–97.

Peacock, Alan T., and Jack Wiseman. *The Growth of Public Expenditures in the United Kingdom*. New York: National Bureau of Economic Research, 1961.

Pechman, Joseph, ed. *What Should Be Taxed: Income or Expenditure?* Washington, D.C.: Brookings Institution, 1980.

———. *Federal Tax Policy*, 5th ed. Washington, D.C.: Brookings Institution, 1987.

———. *World Tax Reform: A Progress Report*. Washington, D.C.: Brookings Institution, 1988.

Pechman, and Benjamin Okner. *Who Bears the Tax Burden?* Washington, D.C.: Brookings Institution, 1976.

Pigou, Arthur C., *The Economics of Welfare*. London: Macmillan, 1932.

———. *A Study of Public Finance*, 3rd ed. London: Macmillan, 1951.

Plato. *Laws*, v. 736.

Ricardo, David. *Principles of Political Economy and Taxation*, 1817, reprinted. In Abbott, Leonard, *Masterworks of Economics*, vol. 2. New York: McGraw-Hill, 1973.

Rosen, Corey, Katherine Klein, and Karen Young. *Employee Ownership in America: The Equity Solution*. Lexington, Mass.: Lexington Books, 1985.

Roskin, Michael. "Federal Government Deficits: Some Myths and Realities." *American Economic Review*, Papers and Proceedings, May 1982.

Rousseau, Jean Jacques. *The Social Contract*, translated by Charles Frankel. New York: Hafner Publishing Company, 1947, Book I.

Sandler, Todd, and John Tschirhart. "The Economic Theory of Clubs: An Evaluative Survey." *The Journal of Economic Literature, 18*, December 1980.

Sassone, Peter, and William Schaffer. *Cost-Benefit Analysis: A Handbook*. New York: Academic Press, 1978.

Savas, Emanuel S. *Privatization: The Key to Better Government*. New York: Chatam House, 1988.

Schlesinger, Arthur, Jr. "Closing Down the Pentagon Follies." *New York Times*, September 28, 1984.

Schumpeter, Joseph. *Capitalism, Socialism and Democracy*, 3rd ed. New York: Harper Colophon Books, 1975.

Serrin, William. "Employee-Owned Companies and Their Fates." *New York Times*, December 30, 1984. E3.

Shoup, Carl, ed. *Fiscal Harmonization in Common Markets*, New York: Columbia University Press, 1967.

Smith, Adam, *An Inquiry Into the Nature and Causes of the Wealth of Nations*, ed. by E. Cannan. New York: Modern Library, 1937.

Stern, Nicholas. "Optimum Taxation and Tax Policy." International Monetary Fund, *Staff Papers*, June 1984.

Stigler, George J. "The Early History of Empirical Studies of Consumer Behavior." *Journal of Political Economy*, April 1954.

Strassels, Paul N. *The 1986 Tax Reform Act*. Homewood, Ill.: Dow Jones–Irwin, 1986.

Stuart, Charles. "Welfare Costs per Dollar of Additional Tax Revenue in the United States." *American Economic Review*, June 1984.

Tait, Alan. *The Value-added Tax*. New York: McGraw-Hill, 1972.

———. "Is the Introduction of Value-added Tax Inflationary?" *Finance and Development*, June 1981.

Tangi, Vito. "The Underground Economy in the United States: Annual Estimates, 1930–80." International Monetary Fund, *Staff Papers*, June 1983.

Tobin, James. "The Burden of the Public Debt." *Journal of Finance*, December 1965.
United Nations. *Yearbook of National Accounts Statistics*. New York: United Nations, various issues.
United States Government. *Bureau of Labor Statistics*, various issues.
———. Department of Commerce, Bureau of the Census. *Government Finances and Current Population Report*, various issues.
———. Department of Commerce, Bureau of the Census. *Historical Statistics of the United States, Colonial Times to 1970*. Washington, D.C.: Government Printing Office, 1975.
———. Department of Commerce, Bureau of the Census. *Statistical Abstracts of the United States*, various issues.
———. Department of Commerce. *Survey of Current Business*, various issues.
———. Joint Economic Committee. *Economic Indicators*, September 1985.
———. Department of Health and Human Services, Social Security Administration. *History of Social Security*. Washington, D.C.: Government Printing Office, 1988.
———. *Economic Report of the President*, various issues.
Wagner, Adolph. *Financzwissenschaft*, 3rd ed. Leipzig: 1890.
Wachtel, Paul, and John Young. "Deficit Announcements and Interest Rates." *American Economic Review*, December 1987.
Webber, Carolyn, and Aaron Wildavsky. *A History of Taxation and Expenditure in the Western World*. New York: Simon and Schuster, 1986.
Weitzman, Martin. *The Share Economy*. Cambridge, Mass.: Harvard University Press, 1984.
Wicksell, Knut. *Finanztheoritische Untersuchungen*. Studies in Finance Theory, 1896.
———. *Vorlesungen über Nationalökonomie* (1901). Published in English as *Lectures in Political Economy*, Lionel Robbins, ed., 1934.
World Bank. *World Development Report*. New York: Oxford University Press, 1985.
———. *World Debt Tables 1985/1986*. Washington, D.C.: World Bank, 1987.
Wren, Christopher. "China Undergoing a New Revolution." *New York Times*, April 24, 1984, A6.
Xenophon's Works, trans. by C. Ashley and others. Philadelphia: Thomas Wardle, 1843.

Index

ABOUT THE AUTHOR

NICHOLAS V. GIANARIS earned his B.A. at the Graduate School of Economics and Business of Athens, his LL.B. at the University of Athens, and his M.A. and Ph.D. in economics at New York University. He has taught in the United States and abroad. At present he is professor and program coordinator of economics at Fordham University, Lincoln Center, New York.

Dr. Gianaris is a member of the American Economic Association, Royal Economic Society (U.K.), Economic History Association, and American Association of University Professors. Listed in *American Men of Science* and similar volumes, he has also received the NYU Founders Award for scholarly achievements.

He has contributed a number of articles to both U.S. and international economics publications such as *American Economic Review, European Economic Review, and Socioeconomic Planning Sciences*, and has presented panel papers at symposia on the United States, Europe, and other regions. Parts of his book *Economic Development: Thought and Problems* (1978) were translated into French and Spanish by the International Monetary Fund for use in the IMF Institute's courses on financial analysis and policy.

His book *The Economies of the Balkan Countries: Albania, Bulgaria, Greece, Romania, Turkey, Yugoslavia* was published by Praeger in 1982 and reprinted in 1985. His third book *Greece and Yugoslavia: An Economic Comparison* was published by Praeger in 1984, while his fourth book, *Greece and Turkey: Economic and Geopolitical Perspectives* was published in 1988, also by Praeger.